Praise for *Taking a Stand*

"Robert Higgs begins *Taking a Stand* by thanking his students. But his list is much too short, for we are all his students. Often funny, and usually subversive of the conventional wisdom, this book spans a short period (2009–14) in Bob's marvelously productive life. Chapters range from serious engagements with economic affairs to heartfelt eulogies—Bob's 'goodbye' to Manuel Ayau cannot be read without tearing up—to parodies of the rock song 'American Pie' and the poem 'The Raven.' It is hard to convey the depth and value of this timely yet timeless book. But if Francis Bacon could be crossed with P. J. O'Rourke, that would come close."

> —**Michael C. Munger**, Professor of Political Science, Economics and Public Policy, and Director of the Philosophy, Politics, and Economics Program at Duke University

"More than anyone in our time, Robert Higgs wrestles with 'James Madison's Dilemma,' that is, if we have created a government powerful enough to protect our rights and liberties, what is to prevent it from taking away those very rights and liberties? One may not agree with all of his recent musings in *Taking a Stand*, but they are invariably thought-provoking and admirable."

> —**Richard E. Sylla**, Henry Kaufman Professor of the History of Financial Institutions and Markets, New York University

"No voice today for peace and liberty is as clear, as consistent, as learned, as insightful, and—this is important—as passionate and resonant as that of Robert Higgs. The pages of *Taking a Stand* prove me correct."

> —**Donald J. Boudreaux**, Professor of Economics and Director of the Center for the Study of Public Choice, George Mason University; Co-Editor, Café Hayek

"Robert Higgs has been pounding Leviathan since before most of today's libertarians were born. He has awakened new generations of students to the perils of unleashed politicians and lawless bureaucrats. In *Taking a Stand*, his passion and principles continue to fire folks up to stand up for their rights and liberties."

> —**James Bovard**, author, *Freedom in Chains, Lost Rights,* and *Terrorism and Tyranny*

"In his latest book *Taking a Stand*, Robert Higgs laments that his mother should not have let him become an economic historian. That's the only error he makes in 99 pithy chapters that debug a virtual database of statist fallacies for government controls. For example, World War II is not proof that astronomical government spending fixed the economy after decades of New Deal spending failed—but it is proof that when one-fifth of the population is forced to fight in a war or to work to support the war effort, the statistical unemployment rate goes down. Everyone interested in freedom should read this book to understand clearly how economic reasoning and political realism apply to ongoing debates over the ever-increasing control that government exerts on our lives."

—**T.J. Rodgers**, Founder, President and Chief Executive Officer, Cypress Semiconductor Corporation

"Full of fascinating insights, *Taking a Stand* illuminates Robert Higgs's life-long search for the true causes of economic and social problems, by utilizing all possible means: theory, history, literature, and his own experience. Higgs's emphasis on the crucial value of liberty has substantial implications for the future role of government in Asian countries and worldwide."

—**Yuzo Murayama**, Professor and Vice President, Doshisha University, Japan

"Robert Higgs writes with passion and wit. No one cuts to the chase with more precision. Higgs's engaging style makes *Taking a Stand* a pleasure to read."

—**Lee J. Alston**, Ostrom Chair, Professor of Economics, and Director of the Vincent and Elinor Ostrom Workshop in Political Theory and Policy Analysis, Indiana University

"In *Taking a Stand*, Robert Higgs dissects the myth of democratic government, juxtaposing it with the realities of the nation state and its systematic accretion of power, perquisites of office, and control over assets. He strips away comforting illusions of the beneficence of government, pointing out that customary justifications for its existence often conceal a lust for control. He explores the nature and legitimacy of government, its tactics and motivations, and the uncertainty and risks it injects into economic choices of the governed, with specific reference to the prospects for economic recovery in the current political environment. The book is highly readable and accessible to non-economists."

—**Charlotte Twight**, Professor of Economics, Boise State University

"With immensely readable vignettes from a life well lived, Robert Higgs's *Taking a Stand* is a wonderful book."

—**Julio H. Cole**, Professor of Economics, Universidad Francisco Marroquín, Guatemala

TAKING A STAND

INDEPENDENT
I N S T I T U T E

INDEPENDENT INSTITUTE is a non-profit, non-partisan, public-policy research and educational organization that shapes ideas into profound and lasting impact. The mission of Independent is to boldly advance peaceful, prosperous, and free societies grounded in a commitment to human worth and dignity. Applying independent thinking to issues that matter, we create transformational ideas for today's most pressing social and economic challenges. The results of this work are published as books, our quarterly journal, *The Independent Review*, and other publications and form the basis for numerous conference and media programs. By connecting these ideas with organizations and networks, we seek to inspire action that can unleash an era of unparalleled human flourishing at home and around the globe.

100 Swan Way, Oakland, California 94621-1428, U.S.A.
Telephone: 510-632-1366 • Facsimile: 510-568-6040 • Email: info@independent.org • www.independent.org

TAKING
A STAND

Reflections on Life, Liberty, and the Economy

ROBERT HIGGS

Foreword by **Judge Andrew P. Napolitano**

INDEPENDENT
I N S T I T U T E

OAKLAND, CALIFORNIA

Independent Institute
100 Swan Way, Oakland, CA 94621-1428
Telephone: 510-632-1366
Fax: 510-568-6040
Email: info@independent.org
Website: www.independent.org

Cover Design: Denise Tsui
Cover Image: © Steve Babuljak

Library of Congress Cataloging-in-Publication Data

Higgs, Robert.
    Taking a stand : reflections on life, liberty, and the economy / Robert Higgs; foreword by Judge Andrew P. Napolitano.
        pages cm
    ISBN 978-1-59813-204-5 (paperback); 978-1-59813-203-8 (hardcover)
1. Administrative agencies—United States—History. 2. Bureaucracy—United States—History. 3. United States—Economic policy. 4. Welfare—United States—History. 5. Liberty—United States—History. 6. State, The—History. I. Title.
    JK411.H543 2015
    320.973—dc23   2014048979

*To my Ph.D. students at the University of Washington
and the Universidad Francisco Marroquín*

Ted Meeker (in memoriam)
Bob McGuire
Lee Alston
Yuzo Murayama
John Wallis
Price Fishback
Charlotte Twight
Julio Cole
Fritz Thomas

You have made your old professor very proud.

Contents

PART II On Doing Analysis in Political Economy

PART III Money, Debt, Interest Rates, and Prices

PART IV Investment and Regime Uncertainty

PART V Boom, Bust, and Macroeconomic Policy

PART IX Just for Fun

Foreword

IN THE ANNALS of academic fidelity to the Jeffersonian ideal that government is best which governs least, no one commands and deserves more respect than Dr. Robert Higgs, Senior Fellow in Political Economy at the Independent Institute. Bob's masterpiece, *Crisis and Leviathan*, remains the standard scholarly critique of the growth of the federal government from the Roosevelt/Wilson to the Carter/Reagan years. In all of the presidencies encompassed by those bookends, including the bookends themselves, the federal government grew radically and well beyond the boundaries envisioned by the Founders.

I know that while many of my conservative brethren will join gleefully in any critical characterization of the Progressive years as those of rampant government interference in private behavior—behavior not even arguably delegated to the feds by the Constitution—most will blanch at the juxtaposition of the names Carter and Reagan in the same phrase and to prove the same point.

But not Bob Higgs. Bob is utterly faithful to the simple belief that the Declaration of Independence means what it says: our rights come from our God-given humanity and not from the government; and to the natural-law observation that since men and women in or out of government are not angels, we need a universal rule of law—not subject to the vagaries of popular whim—to restrain their impulses to use the coercive powers of government in controlling how others live and to guarantee that there remain areas of human behavior that are immune from governmental surveillance and regulation.

Prior to the War Between the States, the feds largely stayed out of the private affairs of private persons. From the Reconstruction Era to the Progressive

Era, the feds moved in and out of private affairs, started printing money legally, taxed personal income, redistributed wealth, regulated private property, engaged in the least moral, least useful, and most catastrophic of modern American wars—World War I—and set the stage for the post-Progressive Era which has brought us the Welfare State, the Warfare State, and the Administrative State.

From the Roosevelt/Wilson years up to the present day, every President, notwithstanding his public utterances and the adulation of his supporters, has held the view that the Constitution unleashes the federal government to use the powers of government, which are not reason but force, to address any need the President and congressional leaders want to address, using any means they choose, subject only to the express prohibitions in the Constitution, and subject, of course, to what they can get away with politically.

In his lectures all over the world and in his scholarly writings, no one has chronicled all this with more intellectual credibility and using more cogent reasoning than Bob Higgs. Indeed, to legal and economic scholars and to historians who challenge the modern-day behemoth in Washington, D.C., Bob's work is the standard against which others should be measured, and one to which we all refer on a regular basis.

Of the three lamentable governmental states that progressivism has brought upon us, the least understood is the Administrative State. It is here—in the darkness of the perpetual bureaucracy that never changes even when different parties control the White House or Congress—that much mischief to liberty and secret lawmaking is done, all well beneath the radar screen. Why is the pressure in your home shower so weak? Why do office chairs—except in the White House—need to have five legs? Why can't the makers of aspirin describe its uses in advertisements? How can a product be lawful, yet its marketing prohibited? Why can't you catch five lobsters from the oceans for your neighbors' use? Surely Congress never debated and legislated on all those things. Surely water pressure and chair legs and lobsters are not areas of regulation delegated by the Constitution to Congress. Well, who did regulate these things, if only Congress can write federal laws? Doesn't the first article of the Constitution begin "All legislative Powers herein granted shall be vested in a Congress . . . "?

In his academic work, Bob has dissected the government's shrewd secret excesses using its administrative arm; and no one has done so more clearly or more pleasingly. In the pages that follow come similar arguments, but often in a non-academic vein. Be prepared for Bob with his hair let down; for here are essays that show a whimsical, introspective, and personal Bob Higgs. Who would have expected this towering intellect to write about whether the dead can be brought back to life? Who knew that he loves (as I do) Edgar Allen Poe's "The Raven" and Don MacLean's "American Pie" and Leonard Cohen's "Everybody Knows"?

From the myth that the government has derived its powers from the consent of the governed to the role of independent experts in formulating monetary and fiscal policy; from the government's duplicity in announcing the unemployment rate in a given month to how the state entraps us, if you want to see a true polymath at work, a humble giant thinking out loud about whatever thoughts that great mind found worthy of contemplation, these lofty, serious, sad, and illuminating essays will do the unthinkable—they will educate you beyond *Crisis and Leviathan.*

In my own television and academic work, I have attempted to use Bob's fidelity to first principles as a model. I have not always succeeded. Yet, what a joy it has been for me to see that fidelity from a different angle; one just as faithful and beautiful, yet bound to create additional admiration for a good and fearless man's mind and work that I love so much.

Judge Andrew P. Napolitano
New York City

Preface

THIS BOOK COLLECTS almost a hundred short pieces that I have written in recent years, mainly for the Independent Institute's group blog *The Beacon*. All but three of them appeared in 2009 or more recently. Most of them are only a few pages in length.

The topics range widely, reflecting my varied interests and experience. As someone trained in economics, specializing in economic history and political economy, I have had to familiarize myself with a multitude of facts, concepts, theories, and modes of analysis in economic analysis, history, politics, law, and related subjects. As someone who not only taught in universities and colleges at the graduate and undergraduate levels, but also consulted from time to time in law cases and regulatory proceedings, I have acquired more first-hand familiarity with the intersection of government and the economy than I would have gained if I had spent my career entirely in academia. After spending twenty-six years as a full-time professor, I have spent the past twenty-one as an editor, writer, lecturer, and consultant outside the walls of academe (except for brief stints abroad as a visiting professor). The wide range of the subjects dealt with in the pieces collected here reflects the diversity of my own teaching, research, editing, writing, and consulting.

In 2008, my friend and colleague Anthony Gregory approached me about contributing to *The Beacon*, which he was just getting off the ground. At the time, I did not foresee that I would have much to offer, but I agreed to join several others who were contributing, to do my small part. It turned out, however, that I greatly underestimated how much I would end up writing for *The Beacon*. During the past six years, I have made more than 300 posts there, some of them being fairly substantial. The present collection brings together more than a quarter of them: those that seem most substantial, provocative, and out of the ordinary.

The pieces are organized under nine headings, although many of them might have fit just as well under one of the other rubrics. Most of them may be described as analytical commentaries or observations. Most are substantive, dealing with definite actors and events, but a substantial number are more methodological, focusing on how various analysts have dealt with particular subjects or how, in my judgment, analysts can deal most effectively with certain subjects. A substantial number of these pieces pertain to the nature and functioning of the state; many with the economy, both as a whole and in regard to particular sectors or specific aspects of its operation. One section pertains to commentaries on libertarianism, an ideology I have long embraced, though the precise nature of my embrace has changed over the years. Fifteen pieces are obituaries or reminiscences, most of them in the nature of homages I pay to my parents, teachers, and colleagues, as well as to professional peers and ideological comrades with whom I have worked in a common quest. Throughout the collection, I make more personal references to my own experiences and endeavors than would be appropriate in more formal writing; thus the collection has an autobiographical aspect, as well.

Because the pieces were originally written to stand alone, the reader may skip from one to another anywhere in the collection without loss of necessary background. The references and graphical displays add some documentation, but no attempt has been made to provide the same type of citation that one finds in scholarly articles and books. The bite-size commentaries I present here are not simply a hodge-podge of ungrounded opinion, testaments to my idiosyncrasies, but neither do I purport to offer them as scholarly fare. Nevertheless, there is no gainsaying that as a scholar of forty-seven years' standing, I often express myself in a way that reflects that background and learning.

The collection ends with three pieces that I wrote just for fun. If the reader should find these amusing—and perhaps find reasons to smile elsewhere in the book, as well—I shall be especially pleased. Life is grim enough without our burrowing constantly into its darkest recesses.

PART I

Politics and the State

1

It's Who You Know

GOVERNMENTS ARE MANAGED by elites who are beholden to somewhat larger elites for support. Members of the former usually spring from the latter. Whether the nature of rule dictates this sort of cozy arrangement, as pronounced by the Iron Law of Oligarchy,[1] or not, we see this type of tight, inbred elite rule in virtually every society, regardless of its declared ideological commitments and ideals.

In U.S. history, defense and foreign policymaking has exemplified this pattern to a greater degree than anything else. Ever since the United States began to exert itself aggressively on the world stage at the end of the nineteenth century, a relative handful of persons drawn from a common, highly unrepresentative background has tended to call the shots in foreign and defense policymaking. Perhaps this pattern has weakened somewhat in the past two or three decades, but it has certainly not disappeared.

Earlier it was so blatant as to be unmistakable. People at the top of the heap in foreign and defense policymaking often had attended the same exclusive boarding schools, the same universities, and the same law schools. They generally had worked in top law firms or top investment banks in New York City. They had often known one another since boyhood. (Women didn't play in this league until very recently.)

One of the most important figures of the twentieth century in U.S. foreign and defense policymaking was Henry Stimson, who was twice secretary of war (under Taft and then under Franklin Roosevelt and Truman) and once

---

1. "Iron Law of Oligarchy," *Wikipedia,* last modified November 18, 2014, http://en.wikipedia.org/wiki/Iron_law_of_oligarchyf.

secretary of state (under Hoover). Stimson, who epitomized the elite's exclusivity, drew the same sort of people to him, giving them an opportunity to put their noses under the tent of power, where many of them kept themselves until quite recently.

In reading a biography of Stimson by Godfrey Hodgson, *The Colonel: The Life and Wars of Henry Stimson, 1867–1950*, I came across a passage (on pp. 247–48) whose content is so remarkable, not to say astonishing, that I am moved to share it. This passage has to do with the men Stimson took on as his chief subordinates at the War Department after he became secretary there in 1940: Harvey Hollister Bundy, Robert A. Lovett, John J. McCloy, George Harrison, and Robert Patterson.

> Stimson, Bundy, Lovett, [and] Harrison were all members of Skull and Bones [a secret society of students at Yale]. Only McCloy and Patterson of the inner circle were not. Stimson, Bundy, Harrison, McCloy and Patterson were all graduates of the Harvard Law School; only Lovett was not. Stimson, Harrison, Lovett, McCloy, and Patterson were all prominent on Wall Street; only Bundy was not, and he practiced law on State Street, the nearest thing to Wall Street in Boston. All six men were Republicans. The plain fact is that, during a war for democracy conducted by a Democratic President—which was also, more than any previous foreign war in American history, a democratic war in the sense that millions of men from every corner of American life fought it together—the War Department was directed by a tiny clique of wealthy Republicans, and one that was almost as narrowly based, in social and educational terms, as a traditional British Tory Cabinet.[2]

Readers who wish to learn much more about such men, their backgrounds, their thinking, and their leading roles in the conduct of official affairs may wish to read *The Wise Men*,[3] by Walter Isaacson and Evan Thomas.

---

2. Godfrey Hodgson, *The Colonel: The Life and Wars of Henry Stimson, 1867–1950* (New York: Alfred A Knopf, 1990), 247–48.

3. Walter Isaacson and Evan Thomas, *The Wise Men: Six Friends and the World They Made* (New York: Simon & Schuster, 1986).

2

What's the Point of Demonstrating?

THOUSANDS OF AMERICANS have just staged a demonstration[1] in Washington, D.C., to express their displeasure with the growth of government in general and the Obama administration's health-insurance proposals in particular. Such demonstrations are a tradition in this country. The First Amendment, which people usually associate with freedom of speech, religion, and the press, also stipulates that Congress shall make no law abridging "the right of the people peaceably to assemble, and to petition the Government for a redress of grievances." The Founders knew that people would sometimes desire to complain publicly against government policies that affected them adversely. After all, their own revolution had begun amid many such protests against the British government.

So, in this country, people have a constitutionally guaranteed right to demonstrate and petition for redress of grievances, and they often exercise this right. Although the government sometimes tries to control when and how people demonstrate, especially when such protests might prove too visibly embarrassing to the emperor or to one of the two gangs that purport to be competing political parties in what is actually a one-party state, most of the time the rulers seem to appreciate that such demonstrations pose no genuine threat to their control of the state and that the wise course is to allow the peasants to blow off steam. Later, they can be told how fortunate they

---

1. David J. Theroux, "Anti-Big-Government DC Demonstration Draws Huge Crowd: 'Don't Tread on Me,'" The Beacon, September 12, 2009, http://blog.independent.org/2009 /09/12/anti-government-dc-demonstration-draws-tens-of-thousands-dont-tread-on-me/.

are to live in a country where the government permits freedom of speech, assembly, and petition, as if such actions in themselves would feed the baby.

I have considerable experience as a demonstrator. In the late 1960s and early 1970s, I marched and otherwise participated in many protests against the U.S. war in Vietnam. Although I managed to get through all of these experiences without getting my head scarred by a police baton—an achievement of which many of my fellow demonstrators cannot boast—I did learn a fair number of lessons in what we might call "applied political science."

Lesson number one is that the cops do not believe in your First Amendment rights, or any other rights of yours, for that matter. If they find it convenient for their own purposes, which often seem to include nothing more than throwing their weight around, they will yell at you, shove you, threaten you with clubs, dogs, and horses, whack you with their batons, and lob tear gas into your ranks. It's all in a day's work for those who have sworn "to serve and protect." Best you remember, however, that this familiar phrase is short for "serve and protect the state," not for "serve you and protect your rights to life, liberty, and property." Protecting your right to demonstrate peacefully against state policies is not part of the cops' job description.

Lesson number two is that the people in the demonstrations are there for all sorts of reasons, despite what one might suppose from their announced issue(s) as signified by signs, banners, and group statements. I often bemoaned the lack of seriousness in many of the antiwar demonstrators with whom I marched. A great many of the younger ones seemed to be there mainly because demonstrating against the war was, literally, a sexy thing for a college student to do: at the demonstration, one might meet someone suitable for a not-very-subsequent sexual liaison—in plain language, participating in a demonstration served as a reasonably promising avenue to getting laid. Beyond this quite understandable motivation, however, people had all sorts of other reasons for participating. Some fancied themselves radicals out to overthrow the government. Others were worried that children, grandchildren, or other relatives and friends might be drafted, shipped to Vietnam, and killed. Some of us actually cared about the countless hundreds of thousands of Asians being slaughtered by U.S. forces for no good reason. Although we were all against the war in some way, our ways varied widely. The participants in most demonstrations, including the recent one in Washington, no doubt have this same heterogeneous quality. In a protest, however, the enemy of my enemy is my friend.

Lesson number three is that the mainstream media are in league with the government when they report on demonstrations. For example, they will minimize any violence the police use against the demonstrators and exaggerate any violence the demonstrators perpetrate. I recall one protest in particular, where our group included tens of thousands of marchers passing through the streets of downtown Seattle. The police, as usual, were out in force, lining the streets and salivating for a chance to crack some heads. Present also were the undercover agents with their cameras; for some reason, the authorities always wanted lots of photos of us dangerous protesters—college students, hippies, grandmothers, little kids in their mother's arms, and so forth, all obviously dangerous subversives. At this particular protest, the organizers took great pains to instruct everybody about scrupulously avoiding any kind of violence, because we all knew that the media would use it to discredit everything about the event. So we maintained absolute order, or so I thought as I made my way through the streets somewhere in the middle of the long parade. No violence whatsoever did I see. Hooray! The next morning, however, the banner headline in the *Seattle Times* read, "Violence Mars Antiwar Demonstration." Someone, it seems, had broken ranks and smashed a shop window, an occurrence so inconsequential that even I, positioned right in the middle of the affair, had not noticed it. This incident illustrates well what passes for journalistic impartiality and balance in this country. Rest assured that if you are bucking the system, the system's guardians in the news media will smack you down by stigmatizing you as some sort of dangerous hooligan or totally out-of-touch wing-nut. They'll also minimize your group's numbers, again seeking to marginalize and trivialize your efforts.

Lesson number four is that the powers that be don't give a damn about your demonstrations or the reasons that have impelled you to participate in them, except to the extent that your actions create bad press for them and their policies. The minute they conclude that your demonstrations actually imperil their personal grip on power, they will cease to be so accommodating of your First Amendment rights. They might even cook up something called COINTELPRO, whereby they employ every political dirty trick in the book against you, up to and including murder. (If you suppose I'm exaggerating, I suggest you do some research on COINTELPRO[2] and other such government schemes to violate the people's civil rights systematically.) Nowadays, the USA PATRIOT Act lends itself splendidly to broad-gauge surveillance and disruption of peaceniks and other troublemakers.

After the Vietnam War ended, I stopped participating in public demonstrations, not because I thought the government no longer deserved protest and petition for redress of grievances, but because I lost all faith in the efficacy of the demonstrations. I was gaining a sounder appreciation of how the state operates, and as my understanding deepened, I found myself unable to suppose that the people who constitute the state have any interest in doing what might loosely be called "the right thing." As for those of us outside the precincts of the state and its supporting coalition of special-interest groups, the state wants us to buckle under to its dictates, shell out the taxes, fees, and fines it demands from us, and shut up. As long as we faithfully comply with the first two requirements, it is willing to cut us some slack on the third, but only up to the point at which our expressions of grievance might actually weaken its iron grip on power. So, when I see demonstrations like the one that just took place in Washington, I sympathize with the people who've gone to the trouble of protesting against the government's abuses, but I find myself wondering, do these poor souls really think they'll accomplish something by this protest?

---

2. "COINTELPRO," *Wikipedia*, last modified November 1, 2014, http://en.wikipedia .org/wiki/COINTELPRO.

3

Partisan Politics

A Fool's Game for the Masses

BECAUSE I DESPISE POLITICS in general, and the two major parties in this country in particular, I go through life constantly bemused by all the weight that people put on partisan political loyalties and on adherence to the normative demarcations the parties promote. Henry Adams observed that "politics, as a practice, whatever its professions, has always been the systematic organization of hatreds." This marshaling of hatreds is not the whole of politics, to be sure, but it is an essential element. Thus, Democrats encourage people to hate big corporations, and Republicans encourage people to hate welfare recipients.

Of course, it's all a fraud, designed to distract people from the overriding reality of political life, which is that the state and its principal supporters are constantly screwing the rest of us, regardless of which party happens to control the presidency and the Congress. Amid all the partisan sound and fury, hardly anybody notices that political reality boils down to two "parties": (1) those who, in one way or another, use state power to bully and live at the expense of others; and (2) those unfortunate others.

Even when politics seems to involve life-and-death issues, the partisan divisions often only obscure the overriding political realities. So, Democrats say that anti-abortion Republicans, who claim to have such tremendous concern for saving the lives of the unborn, have no interest whatever in saving the lives of those *already* born, such as the poor children living in the ghetto. And Republicans say that Democrats, who claim to have such tremendous concern for the poor, systematically contribute to the *perpetuation* of poverty by the countless taxes and regulations they load onto business owners who would otherwise be in better position to hire and train the poor and thereby to hasten their escape from poverty.

If the unborn children happen to be living in the wombs of women on whom U.S. bombs and rockets rain down in Iraq, Afghanistan, and Pakistan, however, all Republican concerns for the unborn evaporate completely, as do the Democrats' concerns for the poor children living in the selfsame bombarded villages. Both parties' positions would seem to rest on very flexible and selective morality, if indeed either party may be said to have any moral basis at all, notwithstanding their chronic public displays of "moral" wailing and gnashing of teeth.

In any event, the parties' principles of hatred have never passed the sniff test; indeed, they reek of hypocrisy. Thus, while railing against the "corporate rich," the Democrats rely heavily on the financial support of Hollywood moguls and multi-millionaire trial lawyers, among other fat cats. And the Republicans, while denouncing the welfare mother who makes off with a few hundred undeserved bucks a month, vociferously support the hundreds of billions of dollars in corporate welfare channeled to Lockheed Martin, Boeing, and General Electric, among many other companies, via larcenous "defense" contracts, Export-Import Bank subsidies, and countless other forms of government support for "national security" and service to "the public interest" as Republicans conceive of these nebulous, yet rhetorically useful entities.

Notice, too, that although ordinary Democrats and Republicans often harbor intense mutual hatreds, the party leaders in Congress rub shoulders quite amiably as a rule. Regardless of which party has control, the loyal opposition can always be counted on to remain ever so loyal and ready to cut a deal. And why not? These ostensible political opponents are engaged in a process of plunder from which the bigwigs in both parties can expect to profit, whatever the ebb and flow of party politics. At bottom, the United States has a one-party state, cleverly designed to disguise the country's true class division and to divert the masses from a recognition that unless you are a political insider connected with one of the major parties, you almost certainly *will* be ripped off on balance. Such exploitation, after all, is precisely what the state and the political parties that operate it are for.

Yet, rather than hating the predatory state, the masses have been conditioned to love this blood-soaked beast and even, if called upon, to lay down their lives and the lives of their children on its behalf. From my vantage point on the outside peering in, I am perpetually mystified that so many people are taken in by the phony claims and obscurantist party rhetoric. As the song says, "clowns to the left of me, jokers to the right," but unlike the fellow in the song, I am not "stuck in the middle." Instead, I float well above all of this wasted emotion, looking down on it with disgust and sadness. Moreover, as an economist, I am compelled to regret such an enormously inefficient allocation of hatred.

4

Democracy's Most Critical Defect

ALTHOUGH DEMOCRACY NOW comes closer than anything else to serving as a world religion, it has never lacked critics. For millennia those critics, such as Aristotle, had large followings among political thinkers and practicing politicians. Even as late as 1787, when a group of prominent men met in Philadelphia to compose the U.S. Constitution, democracy was viewed with trepidation, and the framers created an apparatus of government in which democracy was hemmed in on all sides, lest the country fall into the much-dreaded condition of "mob rule."

Nowadays, democracy's defects are more likely to be seen as relatively benign—its devotees like to quote Winston Churchill's quip[1] that "democracy is the worst form of government except all those other forms that have been tried from time to time"—or as defects not of democracy itself, but of the party shenanigans and other frictions that keep the democratic system from operating more fully. Thus, people complain of "gridlock" and bemoan a "do-nothing" Congress because these things impede the unrestricted functioning of democracy.

Public choice theorists have written countless articles and books spelling out the manifold ways in which democracy, viewed as a political-decision rule for making collective choices by means of voting, may fail to aggregate the preferences of individual constituents into an outcome that represents the "will of the people." More than sixty years ago, Kenneth Arrow showed[2] that no such aggregation is possible, given certain seemingly appealing restrictions

---

1. "Winston Churchill Quote," *Winston Churchill,* http://www.iwise.com/apNh7.
2. "Social Choice and Individual Values," *Wikipedia,* last Modified October 26, 2014, http://en.wikipedia.org/wiki/Social_Choice_and_Individual_Values.

on the nature of people's preferences, such as transitivity (if A is preferred to B, and B is preferred to C, then C cannot be preferred to A).

None of this theorizing had the slightest effect on the common people's idea that democracy can and should translate the "will of the people" into collective choices; nor has it kept generations of politicians from talking as if such a translation were possible and desirable. (Political practice, in contrast to political rhetoric, has always proceeded in the usual corrupt fashion, featuring scheming plutocrats, privilege-seeking special-interest groups, and the iron law of oligarchy.)[3]

I mention these things only by way of introduction, however, because here I wish to claim that democracy's gravest defect has little or nothing to do with the defects traditionally ascribed to it. I maintain that its severest defect, indeed, a flaw so critical that it gives democracy the potential to destroy civilization, pertains to its effect in corrupting the people's moral judgment.

To see how this corruption comes about, let us begin by recognizing that in many people's eyes, certain government functionaries may legitimately take actions that would be condemned as criminal if anyone else were to take them. If you or I were to threaten a neighbor with violence unless he handed over a specified sum of money, we would be universally recognized as engaged in extortion or attempted robbery. Yet, the functionaries of St. Tammany Parish, the state of Louisiana, and the United States of America routinely obtain money from me in precisely this manner. And although many people subject to such takings may complain that the amounts demanded are excessive, hardly anybody describes the exactions as constituting nothing more than extortion or armed robbery. Why not? Because the functionaries who assess and collect these sums of money—which they style "taxes," not loot, plunder, or swag—are democratically elected "public officials."

From a moral point of view, I am hard pressed to see how their employment status gives them a defensible right to act in ways that everyone would recognize as criminal if undertaken by a private individual. In political theory, a representative democratic government is said to derive its just powers by delegation from the people who are governed, with their consent. I assure you that I have never consented to have the various governments rob me,

---

3. "Iron Law of Oligarchy," *Wikipedia,* last modified November 18, 2014, http://en.wikipedia.org/wiki/Iron_law_of_oligarchy.

especially for the financing of countless activities that I consider to be useless, destructive, or inherently criminal. Regardless of the uses to which a government puts its booty, however, the people cannot justly delegate to political representatives any rights that they themselves do not possess. If I do not have a right to plunder my neighbor, how can I delegate that right to a government functionary who purports to represent me?

The situation is the same with regard to innumerable other actions that governments carry out, including unjust imprisonment, murder, and demands for compliance with so-called "regulations." If you or I were to demand the same actions that regulators commonly prescribe, our demands would be plainly seen to constitute unjustified intimidation and lawless coercion, at best. Likewise, if I were to send a private Predator drone to Pakistan to fire explosive missiles into villages, killing women, children, and other innocent persons, I would be seen as a monstrous mass murderer, and demands would be made that I be apprehended and "brought to justice" or killed. Yet when President Obama causes deaths in this way, no such demands are made. How did Barack Obama come by the right to kill innocent people? By democratic election to the presidency of the United States, of course. Most people actually believe, and act on the belief, that mere election to a political office can endow a person with standing to disregard the moral requirements applicable to people in general. And not only the elected official, but all those officials beneath him in the chain of command—nobody demands that the technician who sits comfortably in the United States and directs the exact operation of the lethal drone be brought to justice; he is, as the saying goes, "only following orders."

In the war-crimes tribunals[4] conducted after World War II, many defendants pleaded not guilty on the grounds that they were only following orders. This defense, however, was ruled inadmissible because the top authorities of the Nazi regime, from Adolf Hitler on down, were themselves viewed as war criminals, albeit unavailable in many instances to stand trial as such. In contrast, none of the military officers and men who carried out the fire bombings of Tokyo, Hamburg, and Dresden were indicted; nor were those who

---

4. "Nuremberg Trials," *Wikipedia,* last modified on November 2, 2014, http://en.wikipedia.org/wiki/Nuremberg_Trials.

dropped the atomic bombs on Hiroshima and Nagasaki; nor were Churchill and Truman (Franklin Roosevelt having already departed this realm of political strife). Strange to say, Hitler himself originally came to power through democratic procedures, which shows that sometimes democracy is not enough to absolve a leader of criminal acts. Winning a war may also prove decisive when innocence and guilt are being decided and punishments administered.

I fully understand how most Americans would react to the preceding observations. They would say that in wartime, certain actions that would be regarded as crimes during peacetime automatically cease to have this character. It's an interesting theory: if the leader, especially a democratically elected one, prosecutes a war, he thereby overturns the entire basis of morality—provided of course that his side wins the war. Killing the innocent, for example, carries no stigma; nor does wanton destruction of property, unjust punishment or imprisonment, and a thousand other actions that would be regarded as flagrant crimes during peacetime.

As the government has grown in this country (and others) during the past century, the scope of government action has widened greatly. Government officials now demand vastly greater sums of money from their subjects, and they demand compliance with vastly more regulations. They and they alone may act in these ways without bringing moral denunciation down on themselves. No wonder they sometimes deport themselves as gods: by their election they have been loosed from the moral bonds that constrain you and me, and, thus unencumbered, they have soared to ever greater heights of criminality and savagery. "When the president does it," Richard Nixon insisted,[5] "that means that it is not illegal." Interviewer David Frost pursued the point, asking: "the dividing line is the president's judgment?" To which Nixon responded, "Yes, and the dividing line and, just so that one does not get the impression that a president can run amok in this country and get away with it, we have to have in mind that a president has to come up before the electorate." Ah, yes, blessed election—that "accountability moment," as George W. Bush

---

5. "Nixon's Views on Presidential Power: Excerpts from a 1977 Interview with David Frost," at www.streetlaw.org/en/Page/722/Nixons_Views_on_Presidential_Power_Excerpts _from_a_1977_Interview_with_David_Frost.

described[6] it—surely covers a multitude of sins. We may think of those sins as democracy in action.

Libertarians often argue about whether they might more successfully recruit followers by showing that a free society works best or by showing that an unfree society is unjust. Most libertarians, as I see the matter, have chosen to base their arguments on utilitarian grounds, often because they despair of ever convincing the average person that government officials chronically, or even intrinsically, violate moral strictures. Although I have no doubt whatsoever that free societies do work better than unfree ones, that they deliver, for example, greater prosperity and more rapid economic progress for the masses, I am skeptical that we can cut deeply into the current mass support for the welfare-warfare-therapeutic state unless we open people's eyes to see that the government actions they now support—and demand ever more of—are utterly immoral because they violate individuals' just rights on a gigantic scale and because the government leaders who propose and implement these measures acquire not an ounce of moral justification from their democratic selection for office. "What works best" remains ever open to dispute, as public policy debate on almost any current issue illustrates: each side has its academic experts, prestigious scientists, or other authorities to prop up its position, and although these two sides rarely offer equally compelling evidence, the lay person can scarcely be expected to see through all of the disinformation and rhetorical flimflam.

Everybody understands, however, without any advanced instruction in the matter, that murder and robbery are wrong, and that no one has a justifiable right to bully his neighbors simply because he does not like the way in which they are conducting their lives. The greatest barrier to libertarian progress continues to be that most people give a moral pass to such criminal actions when democratically elected functionaries take them. This presumed moral immunity by virtue of election to public office is the sheerest superstition—a monstrous mistake in moral reasoning—and if people can be brought to see it for what it really is, they will be able to act more effectively to regain some of their lost freedom.

---

6. Michael A. Fletcher and Jim VandeHei, "Transcript of Bush Interview," *The Washington Post* online, January 16, 2005, http://www.washingtonpost.com/wp-dyn/articles/A12570 -2005Jan15.html.

5

Nothing Outside the State

A POPULAR SLOGAN[1] of the Italian Fascists under Mussolini was, "Tutto nello Stato, niente al di fuori dello Stato, nulla contro lo Stato" (everything for the state, nothing outside the state, nothing against the state). I recall this expression frequently as I observe the state's far-reaching penetration of my own society.

What of any consequence remains beyond the state's reach in the United States today? Not wages, working conditions, or labor–management relations; not health care; not money, banking, or financial services; not personal privacy; not transportation or communication; not education or scientific research; not farming or food supply; not nutrition or food quality; not marriage or divorce; not child care; not provision for retirement; not recreation; not insurance of any kind; not smoking or drinking; not gambling; not political campaign funding or publicity; not real estate development, house construction, or housing finance; not international travel, trade, or finance; not a thousand other areas and aspects of social life.

One might affirm that the state still keeps its hands off religion, but it actually does not. It certifies certain religious organizations as legitimate and condemns others, as many young men discovered to their sorrow when they attempted to claim the status of conscientious objector during the Vietnam War. It assigns members of certain religions, but not members of others, as chaplains in its armed services.

---

1. "Italian Fascism," *Wikipedia,* last modified November 24, 2014, http://en.wikipedia.org/wiki/Italian_Fascism.

Besides, isn't statism itself a religion for most Americans? Do they not honor the state above all else, above even the commandments of a conventional religion they may claim to embrace? If their religion tells them "thou shalt not murder," but the state orders them to murder, then they murder. If the state tells them to rob, to destroy property, and to imprison innocent people, then, notwithstanding any religious strictures, they rob, destroy property, and imprison innocent people, as millions of victims of the wars in Iraq and Afghanistan and millions of victims of the so-called Drug War in this country will attest. Moreover, in every form of adversity, Americans look to the state for their personal salvation, just as before the twentieth century their ancestors looked to Divine Providence.

When the state produces unworkable or unsatisfactory conditions in any area of life, and therefore elicits complaints and protests, as it has for example in every area related to health care, it responds to these complaints and protests by making "reforms" that heap new laws, regulations, and government bureaus atop the existing mountain of counterproductive interventions. Thus, each new "reform" makes the government more monstrous and destructive than it already was. Citizen, be careful what you wish for; the government just might give it to you good and hard.

The areas of life that remain outside the government's participation, taxation, subsidization, regulation, surveillance, and other intrusion or control have become so few and so trivial that they scarcely merit mention. We verge ever closer on the condition in which everything that is not prohibited is required. Yet the average American will declare loudly that he is a free man and that his country is the freest in the world. Thus, in a country where more and more is for the state, where virtually nothing is outside the state, and where, aside from pointless complaints, nothing against the state is permitted, Americans have become ideal fascist citizens. Like the average German during the years that Hitler ruled Germany, most Americans today, inhabiting one of the most pervasively controlled countries in the history of the world, think they are free.

6

Consent of the Governed?

WHAT GIVES SOME people the right to rule others? At least since John Locke's time, the most common and seemingly compelling answer has been "the consent of the governed."[1] When the North American revolutionaries set out to justify their secession from the British Empire, they declared, among other things: "Governments are instituted among Men, deriving their just Powers from the Consent of the Governed." This sounds good, especially if one doesn't think about it very hard or very long, but the harder and longer one thinks about it, the more problematic it becomes.

One question after another comes to mind. Must every person consent? If not, how many must, and what options do those who do not consent have? What form must the consent take—verbal, written, explicit, implicit? If implicit, how is it to be registered? Given that the composition of society is constantly changing, owing to births, deaths, and international migration, how often must the rulers confirm that they retain the consent of the governed? And so on and on. Political legitimacy, it would appear, presents a multitude of difficulties when we move from the realm of theoretical abstraction to that of practical validation.

I raise this question because in regard to the so-called *social contract*,[2] I have often had occasion to protest that I haven't even seen the contract, much less been asked to consent to it. A valid contract requires voluntary offer, acceptance, and consideration. I've never received an offer from my rulers, so I

---

1. "Consent of the Governed," *Wikipedia*, last modified on November 20, 2014, http://en.wikipedi.org/wiki/consent_of_the_governed.

2. "Social Contract," *Wikipedia*, last modified on November 19, 2014, http://en.wikipedia.org/wiki/social_contract.

certainly have not accepted one; and rather than consideration, I have received nothing but contempt from the rulers, who, notwithstanding the absence of any agreement, have indubitably threatened me with grave harm in the event that I fail to comply with their edicts. What monumental effrontery these people exhibit! What gives them the right to rob me and push me around? It certainly is not *my* desire to be a sheep for them to shear or slaughter as they deem expedient for the attainment of their own ends.

Moreover, when we flesh out the idea of "consent of the governed" in realistic detail, the whole notion quickly becomes utterly preposterous. Just consider how it would work. A would-be ruler approaches you and offers a contract for your approval. Here, says he, is the deal.

I, the party of the first part ("the ruler"), promise:

(1) To stipulate how much of your money you will hand over to me, as well as how, when, and where the transfer will be made. You will have no effective say in the matter, aside from pleading for my mercy, and if you should fail to comply, my agents will punish you with fines, imprisonment, and—in the event of your persistent resistance—death.

(2) To make thousands upon thousands of rules for you to obey without question, again on pain of punishment by my agents. You will have no effective say in determining the content of these rules, which will be so numerous, complex, and in many cases beyond comprehension that no human being could conceivably know about more than a handful of them, much less their specific character, yet if you should fail to comply with any of them, I will feel free to punish you to the extent of a law made by me and my confederates.

(3) To provide for your use, on terms stipulated by me and my agents, so-called public goods and services. Although you may actually place some value on a few of these goods and services, most will have little or no value to you, and some you will find utterly abhorrent, and in no event will you as an individual have any effective say over the goods and services I provide, notwithstanding any economist's cock-and-bull story to the effect that you "demand" all of this stuff and value it at whatever amount of money I choose to expend for its provision.

(4) In the event of a dispute between us, judges beholden to me for their appointment and salaries will decide how to settle the dispute. You can expect to lose in these settlements, if your case is heard at all.

In exchange for the foregoing government "benefits," **you, the party of the second part ("the subject"), promise:**

(5) To shut up, make no waves, obey all orders issued by the ruler and his agents, kowtow to them as if they were important, honorable people, and when they say "jump," ask only "how high?"

Such a deal! Can we really imagine that any sane person would consent to it?

Yet the foregoing description of the true social contract into which individuals are said to have entered is much too abstract to capture the raw realities of being governed. In enumerating the actual details, no one has ever surpassed Pierre-Joseph Proudhon, who wrote:

> To be GOVERNED is to be kept in sight, inspected, spied upon, directed, law-driven, numbered, enrolled, indoctrinated, preached at, controlled, estimated, valued, censured, commanded, by creatures who have neither the right, nor the wisdom, nor the virtue to do so. To be GOVERNED is to be at every operation, at every transaction, noted, registered, enrolled, taxed, stamped, measured, numbered, assessed, licensed, authorized, admonished, forbidden, reformed, corrected, punished. It is, under pretext of public utility, and in the name of the general interest, to be placed under contribution, trained, ransomed, exploited, monopolized, extorted, squeezed, mystified, robbed; then, at the slightest resistance, the first word of complaint, to be repressed, fined, despised, harassed, tracked, abused, clubbed, disarmed, choked, imprisoned, judged, condemned, shot, deported, sacrificed, sold, betrayed; and, to crown all, mocked, ridiculed, outraged, dishonored. That is government; that is its justice; that is its morality.[3]

---

3. P-J. Proudhon, *General Idea of the Revolution in the Nineteenth Century*, trans. John Beverley Robinson (London: Freedom Press, 1923), 294.

Nowadays, of course, we would have to supplement Proudhon's admirably precise account by noting that our being governed also entails our being electronically monitored, tracked by orbiting satellites, tased more or less at random, and invaded in our premises by SWAT teams of police, often under the pretext of their overriding our natural right to decide what substances we will ingest, inject, or inhale into what used to be known as "our own bodies."

So, to return to the question of political legitimacy as determined by the consent of the governed, it appears upon sober reflection that the whole idea is as fanciful as the unicorn. No one in his right mind, save perhaps an incurable masochist, would voluntarily consent to be treated as governments actually treat their subjects.

Nevertheless, very few of us in this country at present are actively engaged in armed rebellion against our rulers. And it is precisely this absence of outright violent revolt that, strange to say, some commentators take as evidence of our *consent* to the outrageous manner in which the government treats us. Grudging, prudential acquiescence, however, is not the same thing as consent, especially when the people acquiesce, as I do, only with simmering, indignant resignation.

For the record, I can state in complete candor that I do *not* approve of the manner in which I am being treated by the liars, thieves, and murderers who style themselves the Government of the United States of America or by those who constitute the tyrannical pyramid of state, local, and hybrid governments with which this country is massively infested. My sincere wish is that all of these individuals would, for once in their despicable lives, do the honorable thing—that is, resign their offices, seek forgiveness from their victims, and undertake to make restitution for their damages.

Addendum on "love it or leave it": Whenever I write along the foregoing lines, I always receive messages from Neanderthals who, imagining that I "hate America," demand that I get the hell out of this country and go back to wherever I came from. Such reactions evince not only bad manners, but a fundamental misunderstanding of my grievance. I most emphatically do not hate America. I was not born in some foreign despotism, but in a domestic one known as Oklahoma, which I understand to be the very heart and soul of this country so far as culture and refinement are concerned. I yield to no one in my affection for the Statue of Liberty, the Rocky Mountains, and the amber waves of grain, not to mention the celebrated jumping frog of Calaveras County. So when I am invited to get out of the country, I feel like someone living in a town taken over by the James gang who has been told that if he doesn't like being robbed and bullied by uninvited thugs, he should move to another town. To me, it seems much more fitting that the criminals get out.

7

Why This Gigantic "Intelligence" Apparatus?

Follow the Money

THE WASHINGTON POST published yesterday the first of three large reports[1] by Dana Priest and William M. Arkin on the dimensions of the gigantic U.S. apparatus of "intelligence" activities being undertaken to combat terrorist acts against the United States, such as the 9/11 attacks. To say that this activity amounts to mobilizing every police officer in the country to stop street fights in Camden only begins to suggest its almost unbelievable disproportion to the alleged threat.

Among Priest and Arkin's findings from a two-year study are the following:

> The top-secret world the government created in response to the terrorist attacks of Sept. 11, 2001, has become so large, so unwieldy and so secretive that no one knows how much money it costs, how many people it employs, how many programs exist within it or exactly how many agencies do the same work.

> [We] discovered what amounts to an alternative geography of the United States, a Top Secret America hidden from public view and lacking in thorough oversight. After nine years of unprecedented spending and growth, the result is that the system put in place to keep the United States safe is so massive that its effectiveness is impossible to determine. Some 1,271 government organizations and 1,931 private companies work on programs related to counterterrorism, homeland security and intelligence in about 10,000 locations across the United States. An estimated

---

1. Dana Priest and William M. Arkin, "A Hidden World, Growing Beyond Control," *The Washington Post* online, July 19, 2010, http://projects.washingtonpost.com/top-secret-america/articles/a-hidden-world-growing-beyond-control/.

854,000 people, nearly 1.5 times as many people as live in Washington, D.C., hold top-secret security clearances.

In Washington and the surrounding area, 33 building complexes for top-secret intelligence work are under construction or have been built since September 2001. Together they occupy the equivalent of almost three Pentagons or 22 U.S. Capitol buildings—about 17 million square feet of space.

Many security and intelligence agencies do the same work, creating redundancy and waste. For example, 51 federal organizations and military commands, operating in 15 U.S. cities, track the flow of money to and from terrorist networks. Analysts who make sense of documents and conversations obtained by foreign and domestic spying share their judgment by publishing 50,000 intelligence reports each year—a volume so large that many are routinely ignored.[2]

According to retired admiral Dennis C. Blair, formerly the director of national intelligence, after 9/11 "the attitude was, if it's worth doing, it's probably worth overdoing." I submit that this explanation does not cut to the heart of the matter. As it stands, it suggests a sort of mindless desire to pile mountains of money, technology, and personnel on top of an already enormous mountain of money, technology, and personnel for no reason other than the vague notion that more must be better. In my view, national politics does not work in that way.

As Priest and Arkin report, "The U.S. intelligence budget is vast, publicly announced last year as $75 billion, 2 ½ times the size it was on Sept. 10, 2001. But the figure doesn't include many military activities or domestic counterterrorism programs." Virtually everyone the reporters consulted told them in effect that "the Bush administration and Congress gave agencies more money than they were capable of responsibly spending." To be sure, they received more than they could spend *responsibly*, but not more than they were eager to spend irresponsibly. After all, it's not as if they were spending their own money.

Why would these hundreds of organizations and contracting companies be willing to take gigantic amounts of the taxpayers' money when everyone agrees that the money cannot be spent sensibly and that the system already

---

2. Priest and Arkin, "Hidden World."

in place cannot function effectively or efficiently to attain its ostensible purpose? The question answers itself. It's loot for the taking, and there has been no shortage of takers. Indeed, these stationary bandits continue to demand more money each year.

And for what? The announced goal is to identify terrorists and eliminate them or prevent them from carrying out their nefarious acts. This task is simultaneously a small one and an impossible one. It is small because the number of persons seeking to carry out a terrorist act of substantial consequence against the United States and in a position to do so cannot be more than a handful. If the number were greater, we would have seen many more attacks or attempted attacks during the past decade—after all, the number of possible targets is virtually unlimited, and the attackers might cause some form of damage in countless ways. The most plausible reason why so few attacks or attempted attacks have occurred is that very few persons have been trying to carry them out. (I refer to genuine attempts, not to the phony-baloney schemes planted in the minds of simpletons by government undercover agents and then trumpeted to the heavens when the FBI "captures" the unfortunate victims of the government's entrapment.)

So the true dimension of the terrorism problem that forms the excuse for these hundreds of programs of official predation against the taxpayers is small—not even of the same order of magnitude as, say, reducing automobile-accident or household-accident deaths by 20 percent. Yet, at the same time, the antiterrorism task is impossible because terrorism is a simple act available in some form to practically any determined adult with access to Americans and their property at home or abroad. It is simply not possible to stop all acts of terrorism if potential terrorists have been given a sufficient grievance to motivate their wreaking some form of havoc against Americans. However, it is silly to make the prevention of all terrorist acts the goal. What can't be done won't be done, regardless of how many people and how much money one devotes to doing it. We can, though, endure some losses from terrorism in the same way that we routinely endure some losses from accidents, diseases, and ordinary crime.

The sheer idiocy of paying for "analysis" carried out by legions of twenty-something grads of Harvard and Yale—youngsters who cannot speak Arabic, Farsi, Pashtun, or any of the other languages of the areas they purport to be analyzing and who know practically nothing of the history, customs, folk-ways, and traditions of these places—indicates that no one seriously expects the promised payoff in intelligence to emerge from the effort. The whole business is akin to sending a blind person to find a needle inside a maze buried somewhere in a hillside. That the massive effort is utterly uncoordinated and scarcely able to communicate one part's "findings" to another only strengthens the conclusion that the goal is not stopping terrorism, but getting the taxpayers' money and putting it into privileged pockets. Even if the expected damage from acts of terrorism against the United States were $10 billion per year, which seems much too high a guess, it makes no sense to spend more than $75 billion every year to prevent it—and it certainly makes no sense to spend any money only pretending to prevent it.

What we see here is not really an "intelligence" or counterterrorism operation at all. It's a rip-off, plain and simple, fed by irrational fear and continually stoked by the government plunderers who are exercising the power and raking in the booty to "fight terrorism."

8

Can the Dead (Capitalism) Be Brought Back to Life?

I POSE THIS QUESTION seriously, not as a physiologist, but as an economic historian. I am provoked to raise the question by an advertisement that Amazon sent me recently, calling to my attention a book titled *Can Capitalism Survive? Creative Destruction and the Future of the Global Economy.*[1] Seeing this sales pitch, my immediate reaction was my usual sadly amused reply to such a question: Can capitalism survive? What an odd question! Assuming that capitalism ever existed at all, it has been dead for at least a century.

At first glance, I did not recognize that the book being advertised is one for which, in a sense, I am responsible. It turns out that the "new" book is only an old (portion of a) book, now adorned by a new subtitle and two new introductory paragraphs by the *Newsweek* columnist Robert J. Samuelson. If I reveal that the book's author is Joseph A. Schumpeter, many readers will recognize it immediately as Part II of that famous economist's best-known work *Capitalism, Socialism and Democracy,*[2] first published in 1942, with subsequent editions in 1947 and 1950.

The new book's front cover has a blurb from *Fortune* that declares Schumpeter to have been "the most influential economist of the twentieth century . . . a major prophet." The back cover has an embarrassingly superficial blurb by publisher Steve Forbes that, among other things, describes Schumpeter as "the twentieth century's foremost economist."

---

1. Joseph A. Schumpeter, *Can Capitalism Survive? Creative Destruction and the Future of the Global Economy* (New York: Harper Perennial, 2009).

2. Joseph A. Schumpeter, *Capitalism, Socialism, and Democracy,* Third Edition (New York: Harper Perennial, 1950).

I do not consider Schumpeter entitled to be called the most influential economist of the past century—that distinction unfortunately belongs to John Maynard Keynes, and Milton Friedman surely deserves the second place. As for Schumpeter's rank as a prophet or as the intellectually foremost economist, I would place him below Ludwig von Mises and F. A. Hayek.

Nevertheless, Schumpeter was unquestionably one of the most important economists of his day, and his work has continued for good reason to attract readers ever since his death in 1950. His analysis of the historical dynamics of classic capitalism, which makes up Part II of *Capitalism, Socialism, and Democracy*, though contestable on various grounds, may be, all in all, the best ever written, and it certainly remains among the most thought-provoking. (My own thoughts on Schumpeter's analysis appear briefly in my book *Crisis and Leviathan*,[3] pp. 239–44.)

In the mid-1970s, having read *Capitalism, Socialism, and Democracy* repeatedly and having used it to good effect in my teaching, I sent a proposal to Harper & Row, the publisher. I proposed that Part II of the book be published as a separate work with an introduction by me. I asked for a reasonable royalty on sales of this proposed book. Harper & Row declined my offer. The publisher liked the idea of a stand-alone publication of Part II, with my introduction, but did not want to pay me a royalty. Not long afterward, in 1978, I was surprised to find in the bookstores the very volume I had proposed, with an introduction by Robert Lekachman, who evidently had been willing to work for less than I when he was approached by the publisher. Somewhat pushed out of shape by this pilfering of my idea, I wrote a letter to Harper & Row to let their managers know how unprofessional, at best, I considered their action to be. As I recall—although my memory is foggy in this regard—Harper then sent me a nominal "finder's fee."

(This episode, by the way, was but one of many that led me to propound Higgs's Law of Publishing, which states: All publishers strive to maximize losses, but by virtue of sheer stupidity, some of them screw up so royally that they earn enough income to remain in business.)

---

3. Robert Higgs, *Crisis and Leviathan: Critical Episodes in the Growth of American Government* (New York: Oxford University Press, 1987).

Returning from the foregoing personal digression, what are we to make of the idea that capitalism might survive, indeed, of the idea that it has survived to date, when in fact it has scarcely ever existed and, even when prevailing economic conditions and institutions verged most closely on the capitalist model, sometime between the 1830s and World War I in the United States, they suffered a variety of government interventions and distortions that made the prevailing economic order, like nearly all such orders in reality, a form of "mixed economy"?

My friend Sheldon Richman has been on something of a crusade[4] recently against the defense of *capitalism* by those who favor a free society, which of course includes a free-market economy. He prefers that defenders of freedom avoid the defense of something called capitalism because, first, the term derives in large part from enemies of the free society, such as the Marxists, and, second, because it has always served and continues to serve the enemies of a free society as a perennial object of misplaced responsibility, a (nonexistent) malefactor to be blamed for every economic problem the government's countless interventions bring about.

Thus, most recently, by undertaking a series of decisive interventions stretching from the Fed's mismanagement of monetary policy, to Fannie and Freddie's subsidies of unqualified home buyers, to the self-serving idiocies of Barney Frank, Chris Dodd, and Co., among other ill-fated actions, the government created the complex of interrelated disasters that includes the housing boom and bust, the financial debacle of 2008, and the economic recession since 2007. And who's to blame? That's right: capitalism. Which must then be "reformed" by mountains of additional government interventions laid atop the previously existing mountain, leaving, of course, Barney and Chris sitting pretty as the reformers, and the key troublemakers—the Fed, Fannie, and Freddie—smelling like roses, with the Fed being given even more power, and Fannie and Freddie being fed a diet of hundreds of billions of dollars in ongoing taxpayer-funded bailouts to continue doing the damage they do.

---

4. Sheldon Richman, "Libertarians Against Capitalism," *Free Association*, http://sheldon freeassociation.blogspot.com/2010/01/libertarians-against-capitalism.html.

Perhaps, if we all frankly admitted that capitalism has been as dead as a dodo since 1914, if not even longer, then such factually absurd, ideologically inspired, politically tactical blame-casting would be obviated. It would make no more sense than blaming our economic troubles on the divine right of absolute monarchs, centuries after that doctrine has been abandoned. Perhaps.

So far, however, I have refrained from coming completely onboard Richman's crusade ship. For many proponents of the free society, *capitalism* has always signified the ideal of the free-market society more than it has referred to any of its deeply compromised and distorted instantiations that have occurred historically. These people are understandably reluctant to give up still another cherished shibboleth to their enemies, as they previously surrendered their most positive and important ideological identity as *liberals*. So, even though I rarely use the term *capitalism*, and I strive to make as clear as I can the difference between the ideal free society (which I defend) and the realities of any existing or previously existing society (which I only study), for now, I decline to condemn those who continue to defend *capitalism*. They may be making a rhetorical mistake, as Richman insists, yet their hearts are in the right place. It will be easier to straighten out people's rhetoric in due course than to bring about the change of heart that so many misguided people must experience if even a shred of freedom is to be preserved.

9

The Welfare State Neutralizes Potential Opponents by Making Them Dependent on Government Benefits

FROM TIME IMMEMORIAL—from Etienne de la Boitie to David Hume to Ludwig von Mises—political analysts have noted that because the number of those in the ruling elite amounts to only a small fraction of the number in the ruled masses, every regime lives or dies in accordance with "public opinion." Unless the mass of the people, no matter how objectively abused and plundered they may appear to be, believe that the existing rulers are legitimate, the masses will not tolerate the regime's continuation in power. Nor need they tolerate it, because they greatly outnumber the rulers, and hence whenever they become sufficiently fed up, they have the power—which is to say, the overwhelming advantage of superior numbers—to oust the regime. Even if the regime possesses a great advantage of coercive power, its employment avails the rulers nothing if they must kill or imprison 90 percent of the population, because such massive violence would reduce them to the status of parasites without hosts.

This consideration long seemed to make sense as a critical element of political analysis, and even today one often encounters it. Something akin to it seems to motivate the current Occupy Wall Street movement and its spin-offs in other venues when they represent themselves as members of the (exploited) 99 percent, in opposition to the (exploiting) 1 percent.

Certain long-established trends in the welfare state, however, have progressively weakened the force of this analysis. The main element of these trends is the tremendous growth in the number of people (and in their proportion in the population) who are directly dependent on government benefits to a substantial degree. Researchers at the Heritage Foundation have been tracking this development for several years and have pushed their analysis back for several decades. An index of dependency[1] based on this research increases from 19 in fiscal year 1962 to 272 in fiscal year 2009.

The Heritage index uses information on almost three dozen important federal programs on which Americans depend for cash income and other support—including housing assistance, Medicaid, Medicare, Social Security, unemployment insurance benefits, educational benefits, and farm-income supports—but it is scarcely a comprehensive measure, inasmuch as the total number of federal programs with dependents is gigantic at present. Of course, each such program has government employees and contractors who run it and hence depend on it to earn much, if not all, of their income. Government civilian and military retirees add millions more to the ranks.

The Heritage researchers found that in 1962, 21.7 million persons depended on the programs they included in their index for benefits. By 2009, the corresponding number of dependents had grown to 64.3 million. Adding dependents not included in the Heritage study might easily increase the number to more than 100 million, or to more than a third of the entire population. Thus, the parasites verge ever closer to outnumbering their hosts.

It would be a mistake, of course, to lump all of these dependents into the ruling (exploiting) class. The recipients of old-age pensions, the recipients of unemployment insurance benefits, and the beneficiaries of temporary assistance for needy families are, as a rule, as far from the ruling class as one can get. However, to the extent that those who depend on government programs for substantial parts of their income enter the calculus of ruling and being ruled, they are likely to become, in effect, cyphers. They have approximately zero influence on the real rulers, yet they exert virtually no weight in opposition to those rulers, either. Fear of losing their government benefits effectively neutralizes them in regard to opposing the regime on whose seeming beneficence they rely for significant elements of their real income. Of course, for whatever voting may be worth, they vote directly or indirectly in overwhelming proportion for the continuation and budgetary enlargement of the government programs on which they depend. Hence, they help to produce

1. William W. Beach and Patrick Tyrrell, "The 2010 Index of Dependence on Government," *The Heritage Foundation,* http://www.heritage.org/research/reports/2010/10/the-2010-index-of-dependence-on-government.

seeming legitimacy for those at the top of the ruling hierarchy—a token of their appreciation for the crumbs their political masters drop on them.

As the ranks of those dependent on the welfare state continue to grow, the need for the rulers to pay attention to the ruled population diminishes. The masters know full well that the sheep will not bolt the enclosure in which the shepherds are making it possible for them to survive. Every person who becomes dependent on the state simultaneously becomes one less person who might act in some way to oppose the existing regime. Thus have modern governments gone greatly beyond the bread and circuses with which the Roman Caesars purchased the common people's allegiance. In these circumstances, it is hardly surprising that the only changes that occur in the makeup of the ruling elite resemble a shuffling of the occupants in the first-class cabins of a luxury liner. Never mind that this liner is the economic and moral equivalent of the Titanic and that its ultimate fate is no more propitious than was that of the "unsinkable" ship that went to the bottom a century ago.

10

The Systematic
Organization of Hatreds

IN THE MID-1970S, I began to do consulting work in addition to my academic work. By that time, I had become familiar with how economists generally analyze cooperation and competition, in both the economy and the political realm. Economists put great weight on gains from trade. Nobody, they like to say, walks past a $20 bill he sees lying on the sidewalk. If a situation contains the potential for a trade or other arrangement that will bring gain to a decision maker, he will embrace that trade or arrangement. This market process leads, in the theoretical extreme, to the happy condition known as the Pareto Optimum—the situation in which all potential gains from trade have been captured.

Notice that this view of mankind causes us to think of people as self-interested, but not as vicious. Individuals are seen as, in effect, indifferent to the welfare of their trading or cooperating partners, but intent on making themselves as well off as possible. They do not seek to harm others, but only to benefit themselves (and those about whom they happen to care).

As I launched into my consulting work, which involved various efforts by Washington state and the U.S. government to resolve disputes and to increase the harvestable resource in the Washington salmon fishery and the federally regulated offshore salmon fishery in the Pacific Ocean, I quickly learned that the politicians in Olympia did not fit the model I had mastered in my education as an economist. To be sure, they sought to feather their own nests, by hook and by crook. But, in many important cases, they acted simply to hurt their political and personal enemies—whose ranks, in some cases, were quite large. Often, it seemed, Mr. P was clearly "out to get" Mr. Q, and he was not simply seeking this objective, other things being the same; he was actually out to get Mr. Q even if he had to bear a cost in doing so.

So, despite the formal models and informal rhetoric that economists and other academic specialists employ in their research and writing about politics and government, a critical element tends to be completely overlooked: the powerful role of aversion, dislike, and hatred. Economists represent individual preference orderings as rankings of valued options: good thing A > good thing B > good thing C, and so on. But for political actors, the preference ordering often looks more like: good thing A > hurt person X > good thing B > hurt person Y > good thing C, and so on.

This sort of preference is the political sentiment Vladimir Lenin expressed when he remarked: "My words were calculated to evoke hatred, aversion and contempt . . . not to convince but to break up the ranks of the opponent, not to correct an opponent's mistake, but to destroy him." Closer to home, Henry Adams observed that "politics, as a practice, whatever its professions, has always been the systematic organization of hatreds."

We see the importance of this element of politics clearly in the contemporary conflict between Democrats and Republicans. Given that these two parties are but two wings of the same predatory one-party state that rules the United States, we might well wonder why their intramural feuding often reaches such vitriolic extremes. The short answer is that despite the two parties' general similarity of fundamental positions, they comprise somewhat different sorts of people—different in regard to religious conviction (or the lack thereof), typical social position, culture, background, occupational distribution, urban-rural composition, and ethnic makeup, among other things—and the two groups tend to dislike each other; indeed, in many individual instances, they despise one another. And their political representatives, though more inclined to conspire and cut deals with the other side, also represent their supporters along the hatred dimension. Occasionally, when a politician does not realize that the microphone is live, we hear some honest expression of his true feelings about his political opponents—"enemies" is the more accurate word.

In view of the foregoing, we are well advised to consider that whenever we seek to move a type of decision-making from private life to the realm of politics and government, we are very likely moving it from a world in which hatred is incidental and avoidable to a world in which hatred is central and inescapable. Because a government imposes one rule, one outcome, one state of affairs on everyone subject to its rule, the hatreds that go into the making of that outcome become generalized and infused throughout the entire society. Thus, what economists label a "public good" is often, in the most substantive way, a "public bad." Even if a person does not share any of the component hatreds that political actors express and deploy, no one can avoid living in a politicized world fashioned in such large part by the organized expression of hatred. It is, therefore, small wonder that some of us view the entire apparatus of politics and government as the living embodiment of evil.

Even a devout Christian has no small difficulty in following Christ's admonition to "love your enemies and pray for those who persecute you." But when we live and act in the private realm, we can make our best attempt to love others or at least to tolerate them in peace, and we have many options for avoiding or running away from hateful people and situations; occasionally we may even be able to lead someone, or ourselves, to substitute love, or at least understanding, for hatred.

In politics and government, however, the institutional makeup fosters hatred at every turn. Parties recruit followers by exploiting hatreds. Bureaucracies bulk up their power and budgets by artfully weaving hatreds into their mission statements and day-to-day procedures. Regulators take advantage of artificially heightened hatreds. Group identity is emphasized at every turn, and such tribal distinctions are tailor-made for the maintenance and increase of hatred among individual persons who might otherwise disregard the kinds of groupings that the politicians and their supporters emphasize ceaselessly.

With a sigh, many people accept that politics and government are, at best, necessary evils. I have great doubt that they are necessary, at least in their present form, but I am certain that in this form they are evil.

11

All Men Are Brothers, but All Too Often They Do Not Act Accordingly

IN "THE COMMUNIST MANIFESTO," Marx and Engels tell us that "[t]he history of all hitherto existing society is the history of class struggles." In a sense I agree, although I define the struggling classes differently than they did. In any event, it seems clear enough from what we know about the past ten thousand years or so of human history that people everywhere have been marvelously creative in finding ways to define certain people as members of a class or other group that can and should be treated with contempt, denied equal justice, and exploited without mercy.

Sometimes the groups have been defined along racial or ethnic lines, at other times along religious lines, at still other times along lines of their place of birth or their citizenship status, sometimes by their level or kind of education, sometimes by the language they speak, and so forth, on and on.

When I was a boy, growing up in the San Joaquin Valley of California, I lived in a place where about two-thirds of the population consisted of Mexicans and their native-born children, people who often suffered mistreatment at the hands of the authorities and members of the public. For many of them, the fear of deportation and police abuse was a constant in their lives.

I myself, however, was a member of a different despised class, the migrants from Oklahoma known as Okies. Although these people had previously suffered considerable mistreatment at the hands of the California legislature, police, landowners, and others, by the time my family arrived, in 1951, such mistreatment had greatly moderated, and although I was always aware that we Okies were looked down on by some people for our poverty, our lack of education, and our speech, I never dwelt on such minor lack of respect, and indeed I personally suffered not at all in this regard when I attended the same small-town schools as everyone else and succeeded there academically and athletically without my group membership's holding me back at all.

After I became a professor, I spent much of my time during the first fifteen years of my career engaged in research and writing about American blacks since the War Between the States.[1] This work was often hard to bear because of the nature of the subject. It was not that I was studying people who had low incomes, little education, or other deficiencies, often as a result of their treatment at the hands of the powers that were, especially in the South. It was more because of how the whites in general treated the blacks with contempt and viewed them as inferior by virtue of nothing but their race. This sort of pervasive withholding of basic human respect made my blood boil. As I studied occasions when such disrespect spilled over into the outrages for which the South became justly infamous—lynchings and similar savageries—I often had to struggle to keep my tears from staining my notes.

Nowadays, I have the same reaction to the contempt with which so many Americans treat the migrants from Mexico, Central America, and elsewhere solely because they belong to a different ethnic group, speak a different language, are very poor, or—worst of all—lack the official stamp of government approval that endows them with permission to be here, a right that no peaceful person ought to have been denied in the first place. Reading about the injustices perpetrated so lavishly on these people, especially by police, but also by various vigilantes, nativists, xenophobes, and other yahoos, I find again that my blood boils and my tears well up.

When, oh when, will people finally learn to treat all human beings as their brothers and sisters? Sad to say, I believe the answer is, never.

---

1. Robert Higgs, *Competition and Coercion: Blacks in the American Economy 1865–1914*, Reprint Edition (Cambridge: Cambridge University Press, 2008 [1977]).

12

Once More, with Feeling

Our System Is Not Socialism,
but Participatory Fascism

I CONTINUE TO encounter many discussions in which the author or speaker bemoans the economic order's drift toward socialism or, in some cases, its actual existence as such. If this characterization were simply a matter of linguistic imprecision, it might not matter much. But it is much more than a matter of terminology, because one's understanding of the nature of our current economic order hinges on how we characterize it.

Socialism is a system in which all the major means of production are owned and operated by the state. Except perhaps for small firms or farms, all productive enterprises are state enterprises. All natural resources belong to the state. All resources are allocated and employed as the state dictates, insofar as its dictates can actually be carried out in practice (all such systems display much slack between orders given and actual conduct on the ground, owing to corruption and attempts to "fix" flaws embedded in the state's overall plan).

Obviously the economic order that prevails in the economically advanced countries is not socialism. Indeed, these systems are commonly called capitalistic or market-oriented, notwithstanding the many types of government intervention that pervade their markets—various taxes, subsidies, direct government production, and regulations galore. Some people refer to these systems as "mixed economies," which at least helps us to recognize that they are not market economies in any pure sense, not even in an approximate one. But in calling them mixed economies, we gain no insight into their nature or operation.

For thirty years or so, I have used the term "participatory fascism,"[1] which I borrowed from my old friend and former Ph.D. student Charlotte Twight. This is a descriptively precise term in that it recognizes the fascistic organization of resource ownership and control in our system, despite the preservation of nominal private ownership, and the variety of ways in which the state employs political ceremonies, proceedings, and engagements—most important, voting—in which the general public participates. Such participation engenders the sense that somehow the people control the government. Even though this sense of control is for the most part an illusion, rather than a perception well founded in reality, it is important because it causes people to accept government regulations, taxes, and other insults against which they might rebel if they believed that such impositions had simply been forced on them by dictators or other leaders wholly beyond their influence.

For the rulers, participatory fascism is the perfect solution toward which they have been groping for generations, and virtually all of the world's politico-economic orders are now gravitating toward this system. Outright socialism is a recipe for widespread poverty and for the ultimate dissolution of the economy and the disavowal of its political leadership. Socialism is the wave of the past; everywhere it has been tried seriously, it has failed miserably. Participatory fascism, in contrast, has two decisive advantages over socialism.

The first is that it allows the nominal private owners of resources and firms enough room for maneuver that they can still innovate, prosper, and hence propel the system toward higher levels of living for the masses. If the government's intervention is pushed too far, this progress slows, and it may eventually cease or even turn into economic regress. However, when such untoward conditions occur, the rulers tend to rein in their plunder and intervention enough to allow a revitalization of the economy. Of course, such fettered economies cannot grow as fast as completely free economies can grow, but the latter system would preclude the plunder and control that the political leaders now enjoy in the fettered system, and hence they greatly prefer the slower-growing, great-plunder system to the faster-growing, no-plunder one.

---

1. Chris Matthew Sciabarra, "Higgs and 'Participatory Fascism,'" *History News Network,* http://hnn.us/blog/7849.

Meanwhile, most people are placated by the economic progress that does occur and by their participation in political and legal proceedings that give them the illusion of control and fair treatment. Although the political system is rigged in countless ways to favor incumbent rulers and their key supporters, it is far from dictatorial in the way that Stalin's Russia or Hitler's Germany was dictatorial. People therefore continue to believe that they are free, notwithstanding the death of their liberties by a thousand cuts that continues day by day.

Participatory fascism's second great advantage over socialism is that when serious economic problems do arise, as they have during the past five years, the rulers and their key supporters in the "private" sector can blame residual elements of the market system, and especially the richest people who operate in that system, for the perceived ills. No matter how much the problems arise from government intervention, it is always possible to lay the blame on actors and institutions in the remaining "free enterprises," especially the biggest bankers and other apparent top dogs. Thus, fascistic rulers have built-in protection against popular reaction that the rulers in a socialist system lack. (Rulers under socialism tend to designate foreign governments and capitalists and domestic "wreckers" as the scapegoats for their mismanagement and inability to conduct economic affairs productively and fairly.)

Americans do not like to admit that they live in a system that is most accurately characterized as participatory fascism. They insist that fascism requires death camps, goose-stepping brown shirts, comical yet murderous leaders in funny hats, and others hallmarks of the fascism that operated in Germany and Italy between the world wars. But fascism takes many specific forms. If you wish to see the form that it has increasingly taken in the economically advanced countries during the past century, just look around you.

13

Love, Liberty, and the State

LOVE AND LIBERTY are the basic building blocks with which decent people build good lives for themselves.

Love takes many forms—in personal relations, in work and other creative endeavors, in charity toward the needy, in spiritual commitments that give deeper meaning to life amid its inevitable challenges and losses. Love gives us a reason to continue despite discouragements and difficulties, to keep trying to make still another comeback after we have been crushed in body or spirit.

Freedom provides the spaces we need to express our love, to pursue our passions in regard to where and how we live, to choose our goals freely and pursue them as we think best, to practice the arts and professions that most attract us, to allocate our personal and material means as we please in the service of our own purposes, to live without feeling a constant need to look over our shoulders, lest we incur the wrath of a state functionary or a policeman in search of his next victim.

If we have love and liberty, other things follow naturally, at least as naturally as the laws of nature, society, and economics allow. Liberty gives us room to maneuver as we construct our lives in accordance with our loves.

It is no wonder that the state's essential nature entails its thwarting of love and liberty—nay, even worse—its breeding and fostering of their exact opposites.

States thrive on hatred.[1] In their very establishment, through conquest and the pillaging of conquered people, they make themselves hateful by their own

---

1. Robert Higgs, "Fear: The Foundation of Every Government's Power," *The Independent Review* 10:3 (Winter 2005): 447–66.

violence and cruelty. In the course of their post-conquest histories, when the formerly roving bandits have discovered that stationary banditry pays better than hit-and-run plunder, they hold their odious threats of violence constantly over their subjects' heads to ensure that no one dare resist their rule or their demands for tribute and abasement.

After democracy enters the picture, and political parties form coalitions to seize control of state powers, the parties provoke and enlarge hatred in order to attract and maintain loyal members. They constantly harp on how the overriding element in every political issue boils down to a question of "us" against the hated "them." Societal division and conflict form the fertile soil in which they plant their poisonous proposals for robbing "them" and dividing the spoils among "us." Thus, by keeping the pot of (largely artificial) class, group, sectional, and race conflicts boiling, democratic political parties smash the love that might grow among cooperative and peaceful people working together for their mutual advantage and replace it with spiritual turmoil and restless contempt for everyone outside the party's arbitrary bounds.

Of course, it scarcely needs to be said that this kind of organized hatred goes hand in hand with the state's attacks on people's liberties. Some of these attacks aim at damaging the "others" outside the ruling coalition, but some of them ironically damage almost everyone in the service of augmenting the state's power and splendor—always in order (or so the rulers assert) ultimately to serve the general public interest or to gain some great advantage for the nation as a whole, or at least for everyone except the members of unpopular minorities.

Amid the dishonesty, hatred, and violence inherent in a state's rule, whether under democracy or some other political order, decent people lose the freedoms to express their love in peaceful, creative, and productive ways. Like a muscle, love unexercised tends to atrophy. State-dominated societies are always hate-ridden and spiteful; they turn individuals against one another in countless ways as they crush the liberties that allow positive-sum games to proliferate and establish instead negative-sum games in which if a man does not crush his fellow, that fellow will crush him. Envy and suspicion run rampant. The cheerful good natures that readily develop and sustain themselves among peaceful, free, and prosperous people wither away. The whole world turns into East Germany.

Love and liberty are fundamentally incompatible with the state's existence and operation. This relation exists not because states begin good and eventually go bad, but because the state is intrinsically an organization whose establishment and operation rest on violence and plunder, which in turn foster hatred and the denial of liberties. Hence, under state rule, decent people's attempts to build good lives for themselves encounter a plethora of obstacles put in their paths by state functionaries backed by ruling coalitions. Countless intellectuals have reasoned that if the state would only do X, Y, or Z, it would make good lives possible for the masses. Such reasoning flies in the face of the state's very nature. Sensible people do not invite a viper to live in their home, much less to make it happier.

14

Legitimacy

WHAT IS THE DIFFERENCE between a government and a criminal gang or protection racket such as the mafia? In a word, it is legitimacy.[1] In practice, this vague notion suggests that people view the government—its institutional composition, its personnel, and its conduct—as morally acceptable or proper, whereas they view the mafia—at least in its conduct—as morally unacceptable or improper.

Many governments claim that their legitimacy rests on the Lockean grounds of consent of the governed, but in practice this consent proves to be highly problematic because the governed population is rarely, if ever, presented with the choice of being ruled or not being ruled under the established governmental institutions. Regimes use public education, propaganda, judicial decisions (rendered by the government's own judges), political elections, public hearings, and other artifices to imbue the people with the idea that their rulers are legitimate authorities taking legitimate actions. Many if not all of these justificatory efforts are highly questionable, if not entirely bogus, and none of them represents decisive evidence of the people's consent to be ruled as they are by the rulers who dominate them.

In reality, the so-called consent of the governed consists for the most part of mere acquiescence—a widespread resignation that signifies only that most people would rather endure the government's robbery and bullying than openly resist it at the risk of injury, imprisonment, and death. The people's

---

1. "Political Legitimacy," *Wikipedia,* last modified May 12, 2014, http://en.wikipedia.org/wiki/Legitimacy_%28political%29.

acquiescence, in many cases a sort of sullen, resentful, implicit surrender, hardly endows the rulers with any moral approbation. Indeed, even in the countries with the greatest degree of popular political participation, the bulk of the people may look upon the governing politicians and bureaucrats with ill-concealed contempt and sometimes with openly expressed hatred.

If a government succeeds in remaining in power for a long time, however, many people may come to accept it simply by force of habit. In some eyes, it will be seen as beyond question merely because it has "always been there" and its actions amount to "how things are." People of a conservative cast of mind may actually believe that antiquity alone is not only a sufficient but also a compelling basis for the approval and preservation of established institutions. Even great liberal philosophers such as David Hume and, in our own time, Anthony de Jasay consider rights to be nothing but conventions that have somehow become established over long periods and thereby have acquired their bona fides and their demonstrated evolutionary fitness in a society's successful functioning. To be sure, many people get used to things as they are, even when these things are irrational and abusive.

In any event, the ostensible bright-line demarcation of legitimacy that separates the government from ordinary criminal gangs fades and blurs under close inspection. It does not disappear completely, however, because for some portion of the ruled population, the government's efforts to sell its legitimacy do succeed. These beguiled individuals are the ones who volunteer for service in the government's palace guards—its armed forces, police, and other agencies of physical violence and intimidation—and who willingly send their children to be sacrificed in the government's foreign wars and other adventures. They provide, as it were, legions of "essential idiots," parallel to the "useful idiots" among the intelligentsia, who fight on the government's behalf in the war of ideas and ideologies.

From one country to another, the division of society between the hopelessly beguiled and the merely intimidated varies greatly. All governments seek to move the demarcation line so that a greater proportion of those it rules falls in the former class. Thus all governments carry on ceaseless efforts to convince the people of their competence, good intentions, close representation of the people's desires, and morally impeccable standards of conduct. Although these efforts provide little more than fodder for bitter laughter among individuals with open eyes and unsullied hearts, they succeed often enough to keep the rulers afloat as they continue their plunder and repression. Their prevailing legitimacy, however, is rarely anything more than ersatz or counterfeit as a sound foundation for a government whose composition, personnel, and conduct are generally desired and approved.

15

Political Problems Have Only One Real Solution

ELDRIDGE CLEAVER FAMOUSLY declared, "You're either part of the solution or you're part of the problem."[1] Although I did not agree with this sentiment in its original context, it has more definite applicability in regard to what one might think of as "solving political problems."

Notice, first, that politics consists in the struggle to control the power that allows one party (whether an individual or a group) to impose its preferences on other parties who object to this imposition. Some political struggles involve attempts to make new impositions; others involve attempts to throw off existing, unwanted impositions. Because in our time the state is usually the organization that possesses the greatest coercive power, politics often boils down to a contest over who will control the state and how state authorities will wield their power. Politics, in short, ultimately has to do with the question, Who will be master?

When we recognize that political problems always involve this question, we see immediately that they can have no solution short of complete capitulation by the political losers. Unless they concede that others will be their masters, they will continue to struggle, either overtly or covertly, to turn the tables. Thus, political problems remain perpetually unresolved in any more than a tactical, short-term way. Losers may appear to have given up, but usually if not always they will continue to harbor a desire to throw off their master or some aspect of the master's regime and continue to work in some way toward the attainment of that objective.

---

1. Eldridge Cleaver, *BrainyQuote.com*, http://www.brainyquote.com/quotes/quotes/e/eldridgecl163167.html.

Of course, wherever more than one way of dealing with an issue exists, there is no necessity of resort to politics. If everyone agrees to let each party act as it wishes without coercive interference, a genuine political solution does exist: abandon politics. Of course, many social thinkers deny the feasibility of this solution as a general matter, however much they may concede that many issues can be handled satisfactorily by following the rule, *laissez faire, laissez passer.* If no genuine "public goods" exist (as some theorists[2] maintain), however, then complete individual liberty solves every political problem *ipso facto.* Notice, though, that this "political solution" works only because it rules out genuinely political action entirely.

If one is willing to live and let live, to accept that each party may go its own way and deal with its perceived problems as it prefers, provided only that it allow equal latitude to every other party, then all political problems as such evaporate. The difficulty arises from some parties' insistence on having their own way, however objectionable that way may be to other parties. To return to Cleaver's dictum, adding appropriate amendments: You're either part of the solution (by abandoning participation in politics) or you're part of the problem (of endless political conflict).

---

2. Hans-Hermann Hoppe, "Fallacies of the Public Goods Theory and the Production of Security," *Journal of Libertarian Studies* 9:1 (1989): 27–46.

16

The Power of the State versus the Power of Love

FOR THOUSANDS OF YEARS, philosophers have argued that society must invest great power in the rulers because only great power can hold back the forces of evil—violence, plunder, and disorder. They have often conceded, of course, that this solution does have an unfortunate aspect, namely, that with great power, the rulers themselves may resort to violence and plunder and hence create disorder. This defect of the proposed solution deserves, they have counseled, continuing reflection, but by and large they have dealt with it by whistling and gazing at their sandals.

Meanwhile, all the positive, productive forces of society continued to reside, as they always have, within the people themselves. All the genuine peace, cooperation, production, and order the society enjoyed sprang from the people. So the state was not a solution to a problem the people could not solve for themselves, but itself a problem masquerading as the only solution to problems whose real solutions already lay close at hand, if they existed at all. (Some social "problems" have no "solution," properly speaking; they are merely aspects of unalterable reality—unavoidable risks, trade-offs, and so forth.)

Given that creation has more value than destruction, how did it come to pass that the state—an institution based on violence and plunder—has overridden peaceful cooperation as the dominant factor in social life virtually everywhere on earth? This simple question requires, I think, a complex answer. Yet it seems clear enough that the rulers have used fear—of themselves and of other dangers known and unknown—to terrorize the people and convince them that they were incapable of providing the security that only the state can provide. First through fear alone, then through (complementary) religion, and ultimately through (complementary) ideology, the people's beliefs were twisted into the forms compatible with the rulers, the priests, and the military elite's living at the expense of the plundered masses, who were kept in line more by false beliefs than by raw force.

So it remains today. Fear and fear-mongering lead the people to acquiesce in their rulers' bullying and plundering up to the very margin of the people's toleration. This margin, however, can be pushed out by new fears and new fear-mongering and kept from receding by a constant drum-beat of reminders that people are at great risk and that they must allow the state to exercise new powers to protect them.

Is any feasible alternative conceivable?

Hardheaded people mock the idea that "love is the answer" to the people's dire situation. They insist that evil forces and evil men are afoot in the world, men who care nothing for love and seek only vile ends, and that such malevolence can be fended off effectively only by meeting it with adequate force and violence. Thus does the widening "security gap" fuel a race to the bottom in which the ostensible protectors become more and more indistinguishable from the alleged evil men who seek to hurt us. We see, then, that by meeting evil only with the rulers' upward ratcheting force and violence and their upward ratcheting suppression of our liberties and our means of self-protection, the ultimate goal—a social environment of security and peaceful cooperation—only recedes farther and farther from realization as the state destroys, as it were, one free village after another in order, it claims, to save it.

Jesus said, "Ye have heard that it hath been said, Thou shalt love thy neighbour, and hate thine enemy. But I say unto you, Love your enemies, bless them that curse you, do good to them that hate you, and pray for them which despitefully use you, and persecute you" (Matthew 5:43–44). Of course, people, even most Christians, no doubt, will say that this admonition, however lovely it might sound in a sermon, is utterly impractical and that behaving in accordance with it would leave us entirely at the mercy of those who seek to harm us. Perhaps it would.

Yet here we are, inhabitants of a world divided in countless ways by mutual hatreds, misunderstandings, and yearnings for vengeance. Because each society is subject to a state whose own interests are served by keeping this vicious pot boiling, we have no prospect whatever of ever breaking out of the endless cycle of evil, violence, and retribution. In the process, the whole world forgoes the immense blessings that would flow from mutual cooperation, peace, and tolerance.

Individuals may rest their personal lives on love and thereby find the peace that seemingly evades all philosophical and sociological understanding in relation to social affairs. Whatever wise men and women may understand and practice in their own lives, however, the Hobbesian analysis, to a greater or lesser degree, holds the great thinkers in its iron grip, and those who recommend love are dismissed as muddle-headed and simplistic. Yet, to repeat, here we are, inhabitants of a world made no better by our hanging on the words of the greatest political philosophers, statesmen, and international-relations experts. In their views, the state is a given, and their analyses proceed from its nature and functioning. Perhaps this point of departure is their root error: that they take for granted what most needs to be challenged.

Sophomores sometimes joke, "Yeah, love is the answer, all right, but what is the question?" However unwittingly, they may have stumbled toward the crux of the matter. So long as the state goes along its way—intrinsically a way of violence, plunder, and insolence—and we seek only solutions to our pressing social problems that employ the state as the chief means, we are doomed not to second-best or third-best solutions, but to "solutions" that are really nothing of the sort, but at best only momentary rest stops on the highway to our continuing degradation and ultimate demise. Destruction is what states do (or threaten to do); and destruction is what they will continue to do; it is the nature of the beast. As technology bulks up state powers, the only end of this terrible sequence must be our complete destruction.

Love turns us in the opposite direction. It seeks to build up, whereas the state seeks to overawe and kill in the service of the self-interested elites who control it and at the expense of the people at large. Love knows no need for flaunting its powers, for flexing its violent muscles, for taking vengeance time and again. Love intends the good of the other for its own sake, not as a means toward the end of one's own aggrandizement. Love is patient; power is impatient and easily provoked. Love does not keep score; international rivalries count the score in many, many dimensions. Love leads to inner peace; the nation-state remains always at war, if not against other states, then certainly against its own subjects, on whom it preys ceaselessly in order to gain its own sustenance and to gratify the rulers' vaulting and grandiose ambitions for personal acclaim and merciless power.

Hardheaded people will say, of course, that in socio-political life, love just doesn't work. Well, power in the hands of the rulers surely does work. That's the trouble.

17

State Power
and How It Might Be Undermined

STATE POWER IS the most dangerous force in modern life. State rulers, seeking their own aggrandizement and enrichment, employ this power systematically[1] to plunder and abuse their subjects. Of course, they cannot act in this way without the assistance of many others,[2] among whom some assist willingly, some in return for adequate compensation, and many only under duress.

To maintain their grip on power, state rulers (1) bamboozle as many subjects as possible; (2) co-opt those whose cooperation or support is essential by bribing them with various sorts of payoffs; (3) intimidate those who are not essential and not fooled by threatening them with fines, imprisonment, and other punishments; and (4) kill those who are not essential, are not fooled, and will not bend to intimidation.

Anyone who seeks to stymie or overturn state power must block these state actions or render them less effective. Resisters therefore have many options.

First, they may work to reduce the number of people who succumb to the rulers' bamboozlement by exposing the rulers' lies, spreading truthful information, and revealing the rulers' venality and cynical disregard of the people's natural rights and the general public interest. People may withdraw their children from government schools and teach them at home; they may spread truthful information about the horrors of the state and the glories of

---

1. Robert Higgs, *Delusions of Power: New Explorations of the State, War, and Economy* (Oakland, CA: Independent Institute, 2012).

2. Etienne De La Boetie, *The Politics of Obedience: The Discourse of Voluntary Servitude* (Montana: Kessinger Publishing LLC, 2010). Available at http://mises.org/librarypolitics -obedience-discourse-voluntary-servitude.

freedom by means of the Internet and the World Wide Web. In short, people may use the word processor that is mightier than the Predator drone (formerly the pen that is mightier than the sword) as well as face-to-face communication to reeducate those who have been taught, conditioned, and forced to drink's the rulers' Kool-Aid.

Second, resisters may alter the incentives of those who cooperate or support the state in return for various payoffs. For example, companies that seek contracts with the government or privileges gained via regulation, tariff protection, or other anti-social means might be boycotted. If this effort caught on, companies would be put in a position of having to choose between the profits to be gained by serving the state and the profits to be gained by serving consumers in a free market. Just as today many sellers certify that their produce is organic and thereby gain sales at the expense of sellers who cannot make this claim, sellers might certify, via independent third-party certification agencies in the free market, that they are free of government contamination—that is, that they have neither sought nor accepted any contract or privilege from the government.

Those who are currently co-opted by the state might also be subjected to public condemnation, denunciation, and shunning, not only commercially but socially. If a company works with the government's armed forces or its spy agencies, for example, people might treat its owners, executives, and workers as the untouchables were treated in the classic Indian caste system. No matter how much the government offered in pay and perks, some people might be unwilling to invest in or work for companies if such an association would make them social pariahs.

Third, subjects who are currently intimidated by the state's threats of fines, imprisonment, and other punishments might be encouraged by the proliferation of black markets and by the establishment of organizations dedicated to assisting them in their efforts to escape such punishment. Of course, many people already use the services of lawyers, tax advisers, investment advisers, and accountants to help them avoid taxes. Such services might be expanded greatly to assist people in their efforts to circumvent punitive regulations and other punitive state actions. In the extreme, people might build a virtual "parallel universe" in which their economic and social life could proceed on the free side of a de facto barrier against state intrusion.

Fourth, in response to the state's resort to killing those who will not bend to its intimidation, the best course of action is probably emigration. Truly massive emigration takes many exploitable human beings beyond the effective reach of the tyrants. It also sets in motion a virtuous feedback mechanism in which the population losers have an incentive to lighten their oppression *and* the population gainers have an incentive to maintain a freer economic and social environment in order to attract even more productive people whose activities have wealth-enhancing spillover effects in the destination venue. In the nineteenth and early twentieth centuries, this kind of feedback sustained the transfer of more than 30 million[3] productive people from Europe to the United States and played a major role in the USA's rise to economic predominance in the world. People remain, in Julian Simon's happy turn of phrase, the ultimate resource.

Much more might be said about efforts to undercut the sources of state power. The foregoing discussion barely scratches the surface. My aim here is only to clarify the main sources of state power and to point toward ways in which these sources can be undermined or eliminated in order to expand the scope of genuine freedom.

Addendum: Please note that I have said nothing about the use of violence against the state. In general, I oppose such violence. The rulers of leviathan states such as the USA love nothing more than violent resistance. They can deal with such forms of resistance readily by bringing their overwhelming advantages in the use to violence to bear by means of police and, if need be, military forces. Moreover, in doing so, they can teach the false lesson that they are the true protectors of the public against those who threaten the social order by resorting to violence. They thereby encourage the public to think of the violent resisters as the crazies and of the state authorities and their police as the sane and peaceful ones, notwithstanding that the state is nothing if not a massive, bureaucratically organized means of threatening or wielding violence against innocent people in order to plunder and bully them.

---

3. Robert Higgs, *The Transformation of the American Economy, 1865–1914: An Essay in Interpretation* (New York: John Wiley, 1971), 23–24.

18

All Government Policies Succeed in the Long Run

A CRAZY CLAIM you are probably thinking after reading my title. After all, "failed policies" are a staple of discussions and debates about government actions in the United States. Everybody, regardless of political preferences, has a list of what he regards as the most glaringly failed policies. This way of looking at the matter, however, is all wrong.

People label a policy as a failure because it does not bring about its declared objective. For example, drug policies do not reduce drug use; educational policies do not educate children better; national-security policies do not make Americans more secure; and so forth. The mistake is to take seriously the announced policy objectives, to forget that virtually everything the government does is a fraud. The best way to document the government's nearly unblemished record of policy success is to follow the money. With very little trouble, you will be able to follow the trail to the individuals and groups who benefit from the policy. Occasionally the true beneficiaries do not benefit in the form of augmented income or wealth, but in other forms of reward, yet the principle remains the same.

When I first studied economics and began to practice as an economist, back in the sixties and seventies, I learned how markets and the market system as a whole operate. With this understanding in mind, I was able to identify a number of reasons why a particular policy might fail: it might be based on insufficient or incorrect information; it might give rise to unintended consequences; it might receive inadequate funding for its implementation; it might be based on unsound theory or mistaken interpretation of historical experience; and so forth.

Analysts who approach the question of failed policies along these avenues can rest assured that they will never lack for new studies to perform and new measures to propose to legislators, regulators, administrators, and judges. For example, if government fiscal or monetary policy fails to stabilize the economy's growth because it derives from unsound macroeconomic theory, then the analyst attempts to identify the ways in which the received theory is unsound and to formulate a sounder theory, on the basis of which a more successful policy may be carried out. This sort of back and forth between theoretical tinkering and policy appraisal fills many pages in mainstream economics journals.

But it's all a waste of time insofar as the attainment of the ostensible policy objectives is concerned, because these objectives are not the policy-makers' real objectives, but only the public rationales they use to disguise their true objective, which invariably is to bring about the enrichment, aggrandizement, and other benefit of the politically potent individuals and interest groups that pack the decisive punch in the policy-making process—for example, those who can most effectively threaten legislators with affirmative punishments or the withdrawal of financial support for the legislators' reelection if the string pullers' interests are not served.

Almost twenty years ago, I wrote an article on this subject called "The Myth of 'Failed' Policies,"[1] commenting briefly on how seven different areas of important, obvious policy failure illustrate my thesis. Looking back at my 1995 article, I can say now that in each case the apparent "failure" and the actual success have only grown. In each case, much more money is being poured down the rat hole of a failed policy now than was being poured down it then—which is only to say that the American political process is at least as corrupt now as it was then, and probably even more so. Despite various surface changes in policy details, none of the ostensible "failures" has been repaired in the least, even though the apparent failure has become only more blatant and undeniable.

Many people, for good reason, have concluded that the surest test of whether a politician or public official is lying is to ask, Are his lips moving?

---

1. Robert Higgs, "Myth of 'Failed' Policies," *The Free Market* 13, no.6 (1995).

An equally simple test may be proposed to determine whether a seemingly failed policy is actually a success for the movers and shakers of the political class. This test requires only that we ask, Does the policy remain in effect? If it does, we can be sure that it continues to serve the interests of those who are actually decisive in determining the sorts of policy the government establishes and implements. Now, as before, "failed" policies are a myth in regard to all policies that persist beyond the short run. The people who effectively run the government, whether from inside or outside the beast, do not run it for the purpose of hampering the attainment of their own interests; on the contrary. Everything else in the policy process is, as Macbeth would put it, "a tale told by an idiot [augmented by economists, lawyers, and public-relations flacks], full of sound and fury signifying nothing."

19

Crisis of Political Authority? I Wish!

IN MY CAPACITY as the longtime editor of *The Independent Review* (reduced in 2013 to the harmless status of Editor at Large), I have often received unsolicited copies of recently published books from the publishers, who hope to obtain reviews that will help them drum up sales. Today's mail delivery brought me such an unrequested volume, a book titled *The End of Authority: How a Loss of Legitimacy and Broken Trust Are Endangering Our Future,* by Douglas E. Schoen.[1]

Skimming quickly, I found that the book deals with what the author calls "a crisis of governance, a crisis of legitimacy, and, indeed, a crisis of authority." "All around the world," he declares, citizens "have lost confidence in those charged with the responsibility of governing them." (Notice the language, "those charged with the responsibility," rather than "those who, by hook and by crook, have impudently imposed themselves on their exploited subjects.") In this dire situation, Schoen intends his book "to offer clear, unambiguous solutions" to this allegedly urgent problem (p. 245).

My first reaction was, "Crisis of Authority? I wish." Although ruling elites may be distressed by the various expressions of discontent and even outrage being expressed by particular groups of (what they surely take to be) trouble-makers, they are accustomed to a certain amount of discontent and rebellion. Suppressing such outbreaks and pounding, tricking, or soothing people back into line are all in a day's work for the rulers. Given the ruling elites'

---

1. Douglas E. Schoen, *The End of Authority: How Loss of Legitimacy and Broken Trust Are Endangering Our Future* (Lanham, MD: Rowman & Littlefield Publishers, 2013).

disproportionate possession of wealth, connections, and firepower, they usually succeed, and I expect that in most cases those who are feeling pressed today will, sooner or later, succeed in reining in their restive populations. The Arab Spring will turn to Arab Summer, Arab Fall, and Arab Winter. The Tea Partiers will lose interest and drift away—many have already been coopted or politically disarmed by the established major parties. The little bands of libertarians will squander their energies, feuding with their fellows and arguing about not-so-pressing issues in lifeboat ethics. The European rioters will be tear-gassed, sprayed with fire hoses, and beaten about the head and shoulders until they find better uses for their time and energy.

Douglas Schoen clearly writes as a friend of the international elite, for whom he has worked in the past as a pollster, consultant, and strategist.[2] One has only to consider what he takes as a given, namely, that existing Establishment institutions deserve to occupy their powerful positions in social and economic life and ought to be reconfigured to exercise their powers more effectively—that is, in a way that gives rise to fewer troublesome reactions from the peasantry.

Well, one man's treasure is another man's trash. I have a different view of the situation. I perceive that the existing institutions—above all, the various nation states—have highly problematic legitimacy. To speak more bluntly, the state in particular has none at all, aside from the somnolent or distracted acquiescence of the mass of its subjects. If there really were a crisis of authority for the state per se, I could only say, thank God, it's about time; bring it on! A few thousand years of people's being bullied, plundered, humiliated, and even killed by their loving masters is more than enough, and the subjects can scarcely move fast enough to suit me in challenging this immoral domination.

Even before I opened the book, I had a strong premonition that I would find its message impossible to swallow. Four blurbs on the dust jacket express high praise for the author and the book. The blurbs are signed by former U.S. president Bill Clinton, former Canadian prime minister Brian Mulroney, former Polish president Aleksander Kwasniewski, and publisher Steve Forbes. If such persons actually approved of what Schoen has to say, I knew with almost

---

2. "Douglas Schoen," *Wikipedia*, http://en.wikipedia.org/wiki/Douglas_Schoen.

complete certainty that I would not approve. Call me an incurable skeptic, but I simply cannot imagine that anything good could come from the current masters of the world, the very people who have contributed so magnificently to the world's present horrors.

PART II

On Doing Analysis
in Political Economy

20

Ten Rules for Understanding
Economic Development

SINCE WORLD WAR II, concern about economic development has reached unprecedented heights. Academic writers, periodical editors, foundation directors, and governmental officials have expended much time and effort in attempting to understand why economic development occurs, why it proceeds more or less rapidly, and how to hasten it where it appears too slow. Unfortunately, as a distinctive field of economic development studies has emerged, complete with textbooks and scholarly journals, a body of misconceptions and myths also has emerged to diminish the potential fruitfulness of these efforts to understand the process of economic change.

Significant progress would result from following ten simple rules of inquiry. Their value is, for the most part, self-evident; but readers familiar with the literature of economic development will recognize that they are more often ignored than obeyed.

1. Do not dichotomize the nations of the world.

Almost all writers have classified the nations of the world (sometimes only the noncommunist world) as either rich or poor, developed or developing, more developed or less developed. This dichotomization is both false and misleading: false because the nations do not fall into two neat camps; misleading because such a division encourages the search for explanations of poverty that, with more or less sophistication, blame it on the rich. In fact, by any measure one cares to use (e.g., income per capita, literacy rate, expectation of life), the nations of the world occupy a continuum, not a dichotomy. The richest and the poorest countries differ starkly, to be sure, but between them lies an enormous variety of intermediate conditions. As one descends from the United States and Sweden through Greece, Mexico, and Turkey, to reach India and Ethiopia, where can a line be drawn to separate rich from poor?

2. Do not personify the nations of the world.

How often does one read that "Brazil has done this, India has done that." Usually, what is meant is that a certain Brazilian or group of Brazilians has done this, a certain Indian or group of Indians has done that. Nations are abstractions; they do not act. Of course, no one openly disputes this obvious fact; and everyone knows that economy of expression sometimes warrants the personification of a national society. Yet such usage subtly supports the implicit and mistaken notion that all members of a nation are alike in essential respects, that all share the same conditions, attitudes, and objectives. Nothing could be further from the truth. Brazilians, like Indians, Thais, or any other people, are diverse in the extreme. They differ greatly in their conditions, attitudes, and objectives. To suppose that "Brazil does such and such" is to overlook the rich diversity of the individuals who, in the aggregate, constitute the Brazilian nation. It is especially important to notice that many individuals and groups in the poorer countries are rich, and many individuals and groups in the richer countries are poor.

3. Do not assume that the poorer nations are not developing.

Writers who set out to explain "economic stagnation" or "low level equilibrium traps" are addressing themselves to rare circumstances. By any accepted measure (e.g., income per capita, literacy rate, expectation of life), most of the poorer nations are currently developing. Moreover, their rates of development compare favorably with those experienced either historically or currently by the richer countries. This rapid change is not an artifact of social accounting. Close observers of such countries as Egypt and Peru (supposedly slowly developing countries) report sweeping changes in the mode of economic life. In such places as Thailand and Mexico the rapid pace of change is even more obvious. To picture the poorer economies as tradition-bound, stagnant, and resistant to change is to accept a false description of current reality. Only a few backwaters remain to fit this long-accepted characterization.

4. Do not conceive of development as solely economic.

Economic development revolves around the growth of economic productivity, but such growth takes place as a result of changing human actions. Changes in economic behavior cannot be viewed in isolation from other dimensions of human action. People raise their productivity in order to gain comfort, wealth, status, power, and security, the principal impetus varying from one individual to another. The incentives that encourage or discourage productivity-raising behavior emerge from the institutional, cultural, and historical environment in which the individuals act. Changes in this environment must precede wide involvement in the search for higher productivity. Perhaps the impetus comes from contact with another culture or from foreign technical knowledge, from new religions or novel organizational schemes. In any event, economic changes grow out of changes in the noneconomic environment. Human behavior forms a whole. To imagine economic development occurring without corresponding developments in the rest of society is grotesque.

5. Remember that economic development is inherently disruptive and costly.

While economic development augments the comfort, wealth, status, power, and security of some people, it concomitantly diminishes these desirable things for other people. One man's innovation often implies another man's obsolescence. And as individuals, few can escape the varied, undesirable side effects of the development process. In *The Constitution of Liberty*, F. A. Hayek expressed this problem eloquently:

> It is not certain whether most people want all or even most of the results of progress. For most of them it is an involuntary affair which, while bringing them much they strive for, also forces on them many changes they do not want at all. The individual does not have it in his power to choose to take part in progress or not; and always it not only brings

new opportunities but deprives many of much they want, much that is dear and important to them. To some it may be sheer tragedy, and to all those who would prefer to live on the fruits of past progress and not take part in its future course, it may seem a curse rather than a blessing.[1]

6. Do not postulate that economic development is the sole objective of some (any) relevant decision maker.

Simply put, people value many things, and economic development is only one of them. As Peter Bauer has insightfully observed:

> Conventional incomes could be increased by forcing people to work longer hours or to transfer to more lucrative but also more arduous or for some other reason less-preferred occupations. Housewives could be forced to go into paid employment. In fact countless people in rich and poor countries could be compelled to increase their conventional incomes by forcing them to give up working habits, attitudes and beliefs which they cherish. It is bizarre to say the least to describe people as irrational for not trying to maximize conventionally measured incomes. It is an approach which disregards people's own preferences in such matters as life expectation, possession of children, working habits, personal values and social mores, including personal preferences for leisure and contemplation against higher conventional incomes; it also disregards considerations of national security.[2]

7. Do not project your own tastes and values onto others.

To assume that everyone wants what I want, and will bear the same cost to get it, is certain to mislead. Tastes and values differ enormously among the people of the world. If the poor Indians would only eat their sacred cows, they could avert the threat of starvation—advice that is easy for me to give, but rather difficult to take for people deeply committed to the inviolability of all

---

1. F. A. Hayek, *The Constitution of Liberty* (Chicago: University of Chicago Press, 1960), 30.
2. P. T. Bauer, *Dissent on Development*, rev. ed. (Cambridge, Mass.: Harvard University Press, 1976), 200.

animal life. A long and laudable list of human values (e.g., loyalty to family members in Latin America, devotion to a contemplative style of life in Asia, adherence to tribal customs and traditions in Africa) has been held up by development enthusiasts as "barriers to progress." How narrow our vision; how insensitive our appreciation of the values of others.

8. Do not assume that comprehensive governmental programs are necessary to create or accelerate development.

All the countries of Western Europe and their offshoots in the New World, as well as Japan, managed to develop without comprehensive governmental planning. Many poorer countries (e.g., Spain, Mexico, Taiwan, South Korea, Thailand) also are doing so. Yet the notion is widely accepted that development requires comprehensive governmental planning. Ultimately, the case for comprehensive planning reduces to the simple fact that some (including the planners) wish to coerce others to do what will not be done voluntarily.

If people want economic development enough to bear its costs, they voluntarily take the actions that promote it. They migrate to locations of superior economic opportunity, innovate on farms and in factories, obtain better educations. If they do not consider the net gains sufficient, they will abstain from such actions. How ironic, then, that the planners should attempt to "improve the welfare of the people" by compelling them to bear costs that, in the people's own judgment, outweigh the corresponding benefits.

9. Do not assume that governments are impartial and benevolent agencies to promote the public interest.

Governmental officials are not, in general, disinterested humanitarians. More commonly, they are self-interested bureaucrats, politicians, soldiers, and dictators. In any event, they are members of the society they rule, and they bring to their respective offices the preferences and loyalties characteristic of their own class, religion, region, and ideology. Even if the rulers sincerely wished to promote the "public interest," however, they could not do so. The public has many interests; indeed every individual possesses a unique and multifarious set of interests.

It is sometimes said that people do not know how best to serve their own interests, and that therefore the government must act to fill this gap in knowledge. Of course, a governmental official may know something that I do not know and could benefit from knowing. But the converse is also a possibility. In particular, my precise circumstances and desires, ever changing as they are, can hardly be known to anyone but me. The same can be said, of course, for almost every individual.

Governmental officials simply cannot be relied upon to possess superior knowledge. As Hayek says, "Compared with the totality of knowledge which is continually utilized in the evolution of a dynamic civilization, the difference between the knowledge that the wisest and that which the most ignorant individual can deliberately employ is comparatively insignificant."[3] And even if governmental officials did possess superior knowledge, they could not, for obvious reasons, be relied upon to put that knowledge to good use. As Scott Gordon once put it, "How much enthusiasm for statism would evaporate if one were to assume that the government will be run by people like Haldeman and Ehrlichman?"[4]

10. Do not forget history.

If this rule were strictly followed, the others would be largely superfluous. Yet development economics, a quintessentially historical subject, has been practiced mainly by researchers with neither much knowledge of nor interest in history. Economic development, however, is a historical process. To neglect history is to neglect the facts of the matter. And an empirical study that neglects the relevant facts is an absurdity.

---

3. Hayek, *Constitution*, 30.

4. Scott Gordon, "Review of *Business Civilization in Decline*, by Robert L. Heilbroner," *Journal of Economic Literature* 15 (March 1977), 103.

21

Underappreciated Aspects of the Ratchet Effect

OVER THE YEARS, as I have defended my hypothesis about the *ratchet effect* of national emergencies in U.S. history since the Progressive Era (when the ideological conditions for the full operation of this effect were established), I have encountered many doubters and critics. My fellow economists have been especially disposed to reject my hypothesis.

The economists sometimes dismissed my idea on the grounds that national emergencies are simply transient or abnormal events—outliers, as the econometricians call them—that should either be purged from a long time series or be treated as stochastic deviations from a long-run trend caused by more "fundamental" factors, such as demographic shifts or changes in the franchise. At times, the economists dismissed my hypothesis because, they maintained, it fails to fit every case in every country in every period of history; as puerile positivists, they concluded that the hypothesis is wrong because a correct hypothesis must be, in effect, a flawless law of history. Most often, perhaps, the economists pooh-poohed my hypothesis because they misconstrued it: they took it to be, like the typical economist's model of the growth of government, a hypothesis about government spending and nothing more. So, if a certain crisis did not appear to have had a persistent, long-run effect by increasing the estimated trend level of government spending (often after standardization for increases in population, the gross domestic product, and the price level), then it did not explain, in their eyes, "the growth of government."

I have always insisted that modern government has many facets and that, at minimum, a study of its growth must consider not only government spending (or taxing or employing), but also the government's scope and power. Changes in these latter aspects of government do not leave the same kind of easily retrieved record or numerical data set that economists typically work with—and without which they are more or less at sea or in denial. Over the many years that I have pursued my research into the growth of government, I have repeatedly met with evidence of essential elements of the ratchet effect that lie completely beyond the purview of conventional economic research on this subject.

The most recent such evidence I've encountered appears near the end of Godfrey Hodgson's book *The Colonel: The Life and Wars of Henry Stimson, 1867–1950*.[1] Stimson was one of the most important public (or private) figures of the twentieth century. Among other things, he was the human bridge between the original American imperialists of the late nineteenth and early twentieth centuries (e.g., Elihu Root, Theodore Roosevelt, Leonard Wood) and the Cold War directors and managers of the national security state (e.g., Dean Acheson, John J. McCloy, McGeorge Bundy, Robert Lovett). Many of these postwar movers and shakers had worked for or with Stimson at some point, especially at the War Department when he was secretary of war from 1940 to 1945.

In considering how the postwar defense and foreign-policy Establishment, with its characteristic policy proclivities, had been fostered by such men's engagement in the Big One, Hodgson writes:

> Government service in World War II—in the War Department or other civilian departments for the slightly older men, in the Office of Strategic Services or elite military units for the younger ones—*gave a whole generation of ambitious and educated Americans a taste for power, as opposed to business success, and an orientation toward government service which they never lost.* When they went back to their law offices or their classrooms, they took with them contacts, attitudes and beliefs they had learned in war service.[2]

Ponder this passage, especially the part I have italicized. Here is a legacy of national emergency that no econometrician can tease out of a statistical

---

1. Hodgson, *The Colonel* (New York: Knopf, 1990).
2. Hodgson, *The Colonel*, pp. 384–85, emphasis added.

time series, yet it is the kind of legacy that gives the ratchet effect its greatest substance.

I have emphasized again and again that the legacies of national emergency are not merely fiscal, but also, more critically, institutional and ideological. From Hodgson's observation, we can see both the institutional and the ideological legacies embodied in a generation of highly placed, closely connected individuals who exerted tremendous influence over the apparatus and conduct of U.S. foreign and defense policies for decades after World War II and whose influence may be seen in the government's conduct of foreign and defense affairs even today, though in somewhat attenuated and altered form.

The ratchet effect is a more complex phenomenon than most of my fellow economists seem capable of understanding. To grasp it, one must go beyond economic analysis and even beyond public choice analysis. One must plunge into the domain of historical analysis, where social scientific theories are necessary but not sufficient for our understanding and where one continually meets path dependencies and contingencies whose resolution is anything but determinate, where real human beings, relying on their attitudes, beliefs, and commitments (shaped by their particular experiences, acquaintances, and loyalties) make genuine—that is, not fully predetermined—choices and thereby set in motion new streams of cause and effect that ripple through time and space.

A century before I formulated my ideas about the ratchet effect, the great William Graham Sumner understood its essence clearly when he said, "It is not possible to experiment with a society and just drop the experiment whenever we choose. The experiment enters into the life of the society and never can be got out again." For historians and social scientists, the challenge remains to explicate precisely how this "entering into the life of the society" has occurred as a result of the "experiments" the government has performed during each of the great national emergencies of the past century. Such understanding appears even more imperative at present, as the government launches yet another great experiment.

22

Diagnostics and Therapeutics in Political Economy

SINCE THE EARLY 1980S, I have been lecturing on the growth of government to a wide variety of audiences. In academic seminars and workshops, professors typically ask questions about my explanatory framework, my evidence, alternative explanations, possible counterexamples, and so forth. But when I speak to a friendly lay audience, the first question is typically something along the lines of, "What can we do to turn this thing around?" Academic people, who are accustomed to discussing all sorts of political and economic developments, many of which are none too savory, usually have the ability to distance themselves from any revulsion they may feel about the matters under discussion and to concentrate on how one might best explain the events in question. In social science, "value freedom" is upheld as a standard for the analyst. Market-friendly nonacademic people, in contrast, are often surprised, and appalled, to discover how much the government has grown and many of the means by which political actors have enlarged it, and their immediate orientation is toward action to reverse what they perceive to be a pernicious development. Thus, they bring normative and programmatic concerns directly to the fore. Like Lenin, they demand to know, "What is to be done?"[1]

Because I am often introduced as an authority on government growth, the lay audiences seem shocked and disappointed when I answer the query about how we can stop further government growth by saying that I don't know or, worse, by saying that I don't think we—which is to say, those of us

---

1. Joe Fineberg, George Hanna, Tim Delany and K. Goins, *"What Is To Be Done?: Burning Questions of Our Movement,"* by Vladimir Ilyich Lenin, *Marxists Internet Archive*, http://www.marxists.org/archive/lenin/works/1901/witbd/index.htm.

in the room and all other likeminded people—can do anything significant to deflect the trend toward larger, more tyrannical government.

I often receive similar reactions when I post commentaries on the Internet. Thus, I recently posted a short essay called "Partisan Politics—A Fool's Game for the Masses," and in response, one man wrote: "Quit whining and figure out something better if you're so damn smart." Another wrote: "Okay, Higgs. So what can one do to protect one's person and family and aid in the country's survival?" I commonly hear from people who find my description or analysis beside the point unless I have "an answer" or "a solution" to the problem under discussion. Higgs, they conclude, is "not constructive," and therefore he does not deserve anyone's time and attention.

Although I would be the last to assert that I have a claim on anyone's time or attention, I believe that the solution-demanding response to my commentaries (or anyone else's) betrays a conflation of diagnostics and therapeutics in political economy. The former focuses on finding the causes of a condition or development, the latter on prescribing measures by which the condition can be lessened or eliminated. This distinction is common in the medical profession, where some practitioners specialize in diagnosis and others in various kinds of therapy. In political economy, however, the two activities are often combined. In professional economics journals, countless articles have been published in which the author first lays out his "model," sometimes presents empirical "tests" of some of its implications, and finally draws "policy conclusions"—that is, unsolicited advice to government functionaries as to how they should employ their powers.

Lay people and professionals alike, however, need to appreciate two critical points. First, in social and economic affairs, one man's problem may be another man's solution. The growth of government belongs to this category. Many people are pleased when the government grows, whereas others are outraged. Still others, of course, have no concern one way or the other, so long as their personal ox is not being gored deeply. In short, the normative evaluation of a socioeconomic condition or development may vary greatly among the people involved in it.

Second, even if everyone agrees that a certain condition constitutes a problem, it still may have no generally acceptable solution. Because of the diversity of beliefs, values, and interests in the populace, whatever is done to create a "public good"—that is, a condition that, if established at all, applies equally to everyone—will displease some people. For example, everyone may value "national security" in the abstract, but if in its pursuit some people want the government to go to war against country X, whereas others want the government to steer clear of war with country X, then some people are bound to be dissatisfied, no matter what the government does. Issues of this kind have no generally acceptable solution, owing to uncertainties about the "production function" for certain public goods. One might imagine, of course, that one side persuades the other to change its beliefs, values, or preferences, but unless unanimous agreement is achieved—an extremely unlikely eventuality—a certain number of problems whose solutions are contentious will necessarily always remain.

Since the Great Depression, the American public has generally approved of an active, interventionist federal government. In a perceived crisis, most people want the government to "do something." Of course, most politicians and government functionaries, for perfectly understandable self-serving reasons, are quite pleased to respond to such public demands for action—after all, taking such action promises to butter their bread more thickly. Franklin D. Roosevelt enthusiastically supported an approach whereby the government would "take a method and try it; if it fails, admit it frankly and try another. But above all, try something." Likewise, more recently, despite the great confusion that prevailed about the current recession's causes and about the best means of moderating or reversing it, Barack Obama, soon after taking office, declared, "The time for talk is over. The time for action is now." In both instances the president was presuming that successful therapy can be administered without a sound diagnosis. This presumption is foolish, however, if one's interest lies not in mollifying a bewildered electorate, but in implementing a genuine remedy for the perceived problem.

Furthermore, in dealing with a "problem" such as the relentless growth of government, we must recognize that unlike the automobile mechanic who undertakes to repair a sputtering engine, we are attempting to alter the workings of a socioeconomic process that has hundreds of millions of moving parts, each one with a mind of its own! It is hubristic—a Hayekian "fatal conceit"—to suppose that anyone can control this process in fine detail. The "man of system," Adam Smith sagely observed, "is apt to be very wise in his own conceit."

He seems to imagine that he can arrange the different members of a great society with as much ease as the hand arranges the different pieces upon a chess-board. He does not consider that the pieces upon the chess-board have no other principle of motion besides that which the hand impresses upon them; but that, in the great chess-board of human society, every single piece has a principle of motion of its own, altogether different from that which the legislature might choose to impress upon it.[2]

I am not a "man of system" in the Smithian sense. For me to propose a "magic bullet" to stop the growth of government, as an oncologist might prescribe a certain drug to cure a particular type of cancer, would be ridiculous. Just as one may know a great deal about the origin and development of a particular type of tumor without knowing how to cure it, one may know a great deal about the growth of government without knowing how to stop it. Indeed, curing a cancer is a much simpler task.

Yet one thing we do know: Many Americans now believe many things about their government that are false, and they expect much from the government that the rulers cannot provide. The public at large embraces myths about what the government can do, what it actually does, and how it goes about doing it. Only people enamored of such myths can support, for example, a gigantically expensive health-care "reform" at a time when the present value of the government's promised future Social Security and Medicare benefits alone amounts to several times the current GDP. (I am disregarding here the interested parties who expect to reap short-run pillage from an intrinsically doomed system.) Until more people come to a more realistic, fact-based understanding of the government and the economy, little hope exists of tearing them away from their quasi-religious attachment to a government they view with misplaced reverence and unrealistic hopes. Lacking a true religious faith yet craving one, many Americans have turned to the state as a substitute god, endowed with the divine omnipotence required to shower the public with something for nothing in every department—free health care, free retirement security, free protection from hazardous consumer products and workplace

---

2. Adam Smith, *The Theory of Moral Sentiments*, ed. D. D. Raphael and A. L. Macfie (Indianapolis: Liberty Classics, 1982), 233–34.

accidents, free protection from the Islamic maniacs the U.S. government stirs up with its misadventures in the Muslim world, and so forth. If you take the government to be Santa Claus, you naturally want every day to be Christmas; and the bigger the Santa, the bigger his sack of goodies. This prevailing ideology constitutes probably the most critical obstacle to reductions in the government's size, scope, and power. Getting rid of this ideology will be diabolically difficult, if possible at all.

Analysts of the political economy, such as yours truly, may have some capacity to open people's eyes with regard to the government's true nature and its actual operation. Such diagnostic work is a full-time job, however, so consumers of this analysis should not be surprised if a diagnostician cannot prescribe a sure-fire cure whenever he identifies, describes, or analyzes a problem. Moreover, consumers of opinion and analysis in political economy would be well served by developing a healthy skepticism toward all those who propose a simple cure for the growth of government—flat tax, term limits, constitutional amendment, abolition of the Fed, you name it. The doctor with a panacea just might be a quack.

23

Can the Rampaging Leviathan Be Stopped or Slowed?

IN A RECENT COMMENTARY, "Diagnostics and Therapeutics in Political Economy,"[1] I endeavored to show that an analytical understanding of past growth in the government's size, scope, and power does not permit us to prescribe effective means of stopping or slowing this growth, particularly any simple "silver bullet" remedy, and I specifically disclaimed any personal knowledge of "what is to be done" toward this end. Responses to this commentary, some of them from keenly intelligent friends of mine who insist that diagnostics and therapeutics must be firmly linked, lead me to believe that I did not make myself sufficiently clear.

One respondent wrote, "Higgs must be speaking with tongue in cheek, for a man of his intellect simply must have a few solutions at least." Well, yes, on one level, I have many "solutions" to propose. The problem comes when we ponder why I've just put quotation marks around the word *solutions*. The reason pertains to the links that connect my understanding of why government has grown with measures that might be taken to stop or slow its ongoing growth.

My understanding of the process by which government has grown in the United States and many other countries since the late nineteenth century is not easy for me to summarize briefly. It involves (1) a structural-ideological-political process operating in a persistent manner to produce long-term trends, (2) a crisis-ideological-political process operating during a series of discrete episodes of "national emergency," and (3) interactions between these two processes, which should not be understood as independent of one another, but as

---

1. Robert Higgs, "Diagnostics and Therapeutics in Political Economy," *The Beacon*, October 15, 2009, http://blog.independent.org/?s=diagnostics+and+therapeutics+in+political+economy&submit=go.

identifiable aspects of the single herky-jerky historical evolution—sometimes regular, sometimes erratic—of a politico-economic order. One upshot of this complex process might be seen if we were to examine a series of "snapshots" at, say, thirty-year intervals. Each snapshot would show us a society with a different composition of economic activities, production techniques, occupations, demographic attributes, and so forth, a different composition of ideological identifications, understandings, and loyalties, and a different configuration of political leanings, organizations, and institutions *reflecting these structural and ideological differences*. To oversimplify, we might say that the overall process creates—usually gradually, but occasionally abruptly—a changing set of "vested interests" among the population, but in this characterization we would have to interpret the idea of *vested interests* more broadly than usual, so that it includes not only people's interests in pecuniary payoffs, but also their interests in ideological outcomes of various sorts. (My views in this area have been developed in a series of personal engagements [as a teacher, consultant in regulatory proceedings, and expert witness in legal proceedings] and in a series of research efforts, the most prominent results of which are reported in my books *Crisis and Leviathan, Against Leviathan, Depression, War, and Cold War, Neither Liberty Nor Safety,* and *Delusions of Power,* to which the reader is referred for a more detailed account of my views on this matter, among others.)

Now, with this rather desperately compressed vision of the complex process by which the government has grown as our background, let us return to my "solutions," that is, to my proposals for stopping or slowing further growth of government. In doing so, however, we must recognize that political "solutions" that clash strongly with the currently prevailing array of vested interests (broadly construed) probably cannot be implemented. For me to suppose otherwise would be inconsistent, because doing so would be tantamount to rejection of my own interpretation of how those interests came into being in the course of the historical process just outlined. At least within somewhat flexible limits, a society's socioeconomic structure, ideological postures, and political institutions must cohere. At a particular point in time, many conceivable (and in my view desirable) political reforms are not feasible.

At the moment, many people are enamored of the solution that calls for abolition of the Federal Reserve System. I certainly agree that the Fed has played an integral (but not an indispensable) role in the growth of government in the United States since 1913. But once one has demanded "abolish the Fed" and subsequently found that it is still in operation, what does one do?

Various next steps might be suggested, such as sponsoring lecturers who explain how the Fed has adversely affected economic prosperity, peaceful international relations, and liberty. From time to time, I have myself given such lectures to audiences that ranged from ordinary Americans to social scientists to Latin American bankers, and, of course, many other speakers have presented similar lectures. All right, we've given our lectures, and the Fed is still operating, so what should we do next? Give more lectures, in an attempt to influence the thinking of more people? Or perhaps mount a political movement aimed at abolition of the Fed?

If one chooses the direct political option, where does one get the financing for it? Who will organize it? Who will lead it? What actions will it take? Will it try to place sympathetic candidates on the ballot for election to Congress? Will it attempt to influence sitting members of Congress by bribing them with campaign contributions or by threatening to recruit constituents to vote against them in the next election? My point is that once we select a specific means of stopping or slowing the government's growth, an endless series of follow-up questions presents itself, as we encounter one problem after another, each of which must be solved successfully if we are to make headway.

No doubt the greatest obstacle of all to any such effort is that thousands of organizations are currently working, directly or indirectly, to *promote* further growth of government. A 2005 article[2] in the *Washington Post* placed the number of registered lobbyists in Washington, D.C., at more than 34,750 and reported that their business was booming, creating "a gold rush on K Street." Many of them have well-equipped offices, large capable staffs, including legions of lawyers, and established connections with incumbents in Congress, regulatory agencies, and other government offices, not to mention their friends on the courts. They also have millions upon millions of dollars to pour into their efforts to win friends and influence people, including the same mass electorate that an anti-Fed or other anti-government-growth political movement presumably seeks to influence. At this point in the historical process, anti-Fed

---

2. Jeffrey H. Birnbaum, "The Road to Riches Is Called K Street," *Washington Post* online, http://www.washingtonpost.com/wp-dyn/content/article/2005/06/21/AR2005062101632.html.

proponents face a fabulously wealthy, tightly connected, deeply entrenched conglomeration of opponents who would sooner confine you, me, and all our friends and relatives at Guantanamo for nonstop torture than give up the Fed, which has long served, and continues to serve, their interests exceedingly well. So, yes, we can try to mount a political movement to abolish the Fed, but, given what we are up against, what chance of success do we really have? One in a thousand? One in a million?

Given this reality, if I offer as a "solution" to the ongoing growth of government that we abolish the Fed, my proposal solves nothing. It only raises a series of other difficult questions, each one of which leads to another and another and another. No political realist was surprised when, according to an October 30 Bloomberg report,[3] "Ron Paul, the Texas Republican who has called for an end to the Federal Reserve, said legislation he introduced to audit monetary policy has been 'gutted' while moving toward a possible vote in the Democratic-controlled House." If the powers that be are not even willing to permit a vote on a bill with 308 co-sponsors aimed at making the Fed's decision-making more transparent, does anyone really believe that those same powers would stand idly by while the Fed was abolished?

Nor is abolition of the Fed unique in this regard. One might propose abolition of any number of government departments or agencies—for example, the Department of Education, the Department of Energy, the Food and Drug Administration, the Securities and Exchange Commission, and countless other government bureaus—and find that in each instance one runs up against another fabulously wealthy, tightly connected, deeply entrenched conglomeration of opponents.

One might alternatively propose simply to reduce government spending across the board without trying to reconfigure the government's organization chart. The obstacles here, however, are if anything even greater, because thousands of powerful interest groups are currently seeking to *increase* government spending. Of course, each wants mainly an increase in the portion of government spending that enriches its own members, but the budgetary process has evolved, along with the committee structure of Congress, to facilitate a gigantic logroll, so that each year nearly every predatory interest group of any

---

3. Bob Ivy, "Federal Reserve Policy Audit Legislation 'Gutted,' Paul Says," *Bloomberg.com*, October 30, 2009, http://www.bloomberg.com/apps/news?pid=newsarchive&sid=atc2o1ijLRno.

consequence tacitly agrees to refrain from blocking the other predators if they will refrain from blocking its own raid on the Treasury. Committee chairpersons and ranking minority members are paid off as required to achieve this massive predation. Hillary Clinton used to complain about a "vast rightwing conspiracy," but if one wants to see a genuine mega-conspiracy, one need look no further than the nexus of members of Congress and the thousands of well-organized and well-financed special-interest groups that support these politicians' perpetual reelection in exchange for their direct or indirect channeling of almost unimaginably huge amounts of the public's wealth into these special interests' coffers.

So, yes, one might propose, say, a balanced-budget amendment to the Constitution—indeed, by now this proposal is hoary with age. Political realists understand, however, that getting support for such an amendment is diabolically difficult, and, even if one were to be ratified, the members of Congress would simply install the appropriate smoke and mirrors to conceal their violation of this constitutional restraint, as they installed such circumventions on previous occasions to violate their own rules for spending restraint. Does anyone still recall the Gramm-Rudman-Hollings Balanced Budget and Emergency Deficit Control Act of 1985?[4]

It appears, then, that among the critical difficulties of restraining the growth of government is the obvious fact that even when restraints are enacted into law, the government will not obey that law. Needless to say at this point, constitutional amendments are not worth the parchment on which they are inscribed. After all, the Constitution still contains the Ninth and Tenth Amendments. With those amendments and three or four bucks, you can get a fair-sized latté at Starbucks.

I trust that by this point I need not belabor my point at greater length. To recapitulate: "solutions" to the ongoing growth of government are available for a dime a dozen. I have a bag full of them myself, and every one of them is utterly worthless as a means of achieving the ultimate goal. Every genuine solution must be *carried through*, and any serious solution will require enough people and money to carry out the activities necessary to bring it about. Marshaling people and money may in turn require ideological conversions on a

---

4. The statute's legal citation is 99th Congress, S.1702, Pub.L. 99–177, title II, December 12, 1985, 99 Stat. 1038.

substantial scale, which themselves may require a great many people and a great deal of money, if such conversions are possible at all, given the existing configuration of vested interests (broadly construed).

Moreover, another potent constraint always lurks in the background. Although we need not spend much time at present in dwelling on this issue, the fact remains that if any truly effective measures were approved to rein in the government, the rulers in all likelihood would resort to whatever legal or illegal violence proved necessary to prevent those measures from taking effect. Thus I am quite sure, for example, that if Ron Paul were ever, by a miracle of miracles, to be elected president, he would not live to take the oath of office. Opponents of the government's ongoing growth must bear in mind that we are dealing with violent, heavily armed, utterly unscrupulous people who, if pushed to the brink, will stop at nothing to retain their power and privileges.

I welcome anyone's proposed "solutions" to the ongoing growth of government, and I wish all such proposals success, however much I doubt the likelihood of their success. I do not believe, though, that a substantial prospect of success is necessary to justify one's efforts in resisting the ongoing growth of what is at bottom a gigantic criminal enterprise. To resist its further growth is simply the decent thing to do, regardless of whether one expects to succeed.

And even those who believe, as I do, that the chances of success in such efforts are extremely small can take heart from the knowledge that ultimately this criminal enterprise will attain such bloated size and scope that its own survival will no longer be possible, and it will implode, as the Soviet Union and other similarly overreaching politico-economic orders have imploded. Governments that grow and grow ultimately find that their predation becomes greater than their prey can support, at which point such predators are doomed. Thus the present system of government in this country and in many others contains the seeds of its *own* destruction, even if those of us who abhor it cannot stop or slow its continued growth in the near term.

Some of the younger people among us may live long enough to help in picking up the pieces and beginning anew. One hopes that the new beginning will rest on a less coercive, more voluntary basis than the present system. Otherwise, it will be destined only to trace the same predatory rise that the present system has followed and to arrive at the same self-destruction that ultimately awaits our own politico-economic order.

24

Higgs Is Just a Pessimist

"HIGGS IS JUST A PESSIMIST"—how often I've come across expressions of that sentiment during the past twenty-five years! In certain circles, I have become the butt of jokes—some good-natured, some not—by virtue of my alleged pessimism.

Okay, maybe I am somewhat pessimistic. My wife, who is confident that she knows more about me than I know about myself, says so, and I am certainly not going to take issue with someone who possesses superior knowledge. But my reputation as a pessimist stems not from the kind of knowledge that my wife possesses in special measure, but from my writings over the years about the growth of government and related matters.

In this context, I have been rather puzzled by many of the accusations of pessimism, because whereas I have always tried to rest my expectations on my knowledge of what happened in the past and my understanding of why those events occurred, those who dismiss or depreciate my prognostications seem to me to be lapsing into wishful thinking—groundless optimism, if you will.

When my book *Crisis and Leviathan*[1] was published in 1987, several reviewers took issue with it on the grounds that my forecast—which occupies less than one page at the end of the book—was unduly pessimistic, especially in view of the great transformation that some of them imagined had been wrought by the "Reagan Revolution." What provoked this bizarre focus on three paragraphs in a book of 372 pages? After disavowing any pretense of knowing the future, I wrote that if human society survives (which is always

---

1. Robert Higgs, *Crisis and Leviathan: Critical Episodes in the Growth of American Government* (New York: Oxford University Press, 1987).

iffy, given the prevailing combination of technological power and moral infirmity), we do know one thing:

> We know that other great crises will come. Whether they will be occasioned by foreign wars, economic collapse, or rampant terrorism, no one can predict with assurance. Yet in one form of another, great crises will surely come again, as they have from time to time throughout all human history. When they do, governments almost certainly will gain new powers over economic and social affairs. Everything I have argued and documented in the preceding chapters points toward this conclusion.

For years afterward, I would tell those skeptical of my thesis—people who were convinced that Big Government was gradually being diminished—that the gains in freedom (which, even at the time, I considered to be more than offset by contemporaneous losses) would be swept away overnight at the onset of the next great crisis. When 9/11 occurred, I had occasion to put my views to the test. Was I wrong then? When the current recession came to a head in the financial debacle of September and October 2008, I had another occasion to put my views to the test. Was I wrong then?

I'm not gloating. It's possible that my views are altogether cockamamie and that the huge spurts of government growth after 9/11 and again after the financial debacle of 2008 have occurred for reasons that only appear to validate my views. I don't think so, however: too many of the details fit my scheme. But consider again the matter I raised at the beginning of this essay: was I right (or apparently right) about these events only because these are bad developments, and such developments always seem to confirm the expectations of ex ante pessimists?

In my years as a basketball player, we used to say after a bad shot fell through the hoop that it's better to be lucky than good. Have my well-confirmed expectations about the post-crisis events of the past decade been simply lucky, rather than soundly based?

In my work on the growth of government over the past three decades, I have always rested my conclusions on a combination of facts and theory. I may be wrong about the facts, although those who have disputed my views have not so much claimed that I got the facts wrong as that I misinterpreted them or that I committed sins of omission. I may also be wrong about the theory, but my theoretical views have seemingly proved their mettle in a variety of applications, in their details and their broad contours, and in one historical episode after another in the modern (post-Progressive) ideological era. In sum, I don't believe that my views on the evolution of the U.S. politico-economic order ever did, or now do, simply express my psychological tendency toward pessimism.

So it has always irritated me when my arguments were dismissed or depreciated on the grounds that "Higgs is just a pessimist." Such a reaction strikes me as a sort of ad hominem fallacy. You might as well say that Higgs is wrong about the growth of government because he's a jackass (a trait I am neither confirming nor denying).

This past week, however, we have seen President Barack Obama awarded a Nobel Peace Prize and seen him use the occasion to present the same-old-same-old pseudo-justifications for enlarging the foolish war in Afghanistan and for perpetuating global U.S. hegemony. As if that shameful travesty were not more than enough insult added to our injuries, we have seen Ben Bernanke named *Time* magazine's person of the year, in the wake of the Fed's having placed the U.S. economy in the kind of jeopardy that it has not suffered since World War II. If you wanted to invent news items to illustrate the black absurdity of our political and ideological situation, you could not have come up with nastier ones.

These sorts of events rarely come as a surprise to me, however: they fit nicely into the analytical narratives I've been writing for decades about where the country is heading and why. But, as always, I may be wrong. So, to keep up your spirits, I recommend that you ask some well-established experts what they think. Chances are that they will reassure you. After all, as everybody knows, Higgs is just a pessimist.

25

My Question for the Doomsters: Then What?

ALTHOUGH I AM reputed to be a cynic, a pessimist, and a bah-humbugger, I am not given to doomsaying in the same way that a growing number of others are. Although I tend to expect, as Thomas Jefferson did, that the natural progress of things will be for liberty to yield and government to gain ground, and for me this course of events will be an unwelcome one, I am not much inclined to predict that, especially in the near term, the economy, society, or government will suddenly "break down," "collapse," or experience some comparably terrible and complete calamity.

I will admit, however, that some of my friends seem mightily inclined toward such doomsaying. It's almost as if they can't wait for the catastrophe to arrive—perhaps because it will demonstrate beyond cavil that the existing order is too corrupt, irrational, and evil to maintain itself. Some people who write or speak along such lines, though, clearly have a vested interest: they are selling something—often precious metals, investment advice, "survival" goods, or "bearish" publications—that they expect to sell more readily to consumers who have acquired a heightened fear of impending economic doom.

Other doomsayers, especially those in the Austro-libertarian camp, may have absorbed their dire expectation from an expression Ludwig von Mises used, "the crack-up boom." By this term, Mises refers to the penultimate stage of hyperinflation, when each acceleration of the money supply only drives the velocity of expenditure higher as people try to exchange any money they hold for real goods as quickly as possible. The culmination occurs when, as Mises writes in *Human Action*, "The monetary system breaks down; all transactions in the money concerned cease; a panic makes its purchasing power vanish altogether."[1] Mises was not simply imagining or theorizing about this sort of development, however; he had seen it with his own eyes in Austria and Germany after World War I. And similar crack-ups have occurred in many other places at various times, including the Confederate States of America during the final year or so of the War Between the States.

Austro-libertarians should note, however, that Mises did not argue that a crack-up boom destroys all economic life. Instead, as he immediately explained, "People return either to barter or to the use of another kind of money." Indeed. Austria, Germany, and the U.S. South did not disappear as a result of their currency's ruin. Although their people suffered grievously from the destructive effects of hyperinflation, most people found a way to survive, and life went on. Eventually, economic life resumed on a new basis after the adoption of a "reformed" or foreign medium of exchange not subject to such rapid increases in supply. Indeed, some people survived even the recent hyperinflation in Zimbabwe, notwithstanding the Mugabe government's best efforts to starve most of them.

Not every forecast of economic catastrophe involves hyperinflation, of course. Some breakdowns are expected to grow out of runaway government spending, growing taxation, oppressive regulation, food shortages, fuel shortages, or natural disasters, such as deadly pandemics or lethal changes in the world's climate. I have yet to encounter a claim that we are all doomed because of an impending beer shortage, but I am a patient man, and I am confident that sooner or later such a scenario will be bruited about.

One aspect that virtually all tales of impending mega-woe have in common is that they end with the catastrophe itself. Bam, crunch, rip, smash, crash: the day of reckoning finally arrives, the dreaded event occurs, and the story ends. *Alles ist kaput.* Maybe somewhere out there in the woods a few cruelly smirking survivalists remain alive, clutching their beloved firearms and muttering, "I told you so." If life continues at all, however, it does so only under conditions that leave the survivors solitary, poor, nasty, brutish, and short of all decent goods and services.

---

1. Ludwig von Mises, *Human Action: A Treatise on Economics,* Third Revised Edition (New Haven, CT: Yale University Press, 1963), 427.

I'm not saying that this sort of thing is impossible. We are talking about human beings and their social interrelations, and from such screwball raw materials, virtually any outcome might conceivably be produced. But such scenarios are dreadfully far-fetched. After all, during the time of the Black Death[2] in the fourteenth century, 30 to 60 percent of the entire population of Europe died, and hundreds of towns simply disappeared after their inhabitants perished or abandoned them in a futile flight from the incomprehensible killer (the refugees inadvertently spreading the disease everywhere they went). Yet Europeans did not die out, and indeed European civilization continued to make slow progress over the long haul, even though the disease became endemic (and episodically epidemic) for centuries.

So, supposing that I accept a horrifying forecast as a point of departure for discussion, my general question for the doomsayers of whatever stripe is: Then what? Do they really believe that when the government can't pay all the pensions and medical bills that it has promised to pay, life will come to an end? Do they believe that when the government defaults on its debt, the economy will cease to function? Do they believe that when the U.S. dollar loses all of its purchasing power, people will not find a new and better medium of exchange for their transactions? And so forth.

One needs to have—and in saying so I feel almost as if I'm having an out-of-body experience—a modicum of faith in people's common sense, creativity, and will to survive and prosper, even in the face of great difficulties and obstacles. If people could keep society running in the aftermath of the Black Death, they surely can keep it running after the U.S. government defaults on its debt. I am not saying that no suffering will occur. Vast socioeconomic adjustments are painful even in the best of circumstances. But people will find a way, life will go on, and eventually some progress will be attained—before governments once again strangle freedom so severely that another calamity occurs. (After all, I cannot imagine that the people who are building the latest Tower of Babel will ever succeed in reaching heaven.)

Years ago, when I lived in Seattle, I sometimes encountered people who seemed terribly worried that because the Northwest's old-growth trees were be-

---

2. "Black Death," *Wikipedia,* http://en.wikipedia.org/wiki/black_death.

ing cut, the so-called Northern Spotted Owl (a bird genetically indistinguishable from the abundant spotted owls in the Rockies, yet somehow imbued with a sacred status) was sure to perish. Try as I might, I could not resist the urge to say to them. "Look, suppose you were a Northern Spotted Owl, and the loggers came along and cut down the tree you were occupying. Would you fall down and die, or would you simply fly to the nearest not-so-old-growth tree and go on living as usual?"

I would be pleased if today's doomsayers felt an obligation to answer a similar question in regard to their own forecasts.

26

Defense Spending Is Much Greater Than You Think

WHEN PRESIDENT OBAMA presented his budget recently for fiscal year 2011, he proposed that the Pentagon's outlays be increased by about 4.5 percent beyond its estimated outlays in fiscal 2010, to a total of almost $719 billion. Although many Americans regard this enormous sum as excessive, few appreciate that the total amount of all defense-related spending greatly exceeds the amount budgeted for the Department of Defense.

In fiscal year 2009, which ended last September, the Pentagon spent $636.5 billion. Lodged elsewhere in the budget, however, other lines identify funding that serves defense purposes just as surely as—sometimes even more surely than—the money allocated to the Department of Defense. On occasion, commentators take note of some of these additional defense-related budget items, such as the Department of Energy's nuclear-weapons program, but many such items, including some extremely large ones, remain generally unrecognized.

Since the creation of the Department of Homeland Security, many observers probably would agree that its budget ought to be included in any complete accounting of defense costs. After all, the homeland is what most Americans want the government to defend in the first place.

Other agencies also spend money in pursuit of homeland security. The Justice Department, for example, includes the Federal Bureau of Investigation, which devotes substantial resources to an anti-terrorist program. The Department of the Treasury claims to have "worked closely with the Departments of State and Justice and the intelligence community to disrupt targets related to al Qaeda, Hizballah, Jemaah Islamiyah, as well as to disrupt state sponsorship of terror."

Much, if not all, of the budget for the Department of State and for international assistance programs ought to be classified as defense-related, too. In this case, the money serves to buy off potential enemies and to reward friendly governments who assist U.S. efforts to abate perceived threats. About $5 billion of annual U.S. foreign aid currently takes the form of "foreign military financing," and even funds placed under the rubric of economic development may serve defense-related purposes indirectly. Money is fungible, and the receipt of foreign assistance for economic-development projects allows allied governments to divert other funds to police, intelligence, and military purposes.

Two big budget items represent the current cost of defense goods and services obtained in the past. The Department of Veterans Affairs, which is authorized to spend about $124 billion in the current fiscal year, falls in this category. Likewise, a great deal of the government's interest expense on publicly held debt represents the current cost of defense outlays financed in the past by borrowing from the public.

To estimate the size of the entire de facto defense budget, I gathered data for fiscal 2009, the most recently completed fiscal year, for which data on actual outlays are now available (see Table 26.1). In that year, the Department of Defense itself spent $636.5 billion. Defense-related parts of the Department of Energy budget added $16.7 billion. The Department of Homeland Security spent $51.7 billion. The Department of State and international assistance programs laid out $36.3 billion for activities arguably related to defense purposes either directly or indirectly. The Department of Veterans Affairs had outlays of $95.5 billion. The Department of the Treasury, which funds the lion's share of military retirement costs through its support of the little-known Military Retirement Fund, added $54.9 billion. A large part of the National Aeronautics and Space Administration's outlays ought to be regarded as defense-related, if only indirectly so. When all of these other parts of the budget are added to the budget for the Pentagon itself, they increase the fiscal 2009 total by nearly half again, to $901.5 billion.

Finding out how much of the government's net interest payments on the publicly held national debt ought to be attributed to past debt-funded defense spending requires a considerable amount of calculation. I added up all past deficits (minus surpluses) since 1916 (when the debt was nearly zero), prorated according to each year's ratio of narrowly defined national security spending—military, veterans, and international affairs—to total federal spending, expressing everything in dollars of constant purchasing power. This sum is equal to 67.6 percent of the value of the national debt held by the public at the end of 2009. Therefore, I attribute that same percentage of the government's net interest outlays in that year to past debt-financed defense spending. The total amount so attributed comes to $126.3 billion.

Adding this interest component to the previous all-agency total, the grand total comes to $1,027.8 billion, which is 61.5 percent greater than the Pentagon's outlays alone.

In similar analyses I conducted previously for fiscal 2002[1] and for fiscal 2006,[2] total defense-related spending was even greater relative to Pentagon spending alone: it was 73 percent greater in fiscal 2002 and 87 percent greater in fiscal 2006. In fiscal 2009, the ratio was held down in large part by the reduced cost of servicing the government's debt, owing to the extremely low interest rates that prevailed on government securities. This situation cannot last forever. As interest rates on the Treasury's securities rise, so will the government's cost of servicing the debt attributable to past debt-financed defense outlays.

For fiscal 2010, which is still in progress, the president's budget estimates that the Pentagon's spending will run more than $50 billion above the previous year's total. Any supplemental appropriations made before September 30 will push the total for fiscal 2010 even farther above the trillion-dollar mark.

Although I have arrived at my conclusions honestly and carefully, I may have left out items that should have been included—the federal budget is a gargantuan, complex, and confusing collection of documents. If I have done so, however, the left-out items are not likely to be relatively large ones. (I have deliberately ignored some minor items, such as outlays for the Selective Ser-

---

1. Robert Higgs, "The Defense Budget is Bigger Than You Think," *San Francisco Chronicle*, January 18, 2004.

2. Robert Higgs, "The Trillion-Dollar Defense Budget is Already Here," Independent Institute, March 15, 2007, http://www.independent.org/newsroom/article.asp?id=1941.

Table 26.1. National Security Outlays in Fiscal Year 2009 (billions of dollars)

Department of Defense	636.5
Department of Energy (nuclear weapons & environ. cleanup)	16.7
Department of State (plus intern. assistance)	36.3
Department of Veterans Affairs	95.5
Department of Homeland Security	51.7
Department of the Treasury (for Military Retirement Fund)	54.9
National Aeronautics & Space Administration (1/2 of total)	9.6
Net interest attributable to past debt-financed defense outlays	126.3
TOTAL	1,027.5

Source: Author's classifications and calculations; basic data from U.S. Office of Management and Budget, *Budget of the United States Government, Fiscal Year 2011* and U.S. Bureau of the Census, *Historical Statistics of the United States, Colonial Times to 1970.*

vice System, the National Defense Stockpile, and the anti-terrorist activities conducted by the FBI and the Treasury.

For now, however, the conclusion seems inescapable: the government is currently spending at a rate well in excess of $1 trillion per year for all defense-related purposes. Owing to the financial debacle and the ongoing recession, millions are out of work, millions are losing their homes, and private earnings remain well below their previous peak, but in the military-industrial complex, the gravy train speeds along the track faster and faster.

27

Which End, if Any, Is Near?

SOME PEOPLE HAVE always occupied themselves in crying out that the end is near. This sort of thing has been going on for millennia. But lately, it seems to me, the volume of such doom-saying has risen markedly. Websites that feature apocalyptic forecasts have grown like weeds on the Web, and at least one well-known libertarian site has shifted from more analytical material to heavy doses of gloom-and-doom. An odd aspect of this increasing tendency toward Chicken-Little-ism is that it now comes for the most part in two completely different versions. Let's call them the Left Version and the Right Version.

The Left Version, of course, has been bombarding us for the past forty or fifty years mainly as a warning of imminent environmental catastrophe—of near-term exhaustion of natural resources, terminal ruin of a hyper-polluted physical environment and, most recently, overheating of the earth's atmosphere with countless attendant climatic disasters. Leftists who peddle this terrifying prospect seek to allay the threat by ceding totalitarian powers to government officials who in their copious wisdom will save the day, if only narrowly and at the cost of our liberties and our modern standard of living.

The Right Version has resided for decades more in the shadows cast by millenarians, goldbugs, and self-anointed financial gurus than in the bright media glow that has illuminated the leftists' prophecies. Recently, however, many more people seem to have concluded that the only sane course is to forsake all hope for the continuation of socioeconomic life as we have known it, and hence that preparation for a complete social and economic meltdown—Greater-than-Great Depression, hyperinflation, dollar collapse—obliges us to stock up on guns, ammo, gold, and a larder full of dried beans and other survivalist goodies.

It is interesting that although many people take an ominous forecast more or less seriously, they have embraced dramatically different conceptions of the nature of the impending doom. Are those who foresee the future so differently living in the same world? If so, how can they have come to such clashing conclusions about the events to come?

The answer, I believe, has to do with ideology,[1] which I have long defined as a somewhat coherent, rather comprehensive belief system about social relations, noting that each such system has four distinct aspects: cognitive, moral, programmatic, and solidary. Ideologies permit people to understand, evaluate, and cope with a social world otherwise too vast and complicated to comprehend. If two persons embrace starkly different ideologies, they can easily arrive at starkly different visions of future developments, even when presented with the same information.

Can objective facts and established scientific theories cut through all of this ideological noise, substituting the pure, harmonious tones of truth for the cacophony of wild-eyed, mutually inconsistent ideologies? No, they cannot. In the determination of human beliefs, ideological outlooks and propensities have the power to override virtually any kind of inconsistent information or knowledge. Decades may pass, yet the Club of Rome remains as convinced as ever that environmental and natural-resource disasters are imminent. Stock markets may soar by multiples while confirmed "bears" never lose their faith that selling short is the road to financial paradise—hedge-fund manager Michael Berger defrauded a multitude of trusting investors, not to mention tricking the government regulators, and drove his firm Manhattan Capital[2] into bankruptcy because he could not surrender his bearish convictions even during a prolonged run-up in stock prices in the late 1990s.

So the answer to my previous question is, yes, different sets of people in effect do live in different worlds, notwithstanding their physical coexistence on

---

1. Robert Higgs, *Neither Liberty nor Safety: Fear, Ideology, and the Growth of Government* (Oakland, CA: Independent Institute, 2007).

2. Chidem Kurdas, "Does Regulation Prevent Fraud?," *The Independent Review*, 13:3 (Winter 2009), 325–43.

planet earth during extended time spans. And therefore you'll have a devil of a time disabusing any of them of their cherished visions. Strange to say, many people fall in love even with their preferred brand of apocalypse. Doomster Paul Erlich might have lost his famous bet with Julian Simon, but he never cried uncle. As Ed Regis wrote in *Wired*:

> A more perfect resolution of the Ehrlich-Simon debate could not be imagined. All of the former's grim predictions had been decisively overturned by events. Ehrlich was wrong about higher natural resource prices, about "famines of unbelievable proportions" occurring by 1975, about "hundreds of millions of people starving to death" in the 1970s and '80s, about the world "entering a genuine age of scarcity."[3]

Yet in 1990, for his having promoted "greater public understanding of environmental problems," Ehrlich received a MacArthur Foundation "genius" award. And so it goes.

If you want to load up on gold, who am I to tell you that you're making a bad bet? I don't know what the price of gold or anything else will be in the future. (I also happen to believe that nobody else knows or can know. Someone who knew the course of future prices could easily and quickly acquire the wealth of Croesus simply by making appropriate transactions in the futures markets.)

What I do know is that for thousands of years, some people have been telling their fellows that the end is near, and although some terrible things did happen from time to time, hardly ever did they prove to be as catastrophic as the prophets' most foreboding warnings had foretold. The sky never rained blood, the oceans never boiled, the ground never rose up to crush squealing humanity between heaven and earth. Of course, as David Hume has taught us, this history is no guarantee that such an apocalypse won't happen. Nevertheless, I am inclined to make my bets on the basis of a somewhat more temperate outlook.

---

3. Ed Regis, "The Doomslayer," *Wired.com*, http://archive.wired.com/wired/archive/5.02/ffsimon_pr.html.

28

Communism's Persistent Pull

PLATO SUPPOSED COMMUNISM—not only of ordinary property, but also of wives and children—to be an ideal social arrangement. Jesus told his disciples to sell all that they owned and give the proceeds to the poor. Through the ages, little sects more numerous than anyone can count have embraced some form of Communism as the basis of their utopian communities. John Lennon's immensely popular visionary song "Imagine" includes the line, "imagine no possessions, it's easy if you try." Even today, when the horrors of communism are known to everyone, social democrats the world over continue to denounce and undermine private property rights and seek to replace them with some form of collectivized property. Since the late nineteenth century, most intellectuals have been hostile to private property rights and have advocated, if not outright communism, at least some "third way" closer to it than to a regime of full-fledged private property.

Why have so many people regarded communism as the most desirable form of social organization?

F. A. Hayek offers a hypothesis in his final book *The Fatal Conceit.*[1] He argues that human beings act in many ways according to genetic predispositions inherited from a long period of development—a million or more years—during which they lived in small bands similar to, and indeed sometimes nothing more than, extended families. The family, of course, is a sort of communist arrangement: its members, especially the younger ones, live not by producing wealth and exchanging the rights to it among themselves, but

---

1. F. A. Hayek, *The Fatal Conceit: The Errors of Socialism* (Chicago: University of Chicago Press, 1991).

by sharing in accordance with at-least-partly altruistic allocations made by the older members. By this means, human beings survived and eventually prospered. Humans who arranged their affairs differently, one presumes, died out, leaving only those who had been molded by and sought to maintain the traditional family arrangement. Little bands and tribes amounted to nothing more than the family writ large and managed their economic affairs accordingly.

When human beings finally began to interact with one another extensively in what Hayek calls "the great society"—the wider world of various tribes and nations and of far-flung markets linking them through commercial exchanges—they retained, according to Hayek, a genetic predisposition to conduct their affairs in the communal fashion of families and small bands from time immemorial. However, Hayek argues further, the altruism and fully shared information that had undergirded the conduct of the family and the band do not, indeed, cannot exist in the great society. Seeking to replicate those primeval arrangements on a vastly greater scale is a futile quest. It represents only "an atavistic longing after the life of the noble savage." At its worst, it gives rise to tragic disasters such as those experienced in the twentieth century in Russia, China, and other similarly collectivized societies.

Hayek's hypothesis is plausible, but I have no idea whether it is the best interpretation of the persistent human longing for some form of communism. This hypothesis, like most such socio-biological explanations, seems to be a "just so story"—it seems to make sense, but we lack a clear means of testing and possibly refuting it.

Other interpretations of the intellectuals' penchant for communism certainly have been advanced.

For example, Ludwig von Mises argues in *The Anti-Capitalist Mentality*[2] that the intellectuals suffer from frustration, envy, and resentment and blame their relatively poor position in the economy and society on "the rich," especially the capitalists who have gained the greatest wealth by serving consumers most successfully in the markets. The other side of the intellectuals' hatred of the free-market system is their yearning for communism or some other system similarly hostile to private property rights.

---

2. Ludwig von Mises, *The Anti-Capitalist Mentality* (Auburn, AL: Ludwig von Mises Institute, 2010 [1956]).

In an essay titled "Why Do Intellectuals Oppose Capitalism?,"[3] Robert Nozick argues similarly that the intellectuals are people who were good at school work but are not good at practical affairs and therefore fail to gain the great wealth and social position achieved by business people and investors who, however unremarkable they might have been as schoolchildren, have what it takes to succeed in the marketplace. The intellectuals, convinced that the smart people (that is, those who were good at school) should run the world and rise to the top of society, harbor intense resentment toward the people who navigate the market most successfully and hence toward the socioeconomic order that accommodates this success.

Many people have taken notice recently that John Lennon was killed thirty years ago, and a great deal of maudlin sentiment has been on display in this regard. Radio stations have hauled out Lennon's recording of "Imagine" to adorn this weepy occasion. Although I consider Lennon to have been a gifted songwriter, I do not recommend him as a political or social philosopher. Nevertheless, I do not condemn "Imagine" in every regard. The music itself is beautiful and beautifully performed, and I cherish the line, "Imagine there's no countries / It isn't hard to do." After all, what is a nation-state but a sort of communism in its own right: a violent suppression of competing private protective agencies by a single, all-encompassing, exceedingly presumptive, and often worthless guardian—and a spectacularly obnoxious one, to boot.

---

3. Robert Nozick, "Why Do Intellectuals Oppose Capitalism?," *Libertarianism.org*, http://www.libertarianism.org/publications/essays/why-do-intellectuals-oppose-capitalism.

29

The Dangers of Samuelson's Economic Method

PAUL A. SAMUELSON died on December 13, 2009, at the age of 94. For more than half a century, he was a towering figure in the economics profession and, to some degree, in the wider world. When I was first learning economics, in the 1960s, Samuelson was held up by my teachers as the greatest living economist—a genius, they used to say— and his way of doing economics was generally regarded as virtually defining how to carry out economic analysis scientifically. In the course of my undergraduate and graduate training, I was never given any reason to doubt that assessment.

Indeed, a memorably painful part of my graduate education consisted of my attempts to read and understand Samuelson's landmark book *Foundations of Economic Analysis,*[1] a treatise in mathematical economic theory, patterned after classical thermodynamics, which set the tone for much of what the cleverest mainstream economists would do for decades to come. The protocol became: build a mathematical model of abstract actors engaged in constrained maximization or minimization of an objective function; prove that the model has a stable equilibrium; show how the model's equilibrium conditions change when its parameters are changed (the so-called method of comparative statics).

I also had the pleasure—if that is the right word—of meeting Samuelson in person once, early in 1968, when I visited the economics department at MIT as a candidate for a job there. At a luncheon seminar with Samuelson and several other members of the department, I experienced firsthand the

---

1. Paul Anthony Samuelson, *Foundations of Economic Analysis* (New York: Atheneum, 1965 [1947]).

famous Samuelsonian wit and arrogance. Although the members of the group bantered and joked at one another's expense during the luncheon, as academics commonly do, it was clear to me that Samuelson's jokes at a colleague's expense dominated a colleague's jokes at his expense. This pecking order came as no surprise to me. I was taken aback, however, that the great man also made jokes at my expense. Of course, as an apprehensive and insecure 24-year-old looking for a job, I made no jokes at anybody's expense, and certainly not at Samuelson's. More than forty years later, and somewhat wiser in the often ill-mannered ways of academia, I remain disappointed that the acclaimed "greatest living economist," a man who only two years later would become the first American to receive the Nobel Prize in economics, chose to make sport of a mere graduate student.

Mathematics Is the Language, Induction Is the Method

Anyone who has read Samuelson's articles and books, however, knows that his arrogance often stands in prominent display. Whether he was the greatest living economist or not, he often expressed himself with the kind of Olympian condescension that strongly suggests he believed himself to be Numero Uno. I was struck by this quality most recently in reading, strange to say, his 1952 article "Economic Theory and Mathematics—An Appraisal." At the end of the first paragraph, Samuelson writes, "I firmly believe in the virtues of understatement and lack of pretension."[2] Upon encountering this affirmation of authorial modesty, I nearly burst out laughing.

Although Samuelson declares that he comes "not to praise mathematics, but rather to slightly debunk its use in economics," the thrust of his article can scarcely be described as debunking. Indeed, in my view, he makes grandiose and indefensible claims on behalf of the use of mathematics in economics. I am no philosopher, but I venture to say also that he makes indefensible claims about mathematics itself—a point that I will leave for better qualified heads to judge. Samuelson's main claim is that "in deepest logic," mathematics and

---

2. Paul A. Samuelson, "Economic Theory and Mathematics—An Appraisal," *American Economic Review* 42:2 (1952).

prose "are strictly identical." My not-very-highly-tutored philosophical hunch is that this claim will no longer be regarded as holding water, if it ever was so regarded. Yet, like many of Samuelson's declarations, it is expressed with the sort of absolute confidence typical of the early generations of logical positivists.

Samuelson maintains that "[e]very science is based squarely on induction—on observation of empirical facts. . . . [D]eduction has the modest linguistic role of translating certain empirical hypotheses into their 'logical equivalents.'" It seems obvious that for him, as for his legions of disciples, an a priori economic theory, such as the praxeological theory that Ludwig von Mises expounds in *Human Action*, does not qualify as science. Although he does not mention Mises in the article, one suspects that he might have had the great Austrian economist in mind when he wrote, "[N]o a priori empirical truths can exist in any field. If a thing has a priori irrefutable truth, it must be empty of empirical content." He then affirms, with characteristic haughtiness, that "at the rough and ready level that concerns the scientist in his everyday work," this view is "widely recognized by scientists in every discipline. The only exceptions are to be found in certain backwaters of economics, and I shall not here do more than point the finger of scorn at those who carry into the twentieth century ideas that were not very good even in their earlier heyday."

Samuelson contra the Austrian School

In the foreword to the 1965 paperback reprint of *Foundations*, Samuelson explicitly identifies Mises in connection with what he what he had previously derided as "certain backwaters of economics":

> Those concerned with general problems of philosophy of science and
> its methodology may find modern economics of considerable interest.
> By this I do not mean that the methodological views of the venerable
> economist Ludwig von Mises are more interesting than the positivistic
> views of his deceased brother, Richard von Mises, the distinguished
> physicist and mathematician. In my view they definitely are not.[3]

---

3. Samuelson, *Foundations,* ix.

One wonders what status Samuelson would accord the Action Axiom— the statement that human beings have ends and use means in conscious attempts to attain those ends. Would he deny that it is apodictically certain a priori? And would he also deny that it is empirically valid?

In a 1957 defense of Misesian methodology, Murray N. Rothbard notes, "Whether we consider the Action Axiom 'a priori' or 'empirical' depends on our ultimate philosophical position." He observes that Mises, taking a Kantian view, regards the axiom as "a law of thought and therefore a categorical truth a priori to all experience." In contrast, Rothbard considers the axiom "a law of reality rather than a law of thought, and hence 'empirical' rather than 'a priori,'" although he concedes that "this type of 'empiricism' is so out of step with modern empiricism that I may just as well continue to call it a priori" for the arguments at issue. He explicates the axiom by saying: "(1) it is a law of reality that is not conceivably falsifiable, and yet is empirically meaningful and true; (2) it rests on universal inner experience, and not simply on external experience, i.e., its evidence is reflective rather than physical; and (3) it is clearly a priori to complex historical events."[4] Samuelson does not deign to consider these issues, opting instead for supercilious derision.

Samuelson does mention one great Austrian economist, indeed, the founder of the Austrian School himself, Carl Menger. His remarks at this point merit extended quotation. "Jevons, Walras, and Menger," he writes, "each independently arrived at the so-called 'theory of subjective value.' And . . . Menger did arrive at his formulation without the use of mathematics. But," he continues,

> I should point out that a recent rereading of the excellent English translation of Menger's 1871 work convinces me that it is the least important of the three works cited; and that its relative neglect by modern writers was not simply the result of bad luck or scholarly negligence. I should also add that the important revolution of the 1870's had little really to do with either subjective value and utility or with marginalism; rather it consisted of the perfecting of the general relations of supply and

---

4. Murray N. Rothbard, "In Defense of Extreme Apriorism," *Southern Economic Journal* 23 (January 1957): 317–18.

demand. It culminated in Walrasian general equilibrium. And we are forced to agree with Schumpeter's appraisal of Walras as the greatest of theorists—not because he used mathematics, since the methods used are really quite elementary—but because of the key importance of the concept of general equilibrium itself.[5]

Samuelson's evaluation, one might venture to say, has matters exactly backward. He fails to see how and why Menger's development of marginal utility and related economic theory is actually superior to the formulations of Jevons and Walras. On this question, the reader can do no better than to consult Jörg Guido Hülsmann's splendid dehomogenization of the three marginalist pioneers' views in his magnificent, recently published biography *Mises: The Last Knight of Liberalism.*

Hülsmann quotes William Jaffé's comments, which are so apt that I quote them again here:

> Menger kept too close to the real world for either the verbal or symbolic formulation of the theory; and in the real world he saw no sharply defined points of equilibrium, but rather bounded indeterminacies not only in isolated bilateral barter but also in competitive market trading. . . . With his attention unswervingly fixed on reality, Menger could not, and did not, abstract from the difficulties traders face in any attempt to obtain all the information required for anything like a pinpoint equilibrium determination of market prices to emerge, nor did his approach permit him to abstract from the uncertainties that veil the future, even the near future in the conscious anticipation of which most present transactions take place.[6]

In this light, we see clearly that Samuelson's positivist insistence that economic science must rest on empirical facts clashes with his expressed preference for abstract, perfect-information general equilibrium, à la Jevons and Walras, in lieu of Menger's utterly realistic foundation for economic reasoning.

---

5. Samuelson, "Economic Theory and Mathematics," 61.

6. Jaffé as quoted in Jürg Guido Hülsmann, *Mises: The Last Knight of Liberalism* (Auburn, AL.: Ludwig von Mises Institute, 2007), 135.

Methodological Monism versus Methodological Dualism

Nothing has done more to render modern economic theory a sterile and irrelevant exercise in autoeroticism than its practitioners' obsession with mathematical, general equilibrium models. Not only does this focus result in the futile spinning of mental wheels by mathematical pseudo-economists, but it has pernicious consequences for policy formulation because, as James M. Buchanan has observed, it gives rise to "the most sophisticated fallacy in economic theory, the notion that because certain relationships hold in equilibrium [in the model] the forced interferences designed to implement these relationships [in the real world] will, in fact, be desirable."[7]

Samuelson writes that although mathematicians occasionally make mistakes, "it is surprising how rare pure mistakes in logic are." To his credit, he then recognizes a highly important point: "Where the really big mistakes are made is in the formulation of premises." He counts it "one of the advantages of the mathematical medium," however, that he and the other model builders "are forced to lay our cards on the table so that all can see our premises." This statement appears at first glance to place mathematical modeling in a favorable light. Yet what advantage is gained if the premises are clearly laid out, seen by everyone to be wholly artificial, otherworldly, or even impossible, and then the deductive game proceeds as if an economic theory based on such premises were perfectly acceptable merely because its premises are so visible and clearly specified? Anyone who has ever mocked the scholastics for counting angels on the head of a pin should try to read an article in the *Journal of Economic Theory* or any other leading outlet for mainstream economic modeling. Talk about a parallel universe!

"There are," Samuelson insists, "no separate methodological problems that face the social scientist different in kind from those that face any other scientist." This claim flies in the face of what everyone ought to sense intuitively: that human beings, who have purposes, choose means of serving them, change their purposes from time to time, and on occasion devise completely new means, differ fundamentally from electrons, molecules, and light waves

---

7. James M. Buchanan, "General Implications of Subjectivism in Economics," in *What Should Economists Do?* (Indianapolis: Liberty Fund, 1979), 83.

(or are they particles?). Mises expounded methodological dualism persuasively in many of his writings. This exposition appears, for example, at the very beginning of his important and unjustly ignored book *Theory and History* (1957), where he notes that given our ignorance of "how external events—physical, chemical, and physiological—affect human thoughts, ideas, and judgments of value," the domain of knowledge is necessarily split "into two separate fields, the realm of external events, commonly called nature, and the realm of human thought and action."

He continues: "The sciences of human action," properly construed, "start from the fact that man purposefully aims at ends he has chosen. It is precisely this that all brands of positivism, behaviorism, and panphysicalism want either to deny altogether or to pass over in silence"—or, as in Samuelson's case, to dismiss with ridicule and scorn as unworthy of economic scientists in the modern age. Sad to say, not all change is true progress, and in modern mainstream economics—which we might justly denominate Samuelsonian economics—much of the change in professional precepts and practices has been manifestly for the worse.

Coda

Having suffered through my Samuelsonian training in graduate school, I immediately began to move away from it once I became an economist. In fact, I increasingly grew to believe that the worst aspects of modern economics owe more to Samuelson than to any other single economist. Eventually I became convinced that the modern mainstream's so-called scientific economics is not truly scientific at all, but a species of scientism—the misapplication of methods developed for the study of material reality to the study of human choice and cooperation.

In 1993, *Reason* magazine invited a number of writers, including me, to contribute a brief entry for a feature called "Know Thy Enemy." The idea was that each of us would "suggest a book published in the last 50 years that is significant because it has helped promote wrongheaded ideas with serious consequences." For my contribution, I selected Samuelson's *Foundations*. If I had to identify such a book today, I still could not think of a more apposite choice.

30

Don't Accuse Me of Blaming America When I Blame the Government

IN DISCOURSE ABOUT public affairs, words matter much more than most people appreciate. We live immersed in language so twisted and abused, in part by the design of interested parties and in part by the sloth of inattentive speakers and listeners, that we often fail to notice or object to linguistic miscarriages that pass for intelligent expression. The examples are legion, but here I have in mind a particular turn of phrase that American conservatives, especially neocons, have employed in recent years as a counter-strike against critics of U.S. foreign and defense policy: They describe such critics as "blaming America" or sometimes as "blaming America first" for attacks against this country or its citizens abroad.

Thus, for example, those who fault U.S. Middle East policies for creating the conditions that caused Muslim fanatics to attack Americans, both at home and overseas, are said to be blaming America for what the policy's defenders' take to be the unprovoked acts of terrorists bent on imposing Sharia on the United States, destroying this country's freedoms, or attaining another such farfetched objective.

Applications to earlier events and policies include use of the expression to fend off the arguments and evidence of those who maintain that the Roosevelt administration waged economic warfare in 1940–41 to provoke a Japanese attack that would justify and lead directly to full-fledged U.S. engagement in World War II; and use of the expression against those who argue that the Truman administration bore at least partial responsibility for the on-set of the Cold War. People accused of blaming America are commonly called "America haters."

Although this riposte to criticism is the rhetorical tactic of first resort for the more simple-minded, flag-waving species of self-anointed patriots, it is by no means their exclusive property. Neocons writing in such elevated outlets as the *New York Times* and the *Washington Post* have not been bashful about smearing their critics as people who "blame America." I noticed this linguistic resort most recently in a commentary by an intelligent, reasonable economist and was shocked that he would embrace this trope while suggesting that "pacifists" and others who criticize U.S. foreign and defense policies are unrealistically imagining that international disputes and warfare can somehow be eliminated from human affairs.

In my view, replying to policy critics by accusing them of "blaming America" is worse than linguistically crude and ideologically twisted; it is stupid.

First, and most important, let us recognize that the U.S. government is not America. Notwithstanding the ease with which politicians and their speechwriters toss around the idea that "America needs X" or "America should do Y," the word America has so many distinct referents that it is extremely ambiguous. In current common usage, *America* may refer to, among other things, the geographic area within U.S. borders; the population residing in this area; the traditions, customs, social practices, and norms that these persons regard as uniquely their own; the ideals that they have long expressed as their foremost aspirations; or a specific group of persons representing the United States in international organizations or competitions (e.g., "America won more medals than any other country in the Olympic games").

Only in discussions of international relations do we automatically understand America to be the same thing as the U.S. government. Thus, when we say that "America entered World War I in 1917," it is understood that the statement means "U.S. government officials, specifically members of Congress and the president, declared the U.S. government to be at war against the German Empire and its allies in 1917." And when we say that "America ratified the United Nations Charter in 1945," we mean that "a majority of the members of the U.S. Senate voted in favor of this treaty."

Notice, however, that if one were to presume that the foregoing use of "America"—that is, the international-relations usage that takes America to be identical to all or part of the U.S. government—were the one being employed, it would make no sense to say that critics of U.S. policy are "blaming

America," because that statement would amount to saying that critics of U.S. government policies are blaming the U.S. government, which is obvious and redundant.

However, it is equally senseless for defenders of U.S. policy to suppose that the policy's critics are blaming America in any of the senses specified in the third paragraph before this one. Critics are not blaming the geographic area, the resident population, the people's traditions and customs, or their foremost ideals.

Critics who are said to be "blaming America" are in fact simply blaming the U.S. government, and defenders of the government's policy who wield this polemical sword are implying either that the government and the people *are* one and the same or that the government indeed bears responsibility for adopting and implementing the policy in question, but should not be faulted for doing so. Either way, the defenders are standing on quicksand.

The government—the collection of politicians, soldiers, hired bureaucrats, and assorted flunkies who devise and carry out U.S. policies—makes mistakes. Of course, many of the actions and policies that sooner or later are generally regarded as mistakes were not mistakes at all, but merely actions and policies that, contrary to official declarations, did not serve the general public's interests, although they served well enough the interests of key government officials and their major supporters. But set aside that class of actions. The government makes mistakes even in its attempts to attain objectives it truly seeks to attain. It cannot help but make such mistakes because its decision makers have limited information, often poor judgment, biases of various sorts in the evaluation of information they do possess, and other shortcomings too numerous to recite.

So, why should anyone suppose that the government simply cannot be mistaken, and hence legitimately criticized for its mistakes? So far as the bulk of the American people are concerned, a great many U.S. foreign and defense policies—from the very beginning of the United States, but especially since the late nineteenth century—have been mistaken. For example, it is very difficult to argue honestly that U.S. engagement in World War I served the general interest of Americans. In ways great and small, Woodrow Wilson's bid to play the role of global messiah had negative repercussions so horrifying that some of them continue to wreak harm to this day (e.g., the creation of artificial, unsustainable state boundaries in the Middle East). It is similarly difficult to argue that the U.S. war in Vietnam was a positive event for the American people at large. And how can anyone mount a strong argument that U.S. engagement in the Middle East since the early 1950s has *not* served to antagonize and destabilize the entire region and turn some of its young people into fanatics bent on revenge against Americans? Indeed, for some of us, who are not flying on pro-government autopilot, it seems that the bulk of the more important U.S. foreign and defense policies, particularly in the past hundred years, has been adverse to the general interest of the American people, however hyped up most of those people might have become when the government plunged into unnecessary wars and the people rallied round the flag, at least in the beginning.

Ambrose Bierce observed in *The Devil's Dictionary*, "In Dr. Johnson's famous dictionary patriotism is defined as the last resort of a scoundrel. With all due respect to an enlightened but inferior lexicographer, I beg to submit that it is the first."[1] H. L. Mencken amended Johnson's dictum by saying, "But there is something even worse: it is the first, last, and middle range of fools." So, no one who criticizes U.S. foreign and defense policy should feel pushed onto the defensive when told that he is "blaming America" or acting as an "America hater." Indeed, it might be best if he broke into laughter to indicate that such a response to his criticism betokens either a juvenile mentality or a shameless willingness to serve as a running dog of the U.S. regime.

I hold myself second to none in my adoration of the amber waves of grain and the purple mountain majesties. I revere the ideal that this nation should serve as a beacon of freedom to the world and a refuge for its huddled masses yearning to breathe free. I weep with pride each time I watch the ailing Lou Gehrig tell the crowd at Yankee Stadium, "Today I consider myself the luckiest man on the face of this earth." I don't blame these beautiful, decent, and admirable aspects of America in the least for the chronic failure of U.S. foreign and defense policy to serve the general public interest.

With regard to the fools, mountebanks, unscrupulous opportunists, and psychopaths who have long played the greatest roles in devising and implementing U.S. foreign and defense policy, however, I hold a quite different and decidedly less favorable opinion.

---

1. Ambrose Bierce, *The Devil's Dictionary, Tales and Memoirs*, ed. S. T. Joshi (New York: Library of America, 2011).

31

Extreme Aggregation Misleads Macroeconomists and the Fed

DESPITE THE ASTONISHING flood of more than a trillion dollars in new commercial-bank reserves that the Fed created in late 2008 and early 2009 when it undertook to rescue the big banks and other institutions from the consequences of their boom-time mistakes, Ben Bernanke has insisted that the Fed can and will contain this inflationary potential, and he has emphasized that inflation remains under control, indeed, that potential *d*eflation presents the greater danger. He rests his case on the evidence of standard macroeconomic indexes.

Standard measures of the money stock, for example, have not increased greatly. The year-to-year change (ending in January 2011) in M2 was only 4.3 percent; the two-year change, only 6.4 percent. For MZM (money zero maturity), the corresponding rates of change were 2.6 percent and 4.4 percent, respectively. Thus it would appear that by historical standards money has grown quite moderately in the past two years.

Bernanke and his supporting cast of monetary economists can also point to corroborating evidence that by historical standards the rate of inflation has been modest. The year-to-year change (ending in January 2011) in the all-items consumer price index (CPI) was only 1.7 percent; the two-year change, only 4.3 percent. The implicit price deflator for GDP, the broadest of all price indexes, reveals even less inflation. This index, which is computed on a quarterly basis, shows a one-year change of only 1.4 percent for the year ending in the fourth quarter of 2010, and a corresponding two-year change of only 1.8 percent.[1]

---

1. I have computed all of the figures mentioned in this article from basic data available at the website maintained by the Federal Reserve Bank of St. Louis, "Federal Reserve Economic Data," at research.stlouisfed.org/fred2/categories/.

The foregoing variables are the ones that macroeconomists and monetary analysts at the Fed consult most often in their analysis of the economy's performance and of the relation between money and inflation. So if Bernanke tells us that inflation is not a problem, he is clearly resting his case on the kinds of evidence that the country's recognized experts in the great universities view as scientifically *de rigueur.*

A serious problem lurks, however, in the way the mainstream experts think about the economy, and hence in the kind of analysis they undertake to assess its current performance and its likely future changes. All too often, they model the macroeconomy as a black box into which flow undifferentiated "labor" services and "capital" services and out of which flows a uniform substance called "output," measured empirically by estimates of real GDP. Units of this output command a price known as the "price level," measured empirically by the GDP deflator; otherwise, prices play no role in the model. The interest rate plays only a limited role as a determinant of the demand for money and as a minor determinant of saving and investment spending. Time is essentially irrelevant. There is no time structure of production in which certain kinds of production must precede others in a process running from raw materials to intermediate goods to completed consumer goods because, as mentioned, such distinctions among different kinds of goods are ignored in favor of positing a single homogeneous "output." Just as time plays no role, and hence the interest rate (the price of goods available now relative to goods available later) plays no role in resource allocation, so location does not matter. It's as though all production took place at a Euclidian point, and therefore no one need worry about, say, the government's injecting "stimulus" money into Connecticut in order to lower unemployment in Nevada.

Although modern macroeconomic models, which have been constructed since the 1930s, vary in many ways, and some of them do not conform to the foregoing description in one way or another, the general approach of macroeconomic analysis fits my description all too well. It is a mode in analysis in which the time structure of production is ignored, interest rates play little or no role in allocating resources between time periods, a single output is produced, and inputs are viewed as homogeneous in kind, quality, and location. If one suspects that such extreme simplification may be squeezing every feature of the Prince of Denmark out of *Hamlet,* one's instincts are alive and well.

Because this approach to thinking about the macroeconomy is essentially timeless—inputs flow in and outputs flow out simultaneously during any arbitrarily defined period of time—the Fed's scrutiny of the economy's performance tends to be extraordinarily focused on the recent past (from which its most up-to-date data come) and the near-term future. Truly long-run considerations scarcely come into play, as the Fed attempts to fine tune its policy instruments at monthly or more frequent intervals to keep the economy on a smooth growth path with a low rate of inflation and a low rate of unemployment—in truth, an impossible task even if performed with the greatest competence, because the number of targets exceeds the number of instruments. So Bernanke is always referring to the most recent report on inflation, for example, to demonstrate that the Fed has taken the optimal policy stance; and he always assures us that whenever new data reveal a deviation from the desired economic conditions, the Fed will take appropriate steps to correct its previous misstep.

Such myopic monetary policymaking has great potential for creating too much monetary stimulus in certain periods, then overreacting by creating too much monetary contraction, thereby introducing or amplifying fluctuations in the economy's real growth or its rate of inflation that would not occur if the Fed did not exist. As Roger Garrison observes, the Fed is a loose cannon on the economy's deck, rolling with great momentum here and there as the ship pitches and rolls and wreaking havoc as it crashes into everything in its compass. Bernanke claims to have absorbed Milton Friedman's teachings about the Fed's responsibility for causing the Great Depression, but he evidently skipped Friedman's class on the day that the professor told the pupils that monetary policy exerts its effects with long and variable lags. Because of these unpredictable lags, the Fed is always, as it were, reacting to information that does not tell the full story about how the economy is already responding, or eventually will respond, to monetary policy changes that extend for a year or more into the past.

One error the Fed makes time and again is failure to recognize until it is too late that it has already built inflation into the system. So we might well wonder whether the Fed is making that very error now. Several indicators suggest strongly that it is doing so.

Inflation does not usually appear equally throughout the economy. Instead, it normally begins in the markets for raw materials and intermediate goods and then works its way to consumer-goods markets, where retailers always explain to irate buyers that they are raising prices only because their cost of goods has risen. If such inflation is occurring now, we can identify it by checking the producer price index (PPI) and some of its components.

Looking first at the overall PPI, we find that the year-to-year change (ending in January 2011) was 5.7 percent, or 4 percentage points greater than the change in the CPI; the two-year change was 12.3 percent, or 8 percentage points greater than the change in the CPI.

Some important components of the PPI have risen even faster. For the PPI for crude foodstuffs and feedstuffs, the one-year change was 20.6 percent, the two-year change, 25.6 percent. The PPI for fuels and power shows a one-year change of 6.5 percent and a two-year change of 33.1 percent. Because food, feed, fuel, and power are so critical to many of the world's poorer countries, these rapid increases in prices have already provoked riots and other displays of desperation throughout the world. It is reasonable to assume that before long the price increases in these markets will have an effect on the rate of increase in consumer-goods prices in the United States and other advanced economies.

We may also look for price changes that reflect market participants' expectation of future inflation and hence their attempts to purchase real goods that might serve as hedges against such price acceleration. Here the most notable indicators include, of course, the price of gold. For the closing gold price in January 2011, the one-year increase was 24.0 percent, the two-year increase, 44.3 percent. Other such indicators come from the stock market, where traders bid up share prices in the expectation of future net income to be earned from the firms' sales of real goods and services. For the Standard & Poor's 500 index, the one-year increase (ending in January 2011) was 19.8 percent, the two-year increase, 55.7 percent.

Bernanke dismisses evidence such as the foregoing by noting, correctly, that the prices of producer goods typically vary more than the prices of consumer goods. In his view, one only muddies the waters of one's analysis of inflation by taking note of producer prices. He might similarly dismiss the zooming prices of gold and corporate stocks as the product of forces unrelated to monetary policy—which they might be, of course, but in the present case I do not think they are.

Bernanke is a celebrated mainstream macroeconomist. His achievements in this field account for his having become Fed chairman in the first place. But his background, training, and research have predisposed him, as it has predisposed almost all mainstream macro and monetary economists, to think about the macroeconomy and about the relation between money and inflation in a way that hides essential elements of what is actually occurring. The root of all of these evils is excessive aggregation. The reigning macroeconomic analysis also has other important flaws, as I have suggested, but however these other problems might be dealt with, as long as mainstream analysts continue to work within the confines of such highly aggregated models, continued failures to understand and control the economy's movements are well-nigh inevitable.

32

Why Do So Many People Automatically and Angrily Condemn Historical Revisionism?

OVER THE YEARS, especially in writing for the general public, as opposed to my professional peers, I have been struck repeatedly by the frequency with which certain conclusions or even entire classes of conclusions elicit not merely skepticism, but angry denunciation. Again and again, I have been called a fool, a traitor, or an America-hater because of my commentaries on history and public affairs. Although I take no pleasure in these denunciations, I find myself not so much depressed as curious about them. I wonder why people react as they do, especially when my commentary rests—as I hope it generally does—on well-documented facts and correct logic.

I surely do not consider myself immune to errors, of course. But if my facts are incorrect, the critic has an obligation to say *why* my facts are incorrect and to state, or at least to point toward, the correct facts. If my logic has run off the rails, the critic has an obligation to state *how* I fell into fallacious reasoning. More often than not, however, the critic resorts immediately to name-calling and to wild characterizations of my statements and my person. Thus I have often been called a socialist, a Marxist, a conservative, an apologist for corporations or the rich, a (modern left) liberal, or something else that by no stretch of the imagination properly describes me or my intellectual or ideological position.

Certain topics are virtually guaranteed to elicit such reactions. When I write about the welfare state and especially about government programs ostensibly aimed at helping the least-well-off members of society, I confidently expect that critics will assail me as a fascist or as an ivory-tower dweller who has no understanding of how poor people really live and no compassion for them. When I write about the Japanese attack on Pearl Harbor in relation to

U.S. economic warfare in 1939–41, I invariably attract angry personal abuse from people of delicate nationalistic sensibilities, from those chronically on the look-out for traitors, and from those who cannot imagine that the nation's leaders, in general, and President Franklin D. Roosevelt, in particular, might have deliberately provoked a Japanese attack or refrained from warning U.S. commanders in Hawaii that an attack was coming.

When people are offended or otherwise greatly displeased by historical analysis, they often employ the term "historical revisionism" as a synonym for falsified, distorted, or doctored accounts that fly in the face of what they, their history teachers, and perhaps even the most respected university historians believe to have been the case.

The irony of such use of the term "historical revision," which makes it practically a swear word, is that revisionism is and always has been an integral part of historical research and writing. As a rule, professional historians do not seek simply to pile up more and more evidence for what historians already generally believe. Historians who proceed in this way cannot expect to make much of a name for themselves. Instead, historians try to find new evidence and new ways of interpreting old evidence that change the currently accepted view. That is, they seek to *revise* the current orthodoxy. In doing so, they need not be ideological mavericks, although those who are may have an additional reason for their revisionist efforts. In short, revisionism is an unremarkable aspect of workaday historical research and writing. Why then do so many readers go ballistic about it?

One reason why revisionists are sometimes seen as subversives stems from the tendency of historians in general to accept the most fundamental aspects of their own society as right and desirable. So, however much political historians may dispute the details of particular campaigns, elections, and policy-making by elected officials—and such disputation runs rampant, to be sure—one hardly expects these historians to conclude that the democratic process itself is little more than a snare and a delusion, a vast apparatus for fooling the masses into believing that they have genuine control over how they are ruled. And however much military and foreign-policy historians may argue with one another about how various wars were entered into and conducted, one hardly expects these historians to conclude that wars almost invariably hurt the mass of the people and benefit, if anyone at all, only the national leadership, its supporting elite, and a ragtag band of hangers-on (which includes, we might note, the "court historians").

When a historian strays outside the 40-yard lines within which the bulk of the historical writing and teaching takes place, however, he is likely to be met with the dreaded accusation that he is not an honest, competent, or "respected" historian, but a revisionist—a writer who seeks to propagate socially destructive and utterly unfounded ideas in order to rend the fabric of national unity and undermine the nation's virtues. Thus one who challenges the standard account of Pearl Harbor can expect not simply to be disbelieved, but also to be personally condemned and vilified. Readers will say that he dishonors the brave men who gave their lives to preserve our freedoms, and so forth. Many people possess a loaded ideological gun with a hair trigger, and the slightest shake suffices to cause them to fire away. Moreover, they shoot first and reserve their fact-checking and more careful thought for later, if indeed they ever reach that stage.

One is tempted to suspect that such quick-draw reactions reveal an underlying lack of confidence in their own beliefs. If my views are so manifestly stupid and anti-social, why respond to them at all? Is it not more sensible to ignore them than to spend time in lavishing calumny on their author? In the age of the Internet, however, many people seem to get their kicks by denouncing and insulting anyone who offends their own sensibilities and their own cherished beliefs. Anyone who seeks examples of ad hominem arguments may easily collect them by the thousands and perhaps by the millions at the websites that feature news and commentary on public affairs. Every species of logical fallacy may be found there in abundance, but my guess is that the ad hominem fallacy occurs more often than any other. Moreover, few people—even seemingly well-educated people—seem to be able to stay on point. So if a revisionist's argument cannot be refuted, his critics freely set up and knock down straw men that they represent as the offender himself. Careful reading is not the most notable activity of those who engage in such flailing away. Many attackers do not even complete their reading, but begin their assault on an author immediately, after having read only a few sentences or paragraphs, as they sometimes admit.

Well, nobody ever promised the revisionist a bed of roses, especially if he challenges ideas that are widely accepted and valued. Americans want to believe that their nation is the greatest that ever was, that they themselves are better than other people in almost every way, including morally. They want to believe that at least some of their government leaders were virtuous and heroic, that their soldiers sacrificed more nobly than the enemy's did, that their country is the last, best hope of humanity, blah, blah, blah. Much of this catalogue of taken-for-granted outlooks and beliefs is ludicrous, but woe unto the writer who laughs out loud at it. "Revisionist, revisionist!" the mobs will cry, expressing the demand that he "get out of the country" and the hope that every species of bad luck and personal misfortune will befall him. If I were one of those social psychologists who enjoy labeling any ideological trait they dislike as a form of mental illness, I might declare that the hair-trigger enemies of historical revisionism are a gaggle of sickos.

33

Where Should the
Burden of Proof Rest?

PERHAPS YOU HAVE been struck, as I have been repeatedly over the years, by the way in which certain disputes are framed. A writer, reporter, or discussant recognizes a difference of views on some matter: A maintains X, and B maintains Y. Yet, even though a difference is acknowledged, the question is resolved by concluding that X must be the case because B has not proven that Y is the case. This conclusion is often reached only on the assumption that A does not, or should not, bear a similar burden of proof.

Libertarians, for example, constantly encounter this situation when they argue against state provision of some good or service currently provided by the state. The libertarians might argue, say, that private suppliers can provide personal security in better quality or at lower cost than the government police can. Critics claim that the libertarians are wrong and note that the libertarians have not conclusively proven that private provision is better. Alternatively, critics sometimes claim that if private provision were actually better it would have already prevailed, conveniently ignoring the various ways in which the government has outlawed or burdened private provision, to preclude or cripple private competition with the state.

Even ostensibly impartial commentators generally lean toward placing the burden of proof on those who challenge the status quo, whether the dispute arises in science, politics, public policy, or any other domain in which an orthodoxy reigns or long-established institutions operate. This bias has a strongly conservative force in the sense that it helps to preserve whatever has gained sway, regardless of how it attained its current domination. Thus replacement of the geocentric model of planetary motion in the solar system with the heliocentric model required more than a century. Copernicus,

Galileo, Newton, and others had to adduce proof that their conception was superior to the Ptolemaic model, which was taken to be correct mainly by virtue of its having been accepted for a very long time.

Likewise, the modern nation-state has been a well-established institution for hundreds of years, during which it has tended to expand its size, scope, and power, ultimately achieving its current near-totalitarian form. People living now are accustomed to what the state is and what it does, and they have difficulty in imagining how alternative arrangements might operate at all, much less how they might operate much more successfully for the general public. Hence ordinary politics takes the form of arguments and policies that move the state back and forth between the 5-yard line and the 4-yard line, not far from the goal line of totalitarianism. The libertarians who propose to move the state back to the 50-yard line, or even to move it all the way to the opposite goal line of statelessness, have difficulty in gaining a hearing for their arguments, much less widespread acceptance of their proposals.

The libertarians' critics invariably respond that the libertarians are utopians, that they seek the impossible, notwithstanding that the modern nation-state did not always exist and that the hopes widely placed in the current nation-state—an institutional arrangement born in and sustained by periodic mass murder and continuous extortion and robbery—themselves testify to a genuinely utopian mindset. People dismiss the panoply of state crimes as aberrations or they adduce ad hoc explanations, rather than face the fact that across the extremely diverse times and places where unspeakably horrible large-scale crimes have been committed, the state has been the common denominator.

Like Winston Churchill, who famously quipped that democracy is the worst form of government except for all of the others, most people now presume—without seriously bearing a burden of proof—that the existing state system is superior to all possible alternatives. The libertarian has good reason to demand: show me. Give me an organized, rational, fact-based argument, not simply the flippant dismissal that I am a dreamer. Copernicus, Galileo, and Newton were widely viewed as dreamers in their day, too.

Morally speaking, it would seem that those who opt in favor of coercive arrangements ought to bear the burden of proof. If the state is such a superior arrangement, by comparison with genuine, voluntary self-government, why must the state be propped up by all of its police and armed forces? Why must people be constantly threatened with imprisonment and death in order to bring forth the revenues that support the state's activities? Walmart does not put a gun to my head to gain my patronage.

Of course, the standard mainstream-economics apology for this threat of violence against unwilling purchasers is that government provides a "public good" and hence must cope with a consequent "free rider" incentive to avoid payment. The trouble is that very little, if any, of what modern governments provide satisfies the criteria for categorization as a public good. The payments the government makes to grandma in her pension are not a public good, nor are the payments that compensate doctors and hospitals for grandpa's medical care, nor are the payments that purchase teachers and buildings to educate my neighbor's kids (while I homeschool my own), and on and on. The "national defense" that serves as the usual example of a government-supplied public good is in fact a ludicrously poor example. Many of us wish the armed forces would cease their current activities in stirring up trouble for Americans around the world, killing innocent people, and destroying property in the service of the military-industrial-congressional complex. I would voluntarily pay to make these hired killers stop what they are doing, come home, and take up honest employment. Some public good!

In truth, the state occupies itself massively in snatching private wealth, transferring much of it to favored supporters, wasting a great deal of it, and retaining the balance to pay its own legions of bullies, do-gooders, and time-servers, as well as its palace guard of police and military forces. This whole vile apparatus has no claim to self-evident superiority to alternative arrangements; it ought to bear the burden of proof for every step it takes; and we ought to recognize that the blackboard proofs proffered by mainstream economists, which compose so-called modern welfare economics, will not feed the baby. This entire body of thought ought to be dismissed as more a corpus of apologetics than a serious attempt to justify the state's pervasively invasive actions in modern life. Much more might be said along these lines, of course, but enough has been said, I hope, to make the case that placement of the burden of proof is utterly crucial in the resolution of disputes, whether they be in science, public policy, or economic analysis. Moreover, we need to be constantly aware that if an arrangement depends on violence or the threat of violence to keep it afloat, it almost certainly has severe deficiencies. Raw force is always the resort of someone who cannot present a persuasive argument in support of his actions. Although the modern state enjoys the support of countless court intellectuals and apologists, it rests firmly on violence in the event that we do not accept the excuses it makes for its crimes. That so many of us fear and loathe the state should in itself be sufficient to indicate that the state, not those of us who long for freedom, should always bear the burden of proof.

34

Politics and Markets

A Highly Misleading Analogy

PROPOSITION: *Putative "public demand," especially as expressed by voting, drives the political-governmental system. Elected officials and hence the bureaucracy subordinate to them may be viewed as perfect agents of the electorate.*

Adherence to this proposition characterizes the bulk of all analysis dealing with the growth of government in the West, regardless of analytical tradition or ideological leaning.[1] This approach displays a professional deformity related to the economist's basic tool of analysis—the theory of markets, with its component theories of demand and supply. Economists, applying their

---

1. Specific citations seem unnecessary, but see virtually any issue of *Public Choice*, as well as these widely cited articles: Allan H. Meltzer and Scott F. Richard, "Why Government Grows (and Grows) in a Democracy," *Public Choice* (Summer 1978):111–18; idem, "A Rational Theory of the Size of Government," *Journal of Political Economy* 89 (October 1981):914–27; idem, "Tests of a Rational Theory of the Size of Government," *Public Choice* 41 (1983):403–18; Sam Peltzman, "The Growth of Government," *Journal of Law and Economics* 23 (October 1980):209–87; idem, "Constituent Interest and Congressional Voting," *Journal of Law and Economics* 27 (April 1984): 181–210; idem, "An Economic Interpretation of the History of Congressional Voting in the Twentieth Century," *American Economic Review* 75 (September 1985):656–75; Gary S. Becker, "A Theory of Competition among Pressure Groups for Political Influence," *Quarterly Journal of Economics* 98 (August 1983):371–400; idem, "Public Policies, Pressure Groups, and Dead Weight Costs," *Journal of Public Economics* 28 (1985):329–47; Thomas E. Borcherding, "The Sources of Growth of Public Expenditures in the United States, 1902–1970," in *Budgets and Bureaucrats: The Sources of Government Growth*, ed. Thomas E. Borcherding, 45–70 (Durham, NC: Duke University Press, 1977); idem, "The Causes of Government Expenditure Growth: A Survey of the U.S. Evidence," *Journal of Public Economics* 28 (1985): 359–82. An even more extreme contribution along these lines is Donald Wittman, "Why Democracies Produce Efficient Results," *Journal of Political Economy* 97 (December 1989):1395–1424.

familiar tools to the analysis of politics, immediately look for analogues. What is the "good" being traded? Who is the "supplier," and who is the "demander"? What is the "price"? The answers seem obvious to economists. Public policy is the good; the elected legislators are the suppliers; the voters are the demanders; votes are the currency with which political business is being transacted. Thus voters "buy" the desired policies by spending their votes; the legislators "sell" policies in exchange for the votes that elect them to office.[2]

Economists view consumer demand in ordinary markets as ultimately decisive for the allocation of resources; hence they speak of consumer "sovereignty," thus importing a political metaphor into economics. Applying their familiar apparatus of thought to politics, economists tend to think that the political system ultimately gives the voters what they want. In the words of the authors of a recent survey of economic theories of the growth of government, "Voters decide which goods the government will provide and which negative externalities the government will correct."[3] Therefore, if the government grows, it does so because that is what the people want.[4] Demand creates its own supply. Voting is ultimately all that matters for determining the growth of government. As Dennis Mueller has observed, "In the public choice literature the state often appears as simply a voting rule that transforms individual preferences into political outcomes."[5]

It is easy—and probably healthy—to mock this view of the political process. Joseph Schumpeter called it "the perfect example of a nursery tale."[6] There are, after all, many significant differences between ordinary markets

---

2. For a straightforward application of such analogues, see Bruce L. Benson and Eric M. Engen, "The Market for Laws: An Economic Analysis of Legislation," *Southern Economic Journal* 54 (January 1988):732–45.

3. Thomas A. Garrett and Russell M. Rhine, "On the Size and Growth of Government," *Federal Reserve Bank of St. Louis Review* 88 (January–February 2006):18, emphasis added.

4. Richard A. Musgrave, "Excess Bias and the Nature of Budget Growth," *Journal of Public Economics* 28 (1985):306; Joseph E. Stiglitz, "On the Economic Role of the State," in *The Economic Role of the State*, ed. Arnold Heertje (Oxford: Basil Blackwell, 1989), 69.

5. Dennis C. Mueller, "The Growth of Government: A Public Choice Perspective," *IMF Staff Papers* 34 (March 1987):142.

6. Joseph A. Schumpeter, *History of Economic Analysis* (New York: Oxford University Press, 1954), 429.

and the "political market."[7] Even Benson and Engen, adherents of this model, describe their output variable as "somewhat artificial and very restrictive" and their price variable as "clearly an incomplete proxy."[8]

Not least of the problems is that voters rarely vote directly for or against policies. Rather, they vote for candidates who run for office. Winning candidates subsequently enact a multitude of policies, many of which neither the voters nor their representatives had considered at the time of the campaign. It is not enough that voters know something about office seekers' general ideological reputation;[9] the devil is in the details. Besides, notwithstanding the elaborate theoretical and econometric attempts to show that politicians are perfect agents,[10] we can easily demonstrate that political representatives frequently act in ways that must necessarily run counter to the dominant preference of their ostensible constituents. We see this disconnect in the U.S. Senate, for instance, every time the two senators who represent the same state split their votes—and such splitting occurs commonly.[11] Remarkably, and quite damningly for models that presume tight linkages between voters and their elected representatives, many of the vote-splitting senators are reelected time and again. So elections are reliable neither as an ex ante check nor as an ex post check on the substantial autonomy of officeholders.

Perhaps the most important case in which legislators and other officials (including many nonelected functionaries) act independently of control by the voters concerns political action during crises. How many voters could possibly have known in the election of 1940 what the elected federal officials would do during their upcoming terms in office, which were to include, depending on the office, some or all of the years of World War II? How many voters in the election of 1972 had any idea how they wished their representatives to deal

7. Robert Higgs, *Crisis and Leviathan: Critical Episodes in the Growth of American Government* (New York: Oxford University Press, 1987), 14–15; Donald J. Boudreaux, "Was Your High School Civics Teacher Right after All? Donald Wittman's *The Myth of Democratic Failure*," *The Independent Review* 1 Spring 1996):115–19.

8. Benson and Engen 1988, 733, 741.

9. As argued by William R. Dougan and Michael C. Munger, "The Rationality of Ideology," *Journal of Law and Economics* 32 (April 1989):119–42.

10. Becker 1983, 1985; Peltzman 1984, 1985; Wittman 1989.

11. Robert Higgs, "Do Legislators' Votes Reflect Constituency Preference? A Simple Way to Evaluate the Senate," *Public Choice* 63 (November 1989):175–81.

with the "energy crisis" of 1973–74 or even that such a crisis would arise? Who anticipated that George H. W. Bush would send U.S. troops to the Persian Gulf to eject the Iraqis from Kuwait? How many, when they cast their ballots for George W. Bush in 2000, anticipated the military invasions and the long, bloody occupations of Afghanistan and Iraq? During crises, government officials, lacking any reliable means of discovering dominant constituent preferences, necessarily exercise considerable discretion. But even if leaders cannot know what "the people" desire, they act nevertheless, often in dramatically important ways.

Once those actions have been taken, the course of events is changed irrevocably in a world of path-dependent historical processes.[12] If U.S. voters in 1940 had preferred that the nation not go to war, it was too late to rectify the legislators' mistake in the election of 1942—the fat was already in the fire. If they preferred the removal of U.S. troops from Iraq in 2004, they were out of luck because neither candidate for the presidency espoused that alternative.

Further, political actions are usually accompanied by carefully crafted rationalizations, excuses, and propaganda emanating from the politicians and their friends who initiated or supported the actions. (How often do politicians admit policy mistakes?) From this vantage point, it is easy to see how political preferences, public opinion, and even the dominant ideology may be altered, becoming more congruent with what has been done and thereby reversing the direction of causality usually assumed in political models.[13]

---

12. Geoffrey Brennan and James M. Buchanan, *The Reason of Rules: Constitutional Political Economy* (Cambridge: Cambridge University Press, 1985), 16, 74; Higgs, *Crisis and Leviathan*, 30–33, 57–74. Karen A. Rasler and William R. Thompson confirm statistically, using Box-Tiao tests, the increasing growth of government spending associated with participation in global wars. See their article "War Making and State Making: Governmental Expenditures, Tax Revenues, and Global Wars," *American Political Science Review* 79 (June 1985), 491–507.

13. On ideology and policy as interactive, see Robert Higgs, "Crisis, Bigger Government, and Ideological Change: Two Hypotheses on the Ratchet Phenomenon," *Explorations in Economic History* 22 (January 1985):1–28; idem, *Crisis and Leviathan*, 67–74; idem, "*Crisis and Leviathan*: Higgs Response to Reviewers," *Continuity: A Journal of History* (Spring–Fall 1989):96–98; and idem, *Depression, War, and Cold War: Studies in Political Economy* (New York: Oxford University Press, 2006), 202–05.

35

Social Science 101

Three Ways to Relate to Other People

MANY YEARS AGO, in a book I've lost along the way (I believe it was *A Primer on Social Dynamics*), Kenneth Boulding[1] described three basic ways in which a person, in the quest to get what he seeks, can approach other people. He can, as it were, say to them:

1. Do something nice for me, and I'll do something nice for you.
2. Do something nice for me, or I'll do something nasty to you.
3. Do something nice for me because of who I am.

The first approach is that of peaceful, mutually beneficial exchange, of "you scratch my back and I'll scratch yours," of positive reciprocity. It is the method by which we conduct the bulk of our economic affairs.

The second approach is that of coercion, of threats to harm others unless they do as we wish, regardless of their own preferences. This is, among other things, the realm of government as we know it. When we say government as we know it, we say violence or threats of violence against all who refuse to comply with the rulers' dictates.

The third approach is that of personal-identity relationships. One person says to another, do what I want you to do because of who I am and who you are—because, for example, I am your father or your teacher or your kinsman.

Boulding argued that all social systems are a blend of these three types of interaction among its individual members. Part of the difficulty of understanding how societies operate arises from the complex ways in which these

---

1. Kenneth Ewart Boulding, *A Primer on Social Dynamics* (New York: The Free Press, 1971).

three types of relationship become entangled with one another and how the nature of this complexity changes over time.

Boulding was an unusually broad-gauge thinker. For him, interdisciplinary thinking came easily. But for most contemporary social scientists, it comes not at all. Most economists think about how markets work, about exchange, and about all of the good and bad consequences the operation of markets may bring about. Most political scientists think about government and politics (the quest for possession or control of coercive power), and about all of the desirable and undesirable consequences of political actions. Identity relations tend to fall within the disciplinary boundaries of psychologists and sociologists, for the most part. This narrow scholarly specialization has both benefits and costs. However, because professional fame and fortune flow mainly to the most outstanding specialists, the brightest people tend to specialize narrowly. There is a reason why hardly anyone outside a particular subfield of economics knows anything about the work of each year's Nobel laureate in economics. If the labor economist knows little or nothing about monetary theory or international trade, even less does the average economist know about political science or psychology.

One area in which I have found a broader appreciation—along the lines of Boulding's three approaches—to be essential has been in my study of ideology.[2] This concept, developed most fully by philosophers, psychologists, sociologists, and political scientists, plays a fundamental role in my explanation of the growth of government in the United States during the past century or so. My thesis is sometimes described as a "crisis theory," but I have been at pains to explain that national emergencies would not have played out as they did had fundamental ideological changes not occurred beforehand as they did. National emergencies give rise to spurts of growth in government's size, scope, and power that are not fully rescinded afterward—that is, they have a "ratchet effect"—only in the context of a widely entrenched collectivist ideology.

Modern collectivist ideology in the United States (and probably in many other countries, as well) is infused with another ideology, namely, nationalism.[3]

---

2. Robert Higgs, "The Complex Course of Ideological Change," *American Journal of Economics and Sociology* 16 (Oct 2008).

3. "Nationalism," *Wikipedia,* http://en.wikipedia.org/wiki/nationalism.

This ideology has been developing in the West for centuries, but it reached its most consequential and destructive heights only in the twentieth century, when German (international) socialists marched off by the millions to die for the fatherland in World War I, and Americans ostensibly devoted to individual liberty marched off by the millions to fight and die in the U.S. state's foreign wars.

One might say that these men acted as they did simply because they were drafted or threatened with a draft, but that claim must be placed in the wider context of these men's submission and involuntary service. Until recent decades, very few men fought because the military paid better than their civilian alternative, but many private contractors came forward to equip and arm these men for fighting only because they found the prospective payoff attractive. The draftees faced a choice between army and prison, so coercion certainly played a vital part in inducing them to report for military service as ordered. Yet many more might have evaded or avoided the draft had their identities been different. Many considered themselves to be, above all, Germans or Americans, and as such they felt that they *should* obey the national government's draft call. To do otherwise would be to betray their very self-identity, not to mention the hostility and ostracism they might expect to elicit from family members, friends, and neighbors psychologically wedded to the same nationalism. Thus the creation and supply of massive armies illustrates well how exchange, coercion, and ideology/identity factors combine and interact in bringing about a definite social outcome.

36

Ten Fallacious Conclusions in the Dominant Ideology's Political Economy

THE DOMINANT IDEOLOGY does much to shape people's views about what is happening in social affairs, why it is happening, and what if anything ought to be done about it. Ideology exerts its force in large part through what we might call its *power of predisposition*, that is, its default conclusions that, on examination, amount to little more than leaps of faith.

For the past century in the United States of America, the dominant ideology has been progressivism. This belief system has not been static, of course, and its specific elements, emphases, and outlooks have changed substantially since the early twentieth century. For example, whereas the early progressives were generally racist, hard imperialist, and eugenicist, today's are generally multiculturalist, soft imperialist, and more inclined to favor jeopardizing the survival of the human race (to save the environment) than to improve it by eliminating the biologically "inferior" people. Nevertheless, through all its emotional and intellectual ups and downs, progressivism has retained one central element: its abiding faith that the state can and should act vigorously on as many fronts as possible to improve society both here and abroad.

As an economist, I note in particular that progressive ideology now embraces the following default conclusions:

1. If a social or economic problem seems to exist, the state should impose regulation to remedy it.
2. If regulation has already been imposed, it should be made more expansive and severe.
3. If an economic recession occurs, the state should adopt "stimulus" programs by actively employing the state's fiscal and monetary powers.

4. If the recession persists despite the state's adoption of "stimulus" programs, the state should increase the size of these programs.

5. If long-term economic growth seems to be too slow to satisfy powerful people's standard of performance, the state should intervene to accelerate the rate of growth by making "investments" in infrastructure, health, education, and technological advance.

6. If the state was already making such "investments," it should make even more of them.

7. Taxes on "the rich" should be increased during a recession, to reduce the government's budget deficit.

8. Taxes on "the rich" should also be increased during a business expansion, to ensure that they pay their "fair share" (that is, the great bulk) of total taxes and to reduce the government's budget deficit.

9. If progressives perceive a "market failure" of any kind, the state should intervene in whatever way promises to create Nirvana.

10. If Nirvana has not resulted from past and current interventions, the state should increase its intervention until Nirvana is reached.

The foregoing progressive predispositions, along with others too numerous to state here, provide the foundation on which the state justifies its current actions and its proposals for acting even more expansively. Progressives see no situation in which the best course of action requires that the government retrench or admit that it can do nothing constructive to help matters. They see the state as well-intentioned, sufficiently capable, and properly motivated to fix any social and economic problem whatsoever if only the public allows it to do so and bears the costs.

It follows that progressives desire a change in the state's size, scope, and power in only one direction, regardless of past and present conditions and regardless of whether previous attempts to implement progressive panaceas have succeeded or failed—indeed, if honestly assessed, virtually all of them have failed, on balance. Progressive faith in the state, however, springs eternal.

It is a great misfortune for modern Western countries, and many others as well, that serious challenges to this currently dominant ideology do not exist. The political parties compete for office, each seeking to direct more of the state's plunder to its supporters, but the ideological differences between the competing parties is almost entirely superficial. All politically potent parties believe in a powerful, pervasively engaged state. They differ only in regard to which specific individuals should steer the Leviathan.

37

Regime Uncertainty

Some Clarifications

PRIVATE INVESTMENT IS the most important driver of economic progress. Entrepreneurs need new structures, equipment, and software to produce new products, to produce existing products at lower cost, and to make use of new technology that requires embodiment in machinery, plant layouts, and other aspects of the existing capital stock. When the rate of private investment declines, the rate of growth of real income per capita slackens, and if private investment drops quickly and substantially, a recession or depression occurs.

Such recession or depression is likely to persist until private investment makes a fairly full recovery. In U.S. history, such recovery usually has occurred within a year or two after the trough. Only twice in the past century has a fairly prompt and full recovery of private investment failed to occur—during the Great Depression and during the past six years.

In analyzing data on investment, we must distinguish gross and net investment: the former includes all spending for new structures, equipment, software, and inventory, including the large part aimed at compensating for the wear, tear, and obsolescence of the existing capital stock; the latter includes the gross expenditure in excess of that required simply to maintain the existing stock. Therefore, net investment is the best measure of the private investment expenditure that contributes to economic growth.

As Figure 37.1 shows, net private domestic fixed investment (a measure that excludes investment in inventories) reached a peak in 2006–2007, declined somewhat in 2008, then plunged in 2009 before reaching a trough in 2010. Although it recovered slightly in 2011, it remained 20 percent below the previous peak, and the pace of its recovery to date implies that another

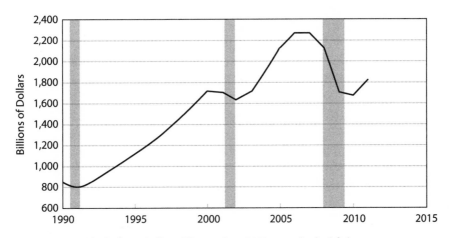

Figure 37.1. Net Private Domestic Investment: Fixed Investment (FPIA)

three or four years will be required merely to bring it back to where it was in 2007. With adjustments for changes in the price level, the projected recovery period would be slightly longer. (Using the price index for gross private domestic investment[1] to obtain real values, we find that real net private domestic fixed investment is now at approximately the same level it had attained in the late 1990s.) To understand why the current overall economic recovery has been so anemic, we must understand why net private investment has not recovered more quickly.

In a 1997 article in *The Independent Review* ("Regime Uncertainty: Why the Great Depression Lasted So Long and Why Prosperity Resumed After the War"[2]) I argued that a major reason for the incomplete recovery of private investment during the latter half of the 1930s was "regime uncertainty." By this, I mean a pervasive lack of confidence among investors in their ability to

1. Federal Reserve Bank of St. Louis, "Gross Private Domestic Investment: Chain-type Price Index, 2014:Q3," http://research.stlouisfed.org/fred2/series/GPDICTPI?cid=21.

2. Robert Higgs, "Regime Uncertainty: Why the Great Depression Lasted So Long and Why Prosperity Resumed After the War," *The Independent Review*, 1:4 (Spring 1997), 561–90.

foresee the extent to which future government actions will alter their private-property rights. In the original article and in many follow-up articles, I documented that between 1935 and 1940, many investors feared that the government might transform the very nature of the existing economic order, replacing the primarily market-oriented economy with fascism, socialism, or some other government-controlled arrangement in which private-property rights would be greatly curtailed, if they survived at all. Given such fears, many investors regarded new investment projects as too risky to justify their current costs.

During the past several years, I have argued that a similar, if somewhat less extreme fear now pervades the business community, which explains at least in part the sluggish pace of the current economic recovery. Other exponents of this view include such prominent economists as Gary Becker, Allan Meltzer, John Taylor, and Alan Greenspan. (Until recently, Austrian economists were more receptive than mainstream economists to the idea of regime uncertainty; see, for example, the recent Mises Daily article by John P. Cochran.[3]) In addition, economists Scott Baker and Nicholas Bloom at Stanford and Steven J. Davis at the University of Chicago have devised an empirical index of policy uncertainty that has remained at extraordinarily high levels since September 2008. However, what most other economists—and all of those in the professional mainstream—have noted is not exactly the same as what I call regime uncertainty, but rather a related, somewhat narrower phenomenon.

Over the years, some economists have urged me to forsake the term "regime uncertainty" and to use instead an expression such as policy uncertainty, rule uncertainty, or regime worsening. I have rejected these suggestions because the idea I seek to convey encompasses more than simply policies or rules. Moreover, regime uncertainly does not necessarily signify only apprehension about potential worsening as a central tendency.

Regime uncertainty pertains to more than the government's laws, regulations, and administrative decisions. For one thing, as the saying goes, "personnel is policy." Two administrations may administer or enforce identical statutes and regulations quite differently. A business-hostile administration

---

3. John P. Cochran, "Malinvestment and Regime Uncertainty," *Mises Daily* online, October 29, 2012, http://mises.org/daily/6245/Malinvestment-and-Regime-Uncertainty.

such as Franklin D. Roosevelt's or Barack Obama's will provoke more apprehension among investors than a business-friendlier administration such as Dwight D. Eisenhower's or Ronald Reagan's, even if the underlying "rules of the game" are identical on paper. Similar differences between judiciaries create uncertainties about how the courts will rule on contested laws and government actions.

For another thing, seemingly neutral changes in policies or personnel may have major implications for specific types of investment. Even when government changes the rules in a way that seemingly strengthens private-property rights overall, the action's specific form may jeopardize particular types of investment, and apprehension about such a threat may paralyze investors in these areas. Moreover, it may also give pause to investors in other areas, who fear that what the government has done to harm others today, it may do to them tomorrow. In sum, heightened uncertainty in general—a perceived increase in the potential variance of all sorts of relevant government action—may deter investment even if the mean value of expectations shifts toward more secure private-property rights.

Regime uncertainty is a complex matter. No empirical index can capture it fully; some indexes may actually misrepresent it. Only the actors on the scene can appraise it, and their appraisals are intrinsically subjective. However, by assessing a variety of direct and indirect evidence, analysts can better appreciate its contours, direction, and impact on private investment decisions.

38

Not Every Intellectual Gunman
Is a Hired Gun

A VENERABLE PIECE of advice in political analysis is "follow the money." However, not many people need to be taught this idea; indeed, in popular journalism and political discourse, it is taken for granted. So the standard way to discredit one's political enemy is to expose that he is being bankrolled by a nefarious interest group or a notorious person or organization. Having thereby smeared the opponent by suggesting that he is anything but disinterested and public-spirited, one gains an important advantage in appealing to the electorate. Of course, both sides can and do play this game. Hence political contests consist in large part of mud-slinging competitions in which the more muddied candidate operates under a dark cloud of suspicion that he is, at least, more corrupt than the other guy.

In part as a spillover from the world of politicking, this same approach has come to prevail in the evaluation of competing public-policy ideas. Thus muckraking journalists seek to gain evidence that, say, a think tank whose studies lend credence to policy X is in fact only an intellectual prostitute paid by interest groups, corporations, or persons who stand to gain from the implementation of policy X. Journalists and commentators on both the left and the right play this game, although because the great majority of journalists are leftists and because big corporations are (incorrectly) believed to be almost always supporters of the Republican Party, the greater part of such follow-the-money smearing arises on the left and tracks the money to corporate sources.

Many nonacademics have come to believe that even in the supposedly ivory-tower precincts of academia, such mercenary corruption dictates the conclusions reached by writers and researchers in the social sciences. Therefore, if an economist writes that, say, government regulation of tobacco products is inefficient, someone is likely to look into whether this economist has received support for his work from tobacco companies or their front groups. If he has done so, his research is likely to be dismissed entirely, regardless of its intellectual quality.

Over the years, I have sometimes been accused of being a hired gun because of my affiliation with the Independent Institute. I have always been torn between irritation and amusement by these accusations—often made as if they are nothing more than obvious facts about my intellectual dishonesty. I am amused because, truth be known, I am not a wealthy man, and I might have put a big payoff to very good use in the support of my family; yet no such payoff, big or small, was ever offered to me. My counter-claim in no way dissuades my accusers, however, because they will present evidence (or a claim that purports to be factual) that the Independent Institute at some time has received a donation (no matter how trifling the amount) from Corporation X, and that my writing has been such that it might well have pleased Corporation X—QED, the accuser supposes. The fact that I have always chosen what to write about and how to write about it, with no intervention whatsoever by anyone at the Independent Institute, carries no weight, or even any credibility, with such accusers. The Independent Institute received money from Corporation X; I received money from the Independent Institute; I wrote something that Corporation X might like; end of story—the story of my utter intellectual corruption. Mine is hardly the only such case. I daresay that hundreds, if not thousands, of other writers and researchers have found themselves in similar circumstances.

When this sort of "exposure" pertains to university professors, it is often even more ludicrous. People outside the universities greatly misunderstand why professors believe and write as they do. Background, training, personal political tendencies, methodological preferences, personal animosities, and most of all ideological convictions—these things may shape what a professor writes and how he writes about it in the social sciences, the humanities, and the law schools. But a definite link between the source of the university's or the writer's income and the content of the writer's work is usually very difficult to document. And even when a link can be shown, the (far more likely) possibility remains that the financial supporter chose to support Professor Y's work because Professor Y was already working along congenial lines, rather than vice versa. Professors are scarcely disinterested intellectual gods, as I know well from my twenty-six years spent in academia. Yet only a few, at most, are simply hired guns willing to reach whatever conclusion the highest bidder will pay them to reach. Exceptions only illustrate the rule.

Libertarian nonacademics often assert that academics are overwhelmingly statist because they work in government-supported institutions. This belief has little foundation. I worked in a large state university for fifteen years. No one ever complained about my anti-statist writings or made any attempt whatsoever to punish or reward me on the basis of my free-market tendencies. I worked also in private colleges for eleven years. The general leftishness of the professoriate there was at least as marked as it had been in the state institution—which, by the way, maintained, among major research universities, one of the world's most free-market-leaning economics departments during my employment there. Professors in the humanities, the social sciences, and the law schools in the United States are overwhelmingly leftish and statist. But no one has to pay them to elicit these ideological tendencies. They are simply fortunate that people like them can find paying employment in institutions where no one will interfere with their self-chosen statist research and writing. The people who fund and administer the public universities are remote from what specifically goes on in them and have little interest in whether 90 percent or 60 percent of the faculty are statists. (They do care about the football team, however, because in many cases it is a major cash cow and the only thing that keeps the alumni supportive of the institution.)

No doubt, many nonacademics will find the foregoing statements hard to swallow. Libertarians in particular seem highly disposed to believe that their ideological opponents must be on the take. In this regard they display the same sort of bias as leftish journalists and muckrakers, only with the direction reversed. But facts are hard things to wish away. The world of think tanks and universities is awash with objectionable activities and modes of thought, but simple intellectual prostitution is a much smaller problem in this world of ideas than most outsiders imagine.

39

Truth and Freedom
in Economic Analysis
and Economic Policymaking

FOR THOUSANDS OF YEARS, philosophers have told us that if we are to live our lives at their best, we should seek truth, beauty, and goodness. Of course, each of these qualities has raised thorny issues and provoked ongoing arguments. That people have carried on such arguments, rather than surrendering themselves to their raw appetites and animal instincts, may be counted a valuable thing in itself, but a final resolution of such deep questions may lie beyond human capacities.

In regard to goodness and beauty, I have nothing worthwhile to add to the discussion. For guidance in seeking goodness, we may look to saints, theologians, moral philosophers, and moral exemplars of our own acquaintance. For demonstrations of beauty, we may turn to nature and to artists, great and small, who have adorned our lives with the grace of music, poetry, and the visual arts. My own professional qualifications, as an economist and an economic historian, do not equip me to contribute anything of value in these areas.

I do feel qualified, however, to speak in regard to truth, because the search for truth has always served as the foundation of my intellectual endeavors. Moreover, my study, research, and reflection within my own professional domains have brought home to me a relationship that others might do well to ponder and respect—a relationship, indeed, an array of relationships, between truth and freedom, such that anyone who seeks the triumph of truth must also seek to establish freedom in human affairs.

When I began my academic career in 1968, my research specialty was the economic history of the United States. I was expected to publish the findings of my research in reputable professional journals. For a young man just beginning to master his field, carrying out publishable research was a daunting task. Thousands of other writers had already contributed to building up the literature in my field, so adding something of enough importance to merit its publication in a good journal was hardly an easy task.

I discovered, however, that one way to proceed was by identifying significant mistakes in the existing literature and correcting them. Moreover, I soon found that many such mistakes had been made. To put this statement in another way, I found that the existing sources often failed to tell the truth about one thing or another, and in some cases the falsehoods propounded by one writer led later writers, who relied on those false statements, to make additional errors of their own. We often think of the scientific or scholarly enterprise as a cooperative process in which the establishment of one truth facilitates the establishment of another, but, unfortunately, the process often works in an adverse way, too, as the establishment of one falsehood fosters the establishment of another.

The errors in my fields of study and research take two main forms: factual and interpretive.

Factual errors arise on a few occasions from deliberate falsification, but they arise far more often from sloppiness in the observation, measurement, transcription, and processing of data. In checking quotations, for example, I often found discrepancies between the words quoted by a writer and the words that appear in the source from which the quotation was taken: some words or punctuation marks were omitted, or other words or punctuation marks were inserted, without any indication being given of such changes. Many writers are simply not careful and therefore make false statements of fact.

For example, I found that in a well-regarded article the increase in U.S. cotton production in the United States between 1850 and 1860, compared to that between 1860 and 1880—an essential fact for the argument being made—had been measured with a large error in part because the original researchers had assumed that a bale of cotton contained the same amount of lint at each of these three dates, whereas the amount of lint per bale had actually increased from 400 pounds in 1850, to 445 pounds in 1860, to 453 pounds in 1880. The researchers had made false statements of fact because they had incorrectly assumed that in the years under consideration a "bale" had signified a constant unit of weight, whereas in fact this unit of measurement had varied over time.[1]

On another occasion, while reviewing a major book by a professor at a leading university, I discovered that whereas the author's findings hinged on simulations derived from a system of simultaneous equations, one of the equations was expressed in a nonsensical form that required incomparable units (physical quantities and dollar values) to be added, and another equation was expressed in a form that produced negative values that made no economic sense. Disturbed by these discoveries, I called the author on the telephone to ask him about the errors. He was surprised by my "careful reading," but he did not seem to be especially crestfallen. Seemingly at a loss to explain how such gross errors got into his book, he assured me that although they were undeniably in the text, they had not been present in the equations he actually used to make his hundreds of simulations. Because I could not see how his equation system could have been altered to make it complete and internally consistent without radical reformulation, I retained a deep suspicion that his big book was nothing more than a monument to the GIGO principle—garbage in, garbage out.[2]

Interpretive errors arise when researchers either apply an unsound theory or apply a sound theory incorrectly in their interpretation of causal relationships. This sort of mistake is much more complex and difficult to resolve than a factual error. Researchers need to master the theory appropriate for application in the area they seek to understand. Honest researchers often disagree about which theories are sound and which are unsound. Many modern economists, for example, proceed as if the role of theory in economics were the same as the role of theory in physics and chemistry. Despite this assumption's wide acceptance, it is incorrect; it fails to take into account the difference between human choices and the movements of molecules, atoms, and subatomic particles; the difference between the action of conscious, purposive beings and

---

1. See Robert McGuire and Robert Higgs, "Cotton, Corn, and Risk in the Nineteenth Century: Another View," *Explorations in Economic History* 14 (April 1977), 169.

2. See Robert Higgs, review of *Late Nineteenth-Century American Development: A General Equilibrium History*, by Jeffrey G. Williamson, *Agricultural History* 49 (October 1975), 690–92.

the behavior of unconscious, purposeless material particles and electrical currents. The positivist assumption that a single explanatory scheme—materialist reductionism—is equally applicable in all sciences is the overarching error that F. A. Hayek called *scientism*. Hayek's mentor Ludwig von Mises argued at length in many of his writings against scientism and in favor of methodological dualism.[3]

In my career in academia, however, I discovered to my dismay that many of my colleagues had little interest in the search for truth, however one might understand or pursue it. For them, their research and publication amounted to a game in which the winning players receive the greatest rewards in salary, research funding, and professional acclaim. They understood that because of cloistered academic inbreeding, economists at the most prestigious universities consider the "smartest guys" to be those who employ the most advanced, complex, and incomprehensible mathematics in their "modeling" and "empirical testing." I observed colleagues who became excited by their discovery of a mathematical theorem that had never been applied in economic research. These economists would look around for a plausible way to use the newly discovered mathematical theorem, to give it the appearance of economic relevance. In this way, mere technique drove research and publication. These economists did not consider, or care, whether the theorem would assist them in the discovery of economic truth; they cared only about showing off their analytical powers to impress their technically less proficient colleagues and journal editors. These colleagues, unfortunately, often did feel intimidated by the authors of articles they could not understand because they did not know the mathematical techniques employed in the exposition. This entire enterprise, which continues even now, consumes valuable time and brainpower in a misguided carnival of intellectually irrelevant one-upmanship.

When we move from the realm of economic research to the realm of economic policymaking, we encounter even more destructive falsehoods. Much modern economic theory, for example, has been used to justify government intervention in the free-market process. We might pause to reflect that this process, which operates as a price system or, seen in another perspective, as a

---

3. See, for example, Ludwig von Mises, *Theory and History: An Interpretation of Social and Economic Evolution* (New Haven: Yale University Press, 1957).

profit-and-loss system, is simultaneously a way of revealing the truth. Thus, for example, a price established on the free market communicates true information to all potential market participants about the exchange value (at the current margin) of a good or service relative to the exchange value of other goods and services. If the government places an excise tax on a good, thereby diminishing the quantity demanded and raising the market price, potential buyers then react to a false signal of the good's true exchange value. If the government pays a subsidy to a good's producers, thereby increasing the quantity supplied and lowering the market price, potential suppliers then react to a false signal of the good's true exchange value. In both cases, changes in the amounts produced give rise to corresponding changes in the amounts of various inputs demanded; and those changes give rise to other market changes; and so on, as the effects of a single government intervention in the market price system ripple outward from their source.

(Those who have studied a little economics in a university may object that according to the theory of "market failure," various deviations from hypothetical "perfectly competitive" conditions may cause market-determined prices to be distorted and outputs to be "inefficient," and in this event the government can intervene with taxes, subsides, and regulations to bring the market into an efficient configuration. What these students probably were not taught, however, is that this theory assumes a great deal that cannot be known by anyone except as it is determined in actual markets. Further, because the actual parameters of demand, cost, and supply functions are unknown [and constantly subject to change] in the real world, the government does not, indeed, cannot know how much to intervene—what amount of tax to collect or how much to pay as a subsidy, for example. Further still, this theory implicitly assumes that the interventionist actions the government takes are themselves without costs. One wonders: how are the tax-and-subsidy agencies and the regulatory bureaucracies supported? Even further still, because in reality such interventions are the creations not of genuine economic experts [themselves helpless enough], but of politicians and their lackeys, the interventions are normally intended to, and do, serve not the purpose of establishing an efficient allocation of resources, but the purpose of promoting the politicians' personal, ideological, and political ends. The entire apparatus of the theory of market failure is a sheer blackboard fantasy, an economic theorist's plaything that has been accepted far too often as a helpful guide to, or justification of, government intervention in the market economy by putatively public-spirited legislators and regulators.)

In reality, the market system tends to foster an efficient allocation of resources—it constantly creates incentives for resource owners to direct their resources away from areas in which those resources have lesser value and toward areas in which they have greater value. Taxes and subsidies, and other government intrusions in the market process in effect falsify the price "signals" that guide market participants in their decisions about how much to buy, how much to sell, how to produce, where to produce, and exactly when to take various actions. If false prices should become established in a free-market system—if, for example, the price of gasoline in one town became greater than the price in a neighboring town by an amount greater than the cost of transporting a gallon of gasoline from one town to the other—entrepreneurs would have an incentive to move the product to the place at which it has a greater value. In doing so, they would cause the lower price to become higher, and the higher price to become lower, and they would move the market toward an efficient allocation of resources. Those old enough to remember the so-called energy crises of the period from 1973 to 1981 in the United States will appreciate immediately how poorly the market system works when such price changes and resource reallocations are forbidden.

Government interference in the price system blunts or destroys the incentives that would otherwise lead entrepreneurs to reallocate resources more efficiently. Taxes destroy the incentive to produce additional amounts of certain goods that, without the tax, would be profitable to produce. Subsidies create the incentive to produce additional amounts of certain goods that, without the subsidy, would be unprofitable to produce. Taxes and subsides, and likewise regulations in various more complex ways, distort the true information inherent in the free market's pricing process. By responding to the false prices of a government-distorted market system, entrepreneurs may enrich themselves, but only at the greater expense of the economy as a whole, not to mention the sacrifice of economic freedom inherent in the government's coercive tax-and-subsidy system.

In this connection, we should recognize that interest rates are key relative prices, and hence government or central bank actions that push interest rates above or below their free–market levels are another way to suppress the truth about economic conditions. Artificially altered interest rates, indeed, are perhaps the most important form of falsification in economic life because they play a key role in inducing the malinvestments whose inevitable bankruptcy heralds the onset of economic busts, creating pervasive economic losses, unemployment of capital and labor, and human suffering that would not have occurred if only the government and the central bank had refrained from interfering in the market's price-setting process.

• • •

In both the realm of economic research and the realm of economic policy, freedom is an essential condition for the generation of truth and thus for the enhanced enjoyment of social life that depends on making use of true, rather than false, information. The academic world of the show-off, pyrotechnic economists who dominate today's mainstream profession would be impossible without the vast government subsidies that support these economists and the institutions in which they perform their wizardry. Given a choice, consumers would not buy their glitzy but worthless research reports. The funds that support this superficially impressive intellectual showmanship must be extorted from taxpayers by threatening them with fines and imprisonment.

In similar fashion, the grossly distorted economy in which—to take but one example among thousands—ethanol producers and corn farmers are enriched at the expense of the direct and indirect consumers of corn throughout the world would be impossible without the huge subsidies and government mandates that have brought the biofuel industry to its present size and configuration. Without the various forms of taxes borne by producers today, many valuable goods and services would be supplied in enormously greater quantities. Work, saving, investment, and technological progress would be much greater and economic growth much faster in a world that relied on true information about relative exchange values, rather than on the false signals brought into being by the government's coercive, politically inspired intrusions.

In economics, as in other areas of life, the pursuit and employment of truth depend on freedom. Every cognizant adult knows that virtually all politicians are habitual liars. Too few of us understand, however, that the free market itself is a grand generator of truth, and that, in general, government intrusion of any kind operates to substitute falsehood for this truth, with devastating consequences for the genuine flourishing of human beings in their social and economic lives.

40

Austrian Economics

The Queen of the Experimental Sciences

MY GREATLY ESTEEMED friend Vernon Smith[1] turned 86 years of age recently. Vernon is, among other things, the leading figure in the development of experimental economics, for which he shared the Nobel Prize in 2002. For various methodological reasons, I have never been a fan of experimental economics. To me, it represents the sort of positivism that Austrian economists reject for good reason.

However, it has struck me recently that Austrian economics itself may be characterized as a kind of experimental economics in that its basic tool of analysis is the *thought experiment*—the careful thinking through of the consequences of hypothetical alternatives. In ordinary experimental science, such as physics, chemistry, and Vernon's experimental economics, one tests hypotheses (whatever their theoretical or other source and however plausible or fantastical they may be a priori) by observing the relation of changes in X to changes in Y, all other relevant things being held constant. The trouble is that, in all cases, one can never be sure that all other relevant things have been controlled. Hence every experiment is inconclusive; its findings are only as good as the controls imposed by the latest experimental setup, and an experiment with better controls may overturn one's current conclusion.

In Austrian economics, in contrast, one deduces the relation of X and Y from first principles so compelling that they are accepted as axioms, especially the Action Axiom (that people purposefully use means to obtain ends desired for the removal of their felt unease). In Austrian thought experiments, all other things whatsoever are held constant by a mental strait jacket that

---

1. "Vernon L. Smith," *Wikipedia*, http://en.wikipedia.org/wiki/vernon_l._smith.

immobilizes them completely. Therefore the deduced relation of X and Y is always as strong as the axioms of analysis, provided that no logical mistakes have been made.

Of course, such thought experiments cannot serve as necessarily effective forecasting devices, because the real world is in constant flux—that is, the "other things" are constantly changing. However, no matter how much they might change, the derived relation of X and Y remains an element of the real world's operation. For example, if the money stock is enlarged, then, all other things being equal, the general purchasing power of a unit of money declines. In an empirical situation, the money stock may be enlarged, yet a unit of money not lose general purchasing power because other things (e.g., the public's demand for money to hold) have changed in an offsetting way. Nonetheless, we may still conclude that in the actual situation we observe, the general purchasing power of a unit of money—whatever it may be—would have been greater had the money stock not risen. Thus we *understand* the workings of the world, at least in some part, even if we cannot *predict empirically* how the world or some specific element of it will change amid its constant flux.

So, all hail Austrian economics—the Queen of the Experimental Sciences. Long live the properly grounded thought experiment!

41

Not All Countries
Are Analytically Equal

ECONOMISTS AND OTHER social scientists have a long history of conducting analyses based on cross-sectional international data. Sometimes these studies examine a handful of countries; sometimes they examine scores of countries. The studies with the larger samples are, it seems, generally viewed as more solidly based than those with smaller samples.

It is common among economists for objections to particular studies to take the form, "But what about country X? It certainly did not follow the pattern your model predicts and your data display." The belief runs deep that only a study that can account for every country's data under the same explanatory setup, whether theoretical or econometric, deserves much respect. Economists seek general explanations, and those that fit every country are commonly regarded as the most general.

All of this seems reasonable as long as we do not spend much time pondering the analytical comparability of the countries. However, when we pause to consider how much countries differ from one another in a great variety of dimensions, we may well begin to wonder whether it makes sense to fit every member of a large group of countries into the same framework of analysis.

Simon Kuznets, who probably did more than any other economist in modern times to systematize the measurements necessary for cross-sectional international analyses and to carry out many such analyses himself, justified the use of nation states as units of analysis by arguing that each such state has unique discretion and importance in setting the policies, laws, and other institutions that form the context of incentives and constraints in which economic actors must operate; hence nation states are better units of analyses than, say, demographic groups, regions, or cities scattered across different states. Even if we concede Kuznets's point, however, it remains true that nation states differ in a host of ways.

Perhaps the most important dimension of difference is the sheer size of population or economic output. Approximately 200 nation states currently exist. Data compiled by organizations such as the United Nations, the World Bank, and the International Monetary Fund are made available to researchers in convenient forms on a regular basis, and hence these data serve hundreds or perhaps thousands of researchers as grist for their analytical mills. Not uncommonly the researcher employs the data for every country for which pertinent data are available in the standard compilations.

In econometric studies it is common for all the individual country observations to enter the analysis with equal weight, regardless of the differences in the countries' size. So, for example, one commonly sees analyses for every country that belongs to the Organization for Economic Cooperation and Development (OECD) or for every country in Latin America. Within the former group, tiny countries such as Estonia, Iceland, and Luxembourg may enter the analysis on equal terms with large countries such as France, Germany, Japan, and the United States. Within the latter group, small countries such as Belize, Honduras, and Uruguay may enter the analysis on equal terms with giants such as Brazil and Mexico.

In statistical analyses, the upshot is that outliers from the calculated central tendencies receive the same weight in the summary statistics (e.g., the coefficient of determination in a regression equation) whether they happen to be Iceland or Germany, whether they happen to be Belize or Brazil. Thus do international cross-sectional statistical studies in effect suppress the identities of the observational units as if they did not matter.

But surely we cannot have equal confidence in the findings of two studies, one of them with Italy and France as the outliers and another with Luxembourg and Denmark as the outliers. Likewise in Latin America, we might well have less satisfaction with a study whose overall pattern cannot account for Brazil and Argentina than with one whose overall pattern cannot account for El Salvador and Belize.

An old colleague and dear friend of mine from days gone by, Morris D. Morris, was a student of Indian economic development. I recall his telling me more than forty years ago that despite the dreary pace of overall Indian development, one saw much stronger performance in Gujarat, and that this region alone had a population comparable to the largest western European states. Morris noted that if Gujarat were listed as a separate country in the international data, its income would place it somewhere in the middle, rather than near the bottom, where India as a whole ranked in those days.

Many of the world's great cities—Mumbai, Shanghai, Sao Paulo, and Mexico City, for example—have populations and economic outputs that place them orders of magnitude above many of the world's smaller countries. And often, as in China today, particular regions may have income levels and rates of economic growth far out of line with those of huge backwater regions where mass poverty and slow rates of growth prevail. Almost all geographically large countries harbor substantial interregional differences, especially in the Third World.

The foregoing commentary is not intended to warrant a conclusion that cross-sectional international studies are worthless. Indeed, they can be revealing and instructive. Yet it behooves everyone who deals with them to bear in mind the incomparability of their units of analysis in population, total output, and other important variables, as well as the internal variation that marks all but the very smallest countries.

After all, you can fit a lot of Denmarks, Omans, and St. Lucias into any one of the world's economic and demographic giants. By treating all of these units of analysis on the same basis, we risk overlooking the truly important patterns because we have implicitly assigned excessive weight to the little fellows.

42

Creative Destruction—
The Best Game in Town

IN HIS JUSTLY famous 1942 book *Capitalism, Socialism and Democracy,* Joseph A. Schumpeter described the dynamics of a market economy as a process of "creative destruction."[1] In his view, innovation—"the new consumers' goods, the new methods of production or transportation, the new markets, the new forms of industrial organization that capitalist enterprise creates"—drives this process. Its most important result is that for the first time in history, the mass of the population in developed countries enjoys a standard of living that even the aristocrats of past ages could scarcely have imagined, much less have actually had.

Yet, as Schumpeter sought to express by his pithy term, the process is not merely creative, but also destructive. As a market economy develops, it necessarily brings about an immense variety of changes in particular demands and supplies, and hence it results in losses as well as profits. For those who rely on selling goods or services in declining or disappearing demand, for those whose locations no longer fit well into emerging spatial patterns of production, for those whose techniques of production no longer represent a means of maximizing net revenues, for those whose skills and experience no longer attract eager buyers in the labor markets—for them and countless others, the process of economic development brings anxiety, disappointment, loss, and in some cases ruin.

---

1. Joseph A. Schumpeter, *Capitalism, Socialism, and Democracy* (New York: Harper Perennial, 2008 [1942]).

The losers take little solace in the thought that their economic displacement or demotion by more competitive workers and producers constitutes the heart and soul of a process by which the entire society, on average, becomes richer. And their plight has always attracted legions of critics who correctly blame the market system for the wreckage. It is simply impossible for the process of economic development to operate without losers. A market economy is a profit-*and*-loss system. Profits signal the desirability (to consumers) of moving resources to new employments; losses signal the desirability (to consumers) of removing resources from current employments. On the one hand, people are drawn by the prospect of heightened economic pleasure; on the other hand, they are repelled by the onset of persistent economic pain. In this way the overall system continually reshapes itself to comport more effectively with the prevailing patterns of demand and supply.

For the losers, the perceived remedy of their plight has often been not to make the necessary personal adjustments as well as possible, but to use force, especially state force, to burden or prohibit the more successful competitors in the market. Thus, the market's critics demand bailouts, subsidies, tax breaks, and corporate and personal welfare of various sorts to soften the blows of the Schumpeterian "perennial gale of creative destruction." Notice, however, that all such attempts to soften the blows also serve to mute or falsify the messages the market system is sending about where resources can be employed most productively in the prevailing circumstances. Amelioration of the suffering softens the blows, to be sure, but it also slows the process by which wealth is being created and introduces wasteful measures that may, especially if they are state-mandated, become entrenched in the politico-economic system and thereby serve as channels for resource waste and as permanent fetters on real progress.

Many critics, of course, have called not for ameliorative measures, but for wholesale abandonment of the market system and its replacement by socialism, fascism, or some other form of state direction of the economic order. For the past two centuries the debates between pro-market and anti-market champions have raged continually with no sign of a final resolution in sight. Nowadays, however, the market's critics call less often for across-the-board abandonment of the market and more often for greater or lesser state intrusions into its fundamental institutions—secure private property rights and genuine rule of law. If enough such partial intrusions accumulate, however, as they have over the past century or more, the system becomes less a market system deflected here and there by the state, and more a state-dominated system deflected here and there by entrepreneurs who operate, legally or illegally, in the system's remaining market-oriented interstices.

In this de facto fascist environment, the resource wastes and misallocations become a growing burden on the system's capacity to generate a high rate of economic growth, indeed, ultimately on its capacity to produce any additions to real wealth. Such overburdened economic orders eventually die a slow death as their vital arteries of innovation and private investment become clogged by subsidies, taxes, regulations, direct state involvement, and other anti-productive buildups. The system then must endure not simply the frustrations and relative impoverishment of a succession of (often only temporary) losers in the process of creative destruction, but the frustration and absolute impoverishment of everyone except perhaps a fortunate few who benefit from the state's channeling loot to them.

What are we to conclude, then, about the process of creative destruction? The main conclusion must be that however painful it may be for those who must make the wrenching adjustments required by the economy's technological progress and changing structure, that pain plays an essential role in motivating the resource reallocation and other adjustments—for example, changes in the types of education, training, and experience people acquire—that make possible an ongoing process of economic development in which, in the course of time, nearly every member of society will be better off. Turning to the state, either for endless ad hoc intrusions or for across-the-board replacement of the market-directed economic order, may eliminate some of the pain associated with the process of creative destruction, to be sure, but only by replacing that process with one of uncompensated destruction, suffocating innovation and other forms of economic creativity and bringing real economic progress to a grinding halt.

It is a sorrowful reality that for the past century or more, people in the West have for the most part turned increasingly away from the economic system whose creativity redeems it and embraced instead systems whose hallmarks are economic irrationality, resource waste, bureaucratic tyranny, and ultimately mass impoverishment. Perhaps the great economic advances in Asia, where the market has been given wider scope in recent decades, will serve as a lesson to Westerners, pulling them back before they allow their governments to plunge them into the mass poverty from which their ancestors pulled themselves by means of the market system in earlier centuries.

43

Thinking Is Research, Too!

BILL PARKER,[1] an old friend of mine who died in 2000, was director of graduate studies in economics at Yale for thirteen years. He told me once about his struggles with his colleagues, who, he believed, were spending too much time on technique and not enough time on substance in teaching their courses. The recalcitrant colleagues maintained that they were teaching the students how to think, but Bill demurred: the students might be learning how to think, he told his colleagues, but they were not learning anything to think *about*.

This recollection fits in the same corner of my brain with something my old and deeply cherished friend (and my colleague as a fellow at Oxford University in 1971–72 and earlier in team-teaching a graduate seminar at the University of Washington in the summer of 1969) Max Hartwell[2] told me more than forty years ago. His colleagues, he complained, groused that he did not do enough research, by which they meant the usual cranking out of mathematical-theoretical models and related econometric effluent. Max's response was to insist that "thinking is research, too!" At the time, occupied as I was in trying to meet the profession's prevailing expectations, I had my doubts—it seemed like too easy an excuse—yet, as my own career has proceeded, I have become more and more convinced that Max had hit the target at its dead center.

I return to this thought frequently, never more so than when I consider how the economics profession has received—or, in far greater degree, not

---

1. "In Memoriam: Yale Economics William N. Parker," *YaleNews,* May 8, 2000, http://news.yale.edu/2000/05/08/memoriam-yale-economist-william-n-parker.

2. Robert Higgs, "R. Max Hartwell, 1921–2009," *The Beacon*, March 17, 2009, http://blog.independent.org/2009/03/17/r-max-hartwell-1921-2009/.

received—my research and writing on what I call regime uncertainty. I first wrote about this topic in 1997 in an article in the first volume of a new journal that I was editing, *The Independent Review*. Although the article contains some material that noneconomists might not understand immediately, it is for the most part nontechnical. It contains no formal mathematical model and no formal econometric estimation. Yet it does contain a great deal of empirical evidence and, to my mind, an analytical argument that has both theoretical substance and a respectable pedigree.

Although this article did not go entirely unnoticed, the mainstream profession paid little or no attention to it. My fellow Austrian economists seemed to find it persuasive, as did some economic historians, but mainstream macroeconomists, so far as I was aware, remained blissfully oblivious to it for many years. Eventually, during the past few years, a few such mainstream analysts took note of it, usually in passing. Meanwhile, the topic of policy uncertainty (a subset of my concept of regime uncertainty) was attracting growing interest from macroeconomists as recovery from the contraction of 2007–2009 proved so slow and, thus far, incomplete.

I continue to believe that the importance of regime uncertainty should be manifest to economists even as I have presented it. *They need only think about it.* They need only inform themselves well of prevailing political and economic conditions, whether during 1935–40 or during 2008–2013, and put themselves imaginatively in the place of a large investor. Does it really stand to reason that such an investor would regard the regime uncertainty manifest in these two episodes as so trivial a consideration that he would choose to disregard it in making his choice to invest or not to invest, especially in long-term projects? To me, the answer is obvious. Even someone completely untutored in economic theory or history should be able to understand that when the predictability of the future security of one's private property rights becomes extremely problematic, with far more margins being "up for grabs" than before, more investors will choose to forgo commitments to long-term projects and to park their money in short-term investments in whose payoff security one can reasonably place relatively greater confidence simply by virtue of the short terms to maturity. To repeat, all one has to do is think about what's going on and how such current and prospective events almost certainly affect investors' thinking.

Yet, mainstream economists appreciate that one earns no professional plaudits for thinking in this way, and, sad to say, one usually incurs no professional disdain or other punishment by disregarding such commonsense thinking altogether. The mainstream profession rewards most highly the "smart guys," the ones who wheel and deal with analytical apparatuses that even many economists do not understand well and cannot themselves employ. At Harvard, Yale, Chicago, Berkeley, Stanford, and similar leading departments of economics, one's publications in top economics journals—and hence one's tenure, pay, promotion, research funding, and professional reputation—gain little or nothing from mere thinking, regardless of how much common sense one embeds in it. The name of the game is pyrotechnics, professional showing off, to impress one's colleagues. Small wonder that mainstream economics has become so disconnected from economic reality over the five or six decades in which such expectations have set the standard for succeeding generations of young economists, each new hotshot being hell-bent on doing something even "smarter" than what his grad school mentors and their contemporaries have done.

There's no arguing with success. The advisability of taking this other-worldly approach has been proved repeatedly by hundreds of young hotshots over the years. But their success hinges entirely on the profession's self-containment, on its insulation from the society that gains so little, indeed, that may actually lose a great deal, from how economists go about their business. To understand why the whole bizarre business continues to thrive, follow the money. It will lead you straight to the treasuries of state and federal governments, where academia constitutes an important player in the fascistic enterprise coordinated by politicians in office and their appointed bureaucrats at agencies such as the National Science Foundation. The payoff to society, however, is entirely another matter. One wonders how long this way of doing economics can survive as the state's relentless expansion eats more deeply into society's capacity to bankroll the silliness of people who would rather solve make-believe economic puzzles than—not to belabor my point—simply think about how the world works.

PART III

Money, Debt, Interest Rates, and Prices

44

Macroeconomic Booms and Busts
Déjà Vu Once Again

CONSIDER THE FOLLOWING commentary on the economic situation:

Foolhardy procedures which are divorced from economic realities, or whose economic implications are not understood by their promoters, do not perforce become sanctified and wise merely by designating them as "action"; tilting at windmills does not draw water.

[W]hen a recovery program, which, while it may appear effective, depends for its efficacy upon much the same kind of "cheap money" inflation which . . . was the main cause of the **recession from 2007 to 2009**, then the present recovery must ultimately prove as illusory as the **boom from 2001 to 2007**, and it is the duty of economists to pierce the veil of illusion.

Certainly the recovery movement to the date of this writing [**December 2010**] is a peculiar one: it is shot through with anomalies. With [**more than 15 million estimated to be**] unemployed . . . with governmental relief rolls still at high levels, . . . there very obviously is something wrong, somewhere.

The fact would seem to be that the authorities who are undertaking the "management" of the current recovery, and congratulating themselves that prosperity is returning because they "planned it so," are utterly oblivious of the fact that recovery is being engineered largely by the same means which produced the last boom—and **recession**. With this difference: whereas the banking system during the **recent**

boom was producing an investment credit inflation by extending credit to business men and corporations, Government is now assuming the role of inducing new deposit currency in the banking system and thereby producing a consumption credit inflation. The Federal Government, instead of private corporations, is issuing the bonds which the banks are now purchasing, thereby inflating the deposit currency structure all over again. These "created" funds are in this instance being used principally to finance consumption expenditures through relief disbursements, make-work projects, and the like. . . . [T]he current inflation tends to conceal and to preserve the fundamental disequilibria which so prolonged the **recession after 2007** and which we are now carrying over therefrom without having once squarely faced the problem of correcting them.

Notice, however, that the foregoing commentary, except for the terms in bold font, was written not yesterday, but, in its final form, in 1937. The authors, C. A. Phillips, T. F. McManus, and R. W. Nelson, placed this commentary, along with a wealth of related evidence and analysis, in their unjustly neglected book *Banking and the Business Cycle: A Study of the Great Depression in the United States.*[1] The quoted passages, which appear on pp. 212–14, originally read as follows:

> Foolhardy procedures which are divorced from economic realities, or whose economic implications are not understood by their promoters, do not perforce become sanctified and wise merely by designating them as "action"; tilting at windmills does not draw water.
>
> [W]hen a recovery program, which, while it may appear effective, depends for its efficacy upon much the same kind of "cheap money" inflation which . . . was the main cause of the Great Depression, then the present recovery must ultimately prove as illusory as the New Era of the 'twenties; and it is the duty of economists to pierce the veil of illusion.

---

1. C.A. Phillips, T.F. McManus, and R.W. Nelson, *Banking and the Business Cycle: A Study of the Great Depression in the United States* (New York: Macmillan, 1937).

Certainly the recovery movement to the date of this writing [February 1937] is a peculiar one: it is shot through with anomalies. With [8 million to 12 million estimated to be] unemployed . . . with governmental relief rolls still at high levels, . . . there very obviously is something wrong, somewhere.

The fact would seem to be that the authorities who are undertaking the "management" of the current recovery, and congratulating themselves that prosperity is returning because they "planned it so," are utterly oblivious of the fact that recovery is being engineered largely by the same means which produced the last boom—and depression. With this difference: whereas the banking system during the 'twenties was producing an investment credit inflation by extending credit to business men and corporations, Government is now assuming the role of inducing new deposit currency in the banking system and thereby producing a consumption credit inflation. The Federal Government, instead of private corporations, is issuing the bonds which the banks are now purchasing, thereby inflating the deposit currency structure all over again. These "created" funds are in this instance being used principally to finance consumption expenditures through relief disbursements, make-work projects, and the like. . . . [T]he current inflation tends to conceal and to preserve the fundamental disequilibria which so prolonged the Great Depression and which we are now carrying over therefrom without having once squarely faced the problem of correcting them.

When policymakers repeat in the early twenty-first century the same mistakes they made in the 1920s and 1930s, and when mainstream economists fail to understand that these policies are misguided now, just as they were then, one can scarcely argue that the mainstream understanding of business fluctuations has advanced at all during the past eighty years. Indeed, the typical macroeconomist today is much inferior to Phillips, McManus, and Nelson, in no small part because today's economists, owing to the high level of aggregation they employ in their theoretical and empirical work, miss what is most important for understanding business booms and busts: policy-induced structural disequilibria and malinvestments.

45

The Continuing Puzzle of the Hyperinflation That Hasn't Occurred

SINCE LATE DECEMBER 2008, the bank prime lending rate—the interest rate banks charge their best corporate customers—has remained steady at 3.25 percent.

Meanwhile, during the same period, the excess reserves that commercial banks hold at the Fed have increased from $2 billion in August 2008 to $1,513 billion in May 2011 (see Figure 45.1).

Ordinarily, one would have expected this development to produce hyperinflation of the general price level. However, the price level has increased quite moderately, and for a while many analysts warned that deflation was the

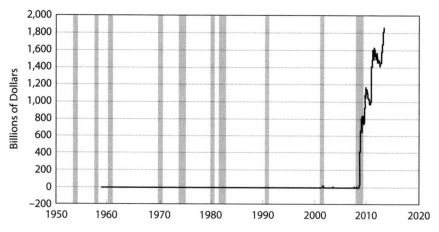

Note: Shaded areas indicate U.S. recessions. 2013 research.stlouisfed.org

Source: Board of Governors of the Federal Reserve System

Figure 45.1. Excess Reserves of Depository Institutions (Discontinued Series) (EXCRESNS)

greater risk. Despite a slight increase in the price level's rate of growth in recent months, the index of prices paid by all urban consumers has increased by only about 6 percent in the three and a half years since the beginning of 2008. Not only has hyperinflation failed to appear; even garden-variety inflation of prices in general has been extremely low by the standard of recent decades.

The preceding combination of events poses a great challenge to economic analysts. How can we explain that the fantastically enormous explosion of bank reserves has not given rise to bank lending that would greatly expand the money stock and thereby drive up prices in general?

The most obvious answer, of course, is that the banks are simply sitting on the reserves, rather than lending them to customers. And why are they doing so? The usual answer is that since late 2008, the Fed has paid the banks a rate of interest on their reserves at the Fed. This interest rate has recently been in the range 0–0.25 percent. Although this is not nothing, it verges very closely on nothing. And if one notes that the purchasing power of money has fallen at least a bit, it is clear that the banks are realizing a negative real rate of return on their holdings of excess reserves at the Fed.

Moreover, they are sitting on the reserves notwithstanding that they appear to have the option of lending at 3.25 percent to their best corporate customers and at higher rates to their less creditworthy customers. Why are they forgoing the opportunity to earn huge sums by switching out of excess reserves at the Fed into commercial loans and investments? The answer would seem to be that that they are so frightened of the risk associated even with loans to their best customers that they are loath to lend. After some volatility up and down and then up again between summer 2008 and early 2010, total loans and investments of all commercial banks have settled for more than a year at a level only about 2 percent greater than their level at the beginning of 2008. This increase of about $200 billion amounts to only a small fraction, about 13 percent, of the increase in their excess-reserve balance at the Fed during the same period.

In these circumstances, some economists have taken to arguing that excess reserves no longer constitute "high-powered money," that they no longer belong to the monetary base, and therefore they have not proved to be the fuel for hyperinflation that nearly all economists would have expected them to be prior to the past four years of anomalous experience.

I am not convinced. First, I am not convinced that these gigantic sums will not, sooner or later, still become the fuel for hyperinflation, or at least for a greatly accelerating rate of general price inflation, which economists expected they would be before the recent recession and all of the government's and the Fed's extraordinary responses to it occurred. Second, I am not convinced that the banks will remain content forever with earning a negative real rate of return on their holdings of $1.5 trillion in excess reserves now languishing at the Fed. If they were to realize only the difference between the rate the Fed is paying them and the rate they would earn by lending these funds exclusively to prime customers—an increase of 3 percent on their return—they would gain an additional $45 billion in income. That's a great deal of potential income to leave lying on the table, and it might be even greater if we factored in the additional income they might earn by lending to less-than-prime customers at greater rates. I understand, of course, that banks are seeking to repair their damaged balance sheets, in light of their recent debacle in real-estate-related investments of various sorts and in conformity with the new Basel requirements for increased bank capitalization. Still, I am not convinced that these considerations can account fully for the very curious conditions now existing in the banking industry.

Of course, my lack of conviction in the new wisdom may be groundless. This time, everything really may be different. But as an economic historian, as well as an economist substantially behind the cutting edge of his profession, I am not ready to latch onto this latest "this time it's different" explanation, at least not until much more time has passed and my skepticism has been proved baseless by long-sustained counter experience. At the moment, the conjunction of recent macroeconomic events still seems to me to pose a great puzzle.

Perhaps part of the answer relates to the regime uncertainty about which I have written from time to time during the past three years, harkening back to my earlier writing about its significance during the second half of the 1930s, during the so-called Second New Deal. It would hardly be astonishing if such worries were now contributing to the extreme risk aversion banks are manifesting. Moreover, perhaps for the same reason, potential borrowers are not exactly clamoring for loans, and indeed many corporations are sitting on huge cash hoards of their own. Interesting times, indeed.

46

Money versus Monetary Base

An Elementary yet Critical Distinction

AS MORE AND MORE people have taken an interest in monetary affairs—especially in the Fed and its various operations—in recent years, many people have joined the discussions related to these matters, especially on the World Wide Web. In reading these posts over the years, in particular in reading the comments on a post I placed recently at *The Beacon*, I have been struck by the frequency with which the writers reveal that they do not understand a basic conceptual matter in regard to money, monetary policy, and the Fed. That matter is the difference between the monetary base and the money stock.

In the data compiled by the Fed and used by analysts in various ways, the *monetary base* (sometimes called "high-powered money" or "base money") consists of currency—that is, Federal Reserve notes, the legally authorized, circulating paper money denominated in U.S. dollars issued by one of the Federal Reserve System's regional banks—plus deposits that commercial banks and other "depository institutions" hold as reserves in accounts at the Fed. This sum is known as the monetary base because it forms the foundation on which commercial banks may extend loans to customers and make investments by means of establishing checking accounts (checkable deposit accounts) for those customers or security sellers.

In a fractional-reserve banking system, such as that in the United States and most other countries, banks are legally required to hold a certain percentage of their deposit liabilities (including those they create as just described) as reserves at the Fed. If they hold more reserves with the Fed than their current accounts require, these reserves are denominated "excess reserves." These may be used, of course, to extend additional loans and make additional investments in securities until the bank has reached a condition in which it has used up all of its legally "excess" reserves.

As a fractional-reserve banking system creates new checking accounts for its customers, it adds to the *money stock*, which is the set of all highly liquid assets that are most readily exchangeable for goods and services. Note, however, that the precise definition of the money stock is necessarily vague: exactly which liquid assets ought to be counted as "money" and which ones ought not to be counted cannot be resolved by finding the "correct" answer; there is no correct answer. What one would wish to count depends on the question one seeks to answer by making reference to the amount of "money" in the system.

Therefore, one finds that many different statistical series[1] are created and employed by economists and financial analysts. These are denominated by acronyms such as M1, M2, M3, MZM, and so forth. There is no conspiracy or attempt to conceal anything in this way of dealing with the data, but only a frank recognition that "money" is not a clear-cut economic entity, and indeed its composition may change—and often has changed in the past—as economic and financial conditions and transaction practices vary.

It is common to say that the Fed and other central banks have the power to "create money out of thin air," that is, out of nothing more than their own declaration that new deposits are now available to a bank at the Fed (often in exchange for a bank's asset or collateral). This common saying, however, is not quite right. In fact, the Fed has the power to create new base money. If the banks that acquire that new base money in their accounts do not use it to make new loans or purchase new investment securities, it simply sits there at the Fed: in that form, it is not money because it is not a balance that can be exchanged directly for goods and services. For the Fed to create money, then, it must have the cooperation of the banks, which use the newly created base money to establish new checking accounts for loan customers or security sellers.

This is the situation to which my previous post called attention: namely, that since August 2008, the Fed has created a fantastically huge addition to the

---

1. Federal Reserve Bank of St. Louis, "Monetary Data: Categories," http://research.stlouis fed.org/fred2/categories/24.

monetary base, about $1.8 trillion dollars, yet the banks have let the lion's share of this additional lending potential sit at the Fed unused, hence untransformed into increases in the money stock.

For example, M2, a commonly used measure of the money stock, has increased by only about $1.244 trillion, or about 16 percent since August 2008. Whereas the "money multiplier" associated with additional base money might normally have been expected to be perhaps 10 or more, turning $1.8 trillion of new base money into $18 trillion of newly created money stock (and thereby triggering hyperinflation), in the present case, the addition to the money stock has actually been *smaller* than the addition to the monetary base—that is, *the money multiplier has been less than one* because of the banks' not making use of the new lending potential this addition provides them.

This difference—this breakage, as it were, of the previously prevailing relation between the monetary base (which the Fed controls) and the money stock (which the Fed and the banking system and its customers jointly control)—is the essence of the puzzle to which I called attention in the previous chapter. Many people have offered plausible explanations for it, but many of the lay commentators' comments are flawed by a failure to appreciate correctly the distinction between the monetary base and the money stock. Intelligent engagement in this discussion requires that one master this elementary yet critical distinction.

47

The Euthanasia of the Saver

IN CHAPTER 24 of *The General Theory of Employment, Interest and Money*[1] (1936), John Maynard Keynes laid out his screwball idea that capital might soon become, or be made to become, no longer scarce; hence no payment would have to be made to induce people to save, and that condition would be splendid inasmuch as it would entail the "euthanasia of the rentier." This stuff really must be seen to be believed; here is the meat of Keynes's discussion in his own words:

> The justification for a moderately high rate of interest has been found hitherto in the necessity of providing a sufficient inducement to save. But we have shown that the extent of effective saving is necessarily determined by the scale of investment and that the scale of investment is promoted by a low rate of interest, provided that we do not attempt to stimulate it in this way beyond the point which corresponds to full employment. Thus it is to our best advantage to reduce the rate of interest to that point relative to the schedule of the marginal efficiency of capital at which there is full employment.
>
> There can be no doubt that this criterion will lead to a much lower rate of interest than has ruled hitherto; and, so far as one can guess at the schedules of the marginal efficiency of capital corresponding to increasing amounts of capital, the rate of interest is likely to fall steadily, if it should be practicable to maintain conditions of more or

---

1. John Maynard Keynes, *The General Theory of Employment, Interest and Money* (New York: Harcourt, Brace, and World, 1965 [1936]).

less continuous full employment—unless, indeed, there is an excessive change in the aggregate propensity to consume (including the State).

I feel sure that the demand for capital is strictly limited in the sense that it would not be difficult to increase the stock of capital up to a point where its marginal efficiency had fallen to a very low figure. This would not mean that the use of capital instruments would cost almost nothing, but only that the return from them would have to cover little more than their exhaustion by wastage and obsolescence together with some margin to cover risk and the exercise of skill and judgment. In short, the aggregate return from durable goods in the course of their life would, as in the case of short-lived goods, just cover their labour costs of production plus an allowance for risk and the costs of skill and supervision.

Now, though this state of affairs would be quite compatible with some measure of individualism, yet it would mean the euthanasia of the rentier, and, consequently, the euthanasia of the cumulative oppressive power of the capitalist to exploit the scarcity-value of capital. Interest today rewards no genuine sacrifice, any more than does the rent of land. The owner of capital can obtain interest because capital is scarce, just as the owner of land can obtain rent because land is scarce. But whilst there may be intrinsic reasons for the scarcity of land, there are no intrinsic reasons for the scarcity of capital. An intrinsic reason for such scarcity, in the sense of a genuine sacrifice which could only be called forth by the offer of a reward in the shape of interest, would not exist, in the long run, except in the event of the individual propensity to consume proving to be of such a character that net saving in conditions of full employment comes to an end before capital has become sufficiently abundant. But even so, it will still be possible for communal saving through the agency of the State to be maintained at a level which will allow the growth of capital up to the point where it ceases to be scarce.

I see, therefore, the rentier aspect of capitalism as a transitional phase which will disappear when it has done its work. And with the disappearance of its rentier aspect much else in it besides will suffer a sea-change. It will be, moreover, a great advantage of the order of events which I am advocating, that the euthanasia of the rentier, of the functionless investor, will be nothing sudden, merely a gradual but prolonged continuance of what we have seen recently in Great Britain, and will need no revolution.[2]

Given the Fed's policy during the past three years of, first, driving short-term interest rates down almost to zero, and, more recently, undertaking Operation Twist, with the intent of driving longer-term interest rates down to levels that, in real terms, equal or fall below zero, we might seriously wonder whether Chairman Ben Bernanke and his colleagues have decided to give a shove to the wheel of history that Keynes longingly anticipated.

However that may be, no one can dispute that people who rely on the earnings on invested funds to support themselves—a situation in which many retired persons in particular find themselves—are now in a world of hurt. Bank savings accounts are paying interest rates of 1 percent or less. Certificates of deposit are paying 0.5 percent to 1.7 percent, depending on the term. U.S. Treasury bonds with terms of 5 to 30 years are yielding in the neighborhood of 1 percent to 3 percent.

In short, the highest yield available to ordinary investors who seek a simple, low-risk investment of their funds is, at best, roughly equal to the rate of inflation—and then, with a 30-year term to maturity, only with substantial risk of capital loss if interest rates should rise. To put the matter another way, all ordinary investors are now being progressively impoverished because the nominal return on their investments falls short of the loss of purchasing power of the dollar during the term of the investment. Getting a positive real rate of return is effectively impossible for the proverbial widows and orphans. Only investors with the knowledge of how to invest in gold, crude commodities, and other such esoteric assets stand any chance of earning positive real returns, and then only with great risk of substantial capital losses.

Given that the Fed's official policy is to drive all interest rates to near zero, one may conclude that the Fed seeks to impoverish the widows, orphans, retired people, and all other financially untutored people who rely on interest

---

2. Keynes, *General Theory*, 375–76.

earnings to support themselves in their old age or adversity. Can a crueler official policy be imagined?

The politicians constantly bark about their solicitude for those who are helpless and in difficulty through no fault of their own. Yet the scores of millions of people who saved money to support themselves in old age now find themselves progressively robbed by the very officials who purport to be their protectors. There are many reasons to oppose the Fed's policy. The reason brought to mind by the official euthanasia of the nation's small savers deserves far more attention than it has received to date.

48

The Fed's Immiseration of People Who Live on Interest Earnings

AS I HAVE NOTED previously,[1] the Fed's policy of acting to hold interest rates well below free-market rates in recent years has had the effect of greatly diminishing the earnings of people who rely on interest income. Such people include especially many retirees who do not wish to hold risky assets with substantial variability of earnings. In the past, many retired people have held the bulk of their wealth in the form of bank certificates of deposit, bonds, and bond-heavy mutual funds, hoping that their incomes would be secure and predictable when they were no longer working. The Fed's actions in recent years have taken a heavy toll on such people's earnings.

As Figure 48.1 shows, personal interest earnings rose substantially from 2004 to 2008, then dropped precipitously when the Fed's new policies took effect in the last quarter of 2008. During the past year, such earnings have more or less stabilized in the neighborhood of $1.2 trillion. However, the present amount is little more than the amount that was earned in the year 2000—eleven years ago.

These data, however, are given in nominal dollars, whose purchasing power has declined substantially over the past decade. As Figure 48.2 shows, the price index for personal consumption expenditures has risen since 2000 by approximately 28 percent. Therefore, the current flow of personal interest income has purchasing power equal to only about 78 percent of the purchasing power of the personal interest income earned eleven years ago. Of course, the

---

1. Robert Higgs, "The Euthanasia of the Saver," *The Beacon*, October 26, 2011, http://blog.independent.org/2011/10/26/the-euthanasia-of-the-saver/.

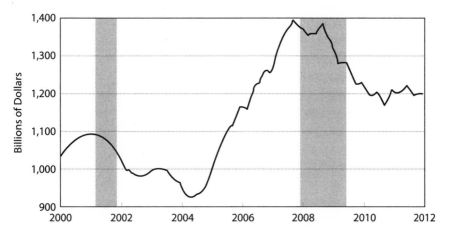

Note: Shaded areas indicate U.S. recessions. 2014 research.stlouisfed.org

Source: U.S. Department of Commerce: Bureau of Economic Analysis

Figure 48.1. Personal Income Receipts on Assets:
Personal Interest Income (PII)

decline since the peak in 2008 has been much greater—in the neighborhood of a one-third drop in real terms.

Defenders of the Fed historically have argued, among other things, that central-bank monetary policies have a sort of neutrality: they affect aggregate demand, the overall price level, and other macroeconomic variables, but they do not attempt to carry out the kind of micromanagement of the economy that Soviet-style central planning attempts. This argument has always been bogus because monetary policy was never—indeed, could not be—neutral. It always had differential effects on different classes of people and different sorts of economic activity, depending in part on who received new infusions of central-bank-enabled money first, second, and later in the process and on how these persons' actions affected ongoing real economic processes. Nonetheless, defenders of the central bank might have argued that at least the Fed did not attempt in any direct way to determine definite changes in the distribution of income, either personal or functional.

Such defenses now ring unmistakably hollow. Even apart from the Fed's entry into clear credit-allocation activities (e.g., buying mortgage-backed securities rather than Treasury bonds alone), it is plain that the Fed is acting in

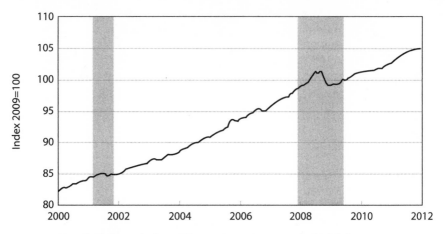

Note: Shaded areas indicate U.S. recessions. 2014 research.stlouisfed.org

Source: U.S. Department of Commerce: Bureau of Economic Analysis

Figure 48.2. Personal Consumption Expenditures:
Chain-type Price Index (PCEPI)

a way that impoverishes a definite class of persons—those heavily dependent on interest earnings for their income—and, moreover, that a policy of keeping interest rates on low-risk assets near zero must eventually wipe out such persons' incomes completely. In that event, people who worked and saved over a working lifetime, taking personal responsibility for guaranteeing their self-sufficiency during their elderly, nonworking years, will be able to survive only at the mercy of the providers of private and public charity.

The link between the Fed's policies and this undeniable effect is too direct and too obvious for anyone, including the Fed's managers, to overlook or misunderstand. We may only conclude, then, that the Fed's managers either (1) want to wipe out the retirees and others who rely heavily on interest earnings or (2) consider these people's immiseration an acceptable price to pay in order to achieve other objectives. Can any decent person approve such policymaking?

49

Extraordinary Demand to Hold Cash

The Mystery Persists

SINCE THE FALL OF 2008, the Federal Reserve System has pumped an almost incomprehensibly large amount of reserves into the commercial banking system—about $1.4 trillion (see Figure 49.1).

In normal circumstances, this action would have given rise to hyperinflation. Of course, not only has no hyperinflation occurred, but scarcely any inflation at all has occurred, and policymakers seem to have lost more sleep in worrying about deflation than about inflation.

By this time, everyone knows that the hyperinflation did not occur primarily because the banks simply held onto their bloated reserve balances rather than using them to extend new loans and make new investments. Whereas

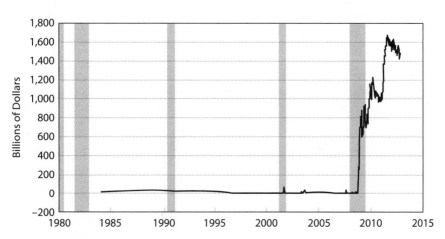

Note: Shaded areas indicate U.S. recessions. 2012 research.stlouisfed.org

Source: Board of Governors of the Federal Reserve System

Figure 49.1. Reserve Balances with Federal Reserve Banks (WRESBAL)

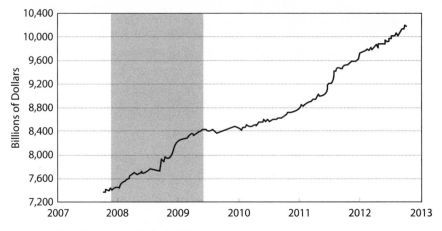

Note: Shaded areas indicate U.S. recessions. 2012 research.stlouisfed.org
Source: Board of Governors of the Federal Reserve System

Figure 49.2. M2 Money Stock (M2)

it used to be the case that increased reserves fairly quickly translated into increased money supply, in the past five years the money supply has increased only moderately and, in certain spells, hardly at all (see Figure 49.2). Additional bank reserves, as such, are not available to the public for making expenditures; hence they have not provided fuel for the spending that would have driven prices up more or less across the board.

However, the money supply has increased somewhat. Indeed, by historical standards, its increase in the past five years—about 38 percent for the M2 measure of money—has been fairly brisk (see Figure 49.2).

Yet this increase failed to give rise to accelerated price inflation in large part because the public has chosen to increase the amount of cash it holds, rather than spends. In technical economic jargon, the money stock's velocity of circulation has fallen substantially—by about 18 percent in the past five years (see Figure 49.3).

The bulk of this decline occurred in 2008, when the financial debacle drove many individuals and firms to flee to the seemingly safest financial asset available amid the tempest of uncertainty—cash. After the winter of 2009, the velocity of monetary circulation rose somewhat, but during the past two years it has resumed its decline. It now stands at the lowest level recorded in more than fifty years (see Figure 49.4).

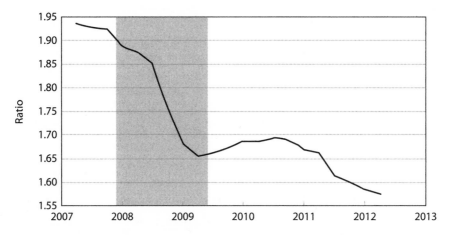

Note: Shaded areas indicate U.S. recessions. 2012 research.stlouisfed.org
Source: Federal Reserve Bank of St. Louis

Figure 49.3. Velocity of M2 Money Stock (M2V)

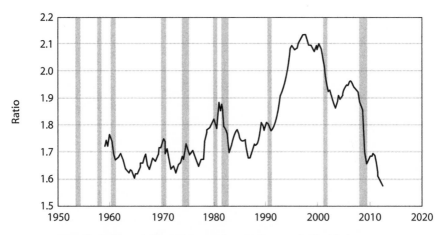

Note: Shaded areas indicate U.S. recessions. 2013 research.stlouisfed.org
Source: Federal Reserve Bank of St. Louis

Figure 49.4. Velocity of M2 Money Stock (M2V)

People ordinarily do not add to their cash balances (relative to their income) unless they believe that alternative assets will have lower risk-adjusted yields than cash. Because cash has a nominal yield of zero, the only way that holding it can have a positive real yield is if its purchasing power increases— that is, if people expect price deflation. Perhaps in the present situation they have not so much expected deflation as they have considered the risks associated with alternative assets to be too great to compensate for their greater expected nominal yield.

I do not claim to have the One True Solution to the puzzle of why the velocity of monetary circulation has fallen so far and, more puzzling to me, why it has not rebounded more from the collapse it experienced during 2008. We live, it seems, in a time of extraordinary apprehensions about the future. Financial, economic, and regime uncertainties abound. Although some people enjoy remarking that fiat money is "just paper" and hence "essentially worthless," the public in general has viewed it in recent years as valuable, indeed, so much so that they have greatly increased their demand to hold it, and they continue to maintain and even to increase this extraordinary demand for the asset with a zero nominal yield.

50

More Monetary Peculiarities of the Past Five Years

TWO MONTHS AGO, I wrote[1] about the extraordinary increase in the demand for money during the past five years, noting in particular the substantial decline in the velocity of the M2 money stock. I also noted that M2 has increased about 38 percent since late 2007. In the present post, I call attention to some peculiarities in how M2 has increased during this period.

M1[2] consists of "(1) currency outside the U.S. Treasury, Federal Reserve Banks, and the vaults of depository institutions; (2) traveler's checks of nonbank issuers; (3) demand deposits; and (4) other checkable deposits (OCDs), which consist primarily of negotiable order of withdrawal (NOW) accounts at depository institutions and credit union share draft accounts." M2[3] consists of M1 plus the following items: "(1) savings deposits (which include money market deposit accounts, or MMDAs); (2) small-denomination time deposits (time deposits in amounts of less than $100,000); and (3) balances in retail money market mutual funds (MMMFs)." Thus, M2 is a fairly broad measure of the funds immediately or quickly available to the holders for making expenditures. For this reason, economists commonly use this measure in their empirical work in macroeconomics and monetary economics in lieu of a variety of available alternative measures of the money stock.

---

1. Robert Higgs, "Extraordinary Demand to Hold Cash—The Mystery Persists," *The Beacon*, Oct 24, 2012, http://blog.independent.org/2012/10/24/extraordinary-demand-to-hold-cash-the-mystery-persists/.

2. Federal Reserve Bank of St. Louis, "M1 Money Stock," updated Nov. 20, 2014, http://research.stlouisfed.org/fred2/series/M1SL?cid=25.

3. Federal Reserve Bank of St. Louis, "M2 Money Stock," updated Dec, 4, 2014, http://research.stlouisfed.org/fred2/series/M2SL?cid=29.

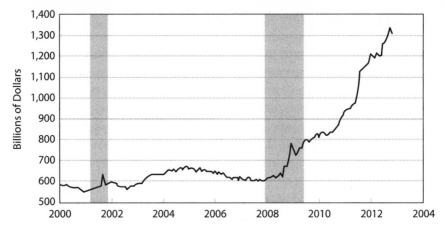

Note: Shaded areas indicate U.S. recessions. 2012 research.stlouisfed.org
Source: Board of Governors of the Federal Reserve System

Figure 50.1. Total Checkable Deposits (TCDSL)

During the past five years (to be precise, during the 59 months from December 2007 to November 2012; likewise hereafter in this post), M2 increased 38.1 percent. The non-M1 part of M2 increased 29.9 percent, which means that the M1 part must have increased much more rapidly than M2 as a whole. Indeed, M1 increased 74.2 percent, or roughly twice as fast as M2.

Moreover, the components of M1 itself grew at very different rates: the currency component grew by $318 billion, or 41.6 percent, whereas total checkable deposits grew by about $700 billion, or 115.2 percent, which is almost three times faster (see Figure 50.1).

When I began my inquiry into the data for this chapter, I had a hunch that I would find that the currency component of M1 had grown most rapidly. I was wrong by a huge margin. In fact, during the past five years, people have continued to pile up money most rapidly not in currency, but in checking accounts. During this period, individuals and businesses have added more money to their checking accounts than they had added in all preceding history.

So the question naturally arises: why? My first thought was that during the recession, many unemployed people had actually shifted to employment in the underground economy and that this shift would be reflected in a big increase in currency holdings. Perhaps such a shift has occurred; after all, currency holdings have increased by almost 42 percent in the past five years. But the gigantic increase in checking account balances, which are completely transparent to various law-enforcement and other government officials, must have a different explanation.

As Figure 50.1 shows, people and firms immediately augmented their checkable balances when the financial debacle occurred in the fall of 2008. Very well, such a flight to liquidity was to be expected in the circumstances. However, after the dust from that crisis settled, especially after mid-2010, the public persisted in rapidly increasing its checkable account balances as if it had acquired an obsession with this form of wealth holding. Why?

We may conjecture that in view of the extraordinary uncertainty[4] associated with asset markets and government actions during these years, people wanted the ability to move quickly without having their funds tied up in riskier and less liquid forms. However, most of them did not need large amounts of currency; indeed, great amounts of currency would have been less secure and convenient than checkable balances in commercial banks and other financial institutions. Thus the unprecedented augmentation of a very liquid yet secure form of assets may be still another reflection of the abnormal uncertainties that have clouded the economic horizon since mid-2008.

---

4. Robert Higgs, "Important New Evidence on Regime Uncertainty," *The Beacon*, Oct 8, 2011, http://blog.independent.org/2011/10/08/important-new-evidence-on-regime-uncertainty/.

51

A Bogus Example of Controlling Inflation with Price Controls

AS THE U.S. GOVERNMENT prepared for and then engaged fully in World War II, it made increasingly stringent efforts to control inflation by imposing price controls. Late in 1942, these controls were strengthened substantially, and from early 1943 through mid-1946, when the controls were allowed to lapse, the consumer price index rose very little (see Figure 51.1). These data have often been trotted out to prove that the government can successfully control inflation if only it makes the laws severe enough and the monitoring agency sufficiently large and powerful.

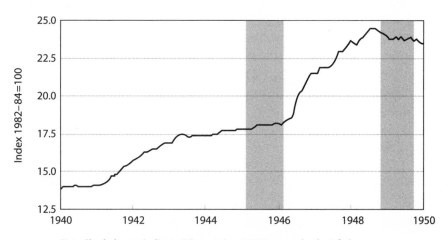

Note: Shaded areas indicate U.S. recessions. 2012 research.stlouisfed.org
Source: U.S. Department of Labor: Bureau of Labor Statistics

Figure 51.1 Consumer Price Index for All Urban Consumers: All Items (CPIAUCNS)

In reality, inflation was not controlled; only the legally revealed prices were controlled. This experience does not require rocket science to understand: if the government makes it illegal and punishable to raise legal prices (or to raise them by more than a stipulated small amount), then sellers will not set legal prices that violate the restrictions.

But legal prices need not be, and during World War II certainly were not, the same as actual prices. Sellers and buyers used a variety of subterfuges to make transactions in violation of the government's price controls. Sellers might reduce the product's quality, as many did at the time; require the buyer to wait longer for an order to be filled; require the buyer to purchase unwanted goods in order to purchase wanted ones; require the buyer to pay for bogus goods, as when tenants were required to pay the landlord a hefty sum as "key money," ostensibly to compensate him for keeping a spare key in case the tenant lost his own key; require the buyer to forgo services normally associated with the goods, such as routine maintenance of rented apartments; or require gifts or other ostensible gratuities not ordinarily given to a seller. Sellers might also simply disregard the posted prices and refuse to sell to anyone except at higher (unlisted and unreported) prices. The methods of evasion were legion.

Milton Friedman and Anna Schwartz and other economists who have made corrections for the understatement of the price level during the war years have shown that even partial corrections are sufficient to establish that the government's price controls were far from the success claimed at the time —claims often gullibly swallowed later by economists and historians. (For sources and more detailed discussion, see pp. 89–93 of my book *Depression, War, and Cold War*.)[1]

Economists are trained in theory, statistics, modeling, and other skills. Historians are trained in the careful scrutiny and interpretation of historical sources. Neither economists nor historians, unfortunately, are trained to use common sense in their work. Postwar proponents of the reimposition of price controls have often pointed to the success of such controls during the war. Yet, despite thousands of employees and an army of volunteer monitors associated

---

1. Robert Higgs, *Depression, War, and Cold War: Studies in Political Economy* (New York: Oxford University Press, 2006).

with the Office of Price Administration and despite the U.S. Attorney General's prosecutory zeal in hauling alleged violators into court, the government's price-control efforts during World War II failed to stem the tide of rising prices set in motion by the huge contemporary increases in the money stock.[2]

Price controls, at most, only create a population of liars. True prices continue to do what the existing economic conditions cause them to do. No one can control the amount of precipitation by passing a law against reporting more than a stipulated amount of rain and snow.

2. Milton Friedman and Anna J. Schwartz, *Monetary Trends in the United States and United Kingdom: Their Relation to Income, Prices, and Interest Rates, 1867–1975* (Chicago: University of Chicago Press, 1982).

52

Monetary Policy and Heightened Price Volatility in Raw Materials Markets

DESPITE THE FED'S breathtaking increase of base money[1] since the autumn of 2008, the money stock as measured by conventional concepts such as M2 has not increased greatly, and hence, as ordinary quantity-theory-of-money thinking would lead us to expect, inflation as measured by conventional concepts such as the consumer price index (CPI) has been fairly tame during the past five years. Between December 2007 and December 2012, the CPI for all items increased only 9.3 percent. As Figure 52.1 shows, this increase represented a continuation of a slow-but-steady inflation trend that extends back to the early 1980s.

This modest consumer-price inflation serves as one of the major bases for the Fed's continued "quantitative easing" and the government's ongoing "stimulus" spending. The idea is that because inflation seems so well contained, additional monetary ease, near-zero interest rates, and huge government deficits will affect primarily output and employment, rather than the price level.

This conventional macroeconomic thinking, however, by virtue of its highly aggregative view and its reliance on macroeconomic models with no place for capital, fails to alert policymakers to other effects—almost certainly pernicious effects—that their policies are creating.

One form of evidence of such effects appears in the certain asset markets, where the rate of price increase has been much greater than it has been in the markets for final consumer goods. As Austrian business cycle thinking

---

1. Robert Higgs, "The Continuing Puzzle of the Hyperinflation that Hasn't Occurred," *The Beacon*, June 23, 2011, http://blog.independent.org/2011/06/23/the-continuing-puzzle-of-the-hyperinflation-that-hasnt-occurred/.

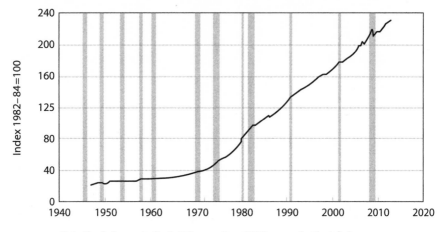

Note: Shaded areas indicate U.S. recessions. 2013 research.stlouisfed.org
Source: U.S. Department of Labor: Bureau of Labor Statistics

Figure 52.1. Consumer Price Index for All Urban Consumers:
All Items (CPIAUCSL)

suggests, these effects have been greatest in the markets for the goods most distant from final consumer products and services, especially in the markets for raw commodities.

As Figure 52.2 shows, the producer price index (PPI) for crude materials has followed a quite different historical path from the CPI. Since World War II, it has passed through four distinct phases: I, no-growth stability from the late 1940s to the early 1970s; II, rapid increase in two bursts between 1972 and 1981; III, no growth (but with much greater variance than in phase I) between 1981 and 2001; and IV, rapid growth with even greater variance from 2002 to 2012.

Austrian thinking associates the rapid run-up of crude materials prices in phases II and IV with a flight from monetary assets, whose real values are falling or expected to fall. Investors seek the safe haven of real assets as the Fed engages in sustained easy-money policies. In addition, producers bid up disproportionately the prices of "early stage" goods required for undertaking the longer-term projects that artificially reduced interest rates encourage.

Whereas the CPI increased by 30.2 percent between December 2001 and December 2012, the PPI for crude materials increased by 166.4 percent during

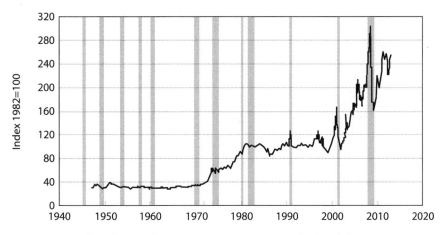

Note: Shaded areas indicate U.S. recessions. 2013 research.stlouisfed.org

Source: U.S. Department of Labor: Bureau of Labor Statistics

Figure 52.2. Producer Price Index:
Crude Materials for Further Processing (PPICRM)

this period. With the onset of the financial panic in the second half of 2008 and the economic contraction that accelerated between mid-2008 and early 2009, the PPI dropped almost by half. Since then, however, crude materials prices have increased relatively rapidly, rising by 58 percent between March 2009 and December 2012, far outpacing the increase in the CPI and maintaining a rate of increase comparable to that between 2002 and mid-2008.

Between the early 1980s and 2007, mainstream economists came to speak of a Great Moderation[2] in business fluctuations and the rate of inflation. They spoke too soon, and they confined their view of price behavior too narrowly. Had they been alive to the importance of asset markets and to the link between monetary policy and price change in these markets, they might have noticed that all was not so well as they imagined when they heaped accolades on "the maestro" Alan Greenspan[3] for having engineered this seeming conquest of inflation and produced this miracle of monetary micromanagement.

2. "Great Moderation," *Wikipedia,* http://en.wikipedia.org/wiki/Great_Moderation.

3. Milton Friedman, "He Has Set a Standard," *Wall Street Journal* online, Jan 31, 2006, http://online.wsj.com/article/SB113867954176960734.html.

As anyone who ponders the movements of the PPI from the late 1940s to the present can see, things are currently far from placid on the price front. In the markets for raw materials, the past decade has been the exact opposite of a "great moderation," and these wild swings have occasioned tremendous difficulties and required wrenching adjustments by many different kinds of producers. Yet scarcely have they made one adjustment when another one has cried out for their attention. Such a violently variable, impossible-to-forecast price environment has necessarily brought about a greater volume of business mistakes and a heightened reluctance to embark on new enterprises and to make new long-term investments in existing firms. For such paralyzing uncertainty, we have policymakers at the Fed and in the federal government to thank.

PART IV

Investment and Regime Uncertainty

53

Regime Uncertainty

Are Interest-Rate Movements
Consistent with the Hypothesis?

REGIME UNCERTAINTY HAS gained increasing recognition as the current economic troubles have persisted with little or no improvement since the economy reached a cyclical trough early in 2009. As described in my 1997 article,[1] regime uncertainty pertains to the likelihood that investors' private property rights in their capital and the income it yields will be attenuated further by government action. Such attenuations can arise from many sources, ranging from simple tax-rate increases, to the imposition of new kinds of taxes, to outright confiscation of private property. Many intermediate threats can arise from various sorts of regulation, for instance, of securities markets, labor markets, and product markets. In any event, the security of private property rights rests not so much on the letter of the law as on the character of the government that enforces, or threatens, presumptive rights. In the latter half of the 1930s, many investors feared that the government would destroy the private enterprise system and replace it with fascism, socialism, or some other extreme transformation of the existing economic order.

In testing my hypothesis, I marshaled three distinct types of evidence: historical documentation of government actions and public reactions; findings of public opinion surveys, especially surveys of businessmen; and evidence from financial markets. The latter seems to some observers, especially to economists, to be the most telling because it is relatively "hard" and quantitative. In any event, it is the sort of evidence economists are accustomed to analyzing.

---

1. Robert Higgs, "Regime Uncertainty: Why the Great Depression Lasted So Long and Why Prosperity Resumed after the War," *The Independent Review* 1 (Spring 1997): 561–90.

My most striking financial evidence for the New Deal episode pertains to the yield curve for corporate bonds, that is, to the spreads between the effective yields on high-grade corporate bonds with various terms to maturity. I found that this yield curve became suddenly much steeper sometime between the first quarter of 1934 and the first quarter of 1935 (a period when the New Deal lurched from its first, or business tolerant, phase to its second, or business hostile, phase) and remained very steep until sometime between the first quarter of 1941 and the first quarter of 1942 (a period when the New Deal handed over the reins to the military and the big-business leaders who, along with the president himself, ran the war-command economy for the duration of the war). I interpreted these extreme spreads as risk premiums on longer-term investments caused by regime uncertainty.

Given the extraordinary scale and scope of the actions the government has taken since mid-2008 and the many expressions of uncertainty (and hence of unwillingness to undertake long-term investments) voiced by businesspeople and others as a result of this flurry of actions—bailouts, unprecedented monetary policies, surges in government spending, and tremendous regulatory undertakings in health care and financial markets, among other things—one wonders whether the corporate bond yield curve shows the same kind of movement it displayed in the face of the regime uncertainty that prevailed from 1935 to 1941.

To pursue this matter, I have examined a number of series on corporate bond yields, by term to maturity, that I constructed from data available at Bondsonline.com.[2] (Normally, when economists analyze "the yield curve," they use data on U.S. Treasury securities. I caution against using such data for the purpose under discussion here. To analyze risks to private property rights as manifested by the risk premiums in bond yields, one must use private bonds, not government bonds.)

I find that back in 2008, before the onset of the financial panic in September, the corporate bond yield curve was rather flat—that is, the yields increased only slightly with term to maturity. At the lower end of the yield curve, yield spreads were tending to narrow slightly until late September. When the panic hit, yields became extremely volatile, especially for the bonds

---

2. *Bondsonline.com*, http://bondsonline.com/Todays_Market/Chart_Center.php?type=C.

with 2 years to maturity (the shortest term in the data), and remained volatile for almost a year. After mid-2009, the volatility diminished greatly.

Examining these data, I find that once this dust had settled, the yield curve for corporate bonds had become substantially steeper. For example, the spread between corporate bonds with 5 years to maturity and corporate bonds with 2 years to maturity increased from roughly 1 percentage point or less before the financial crisis to roughly 2 percentage points since mid-2009. Similar changes occurred in the spread between the bonds with 10 years to maturity or 20 years to maturity and the bonds with 2 years to maturity: the former increased from roughly 1 percentage point to 2–3 percentage points; the latter increased from roughly 2 percentage points to roughly 4 percentage points or more.

Similarly, at the upper end of the yield curve, the spreads widened: between the bonds with 10 years to maturity and those with 5 years to maturity, from roughly a fraction of 1 percentage point to roughly more than 1 percentage point; between bonds with 20 years to maturity and those with 5 years to maturity from roughly 1 percentage point or less to 2–3 percentage points. Finally, the spread between the bonds with 20 years to maturity and those with 10 years to maturity increased from less than 1 percentage point before the crisis to 1–2 percentage points since mid-2009.

Thus corporate bond yields have exhibited three distinct periods: pre-crisis stability with a shallow yield curve; extreme volatility of the yield curve, including some inversions in the latter part of 2008; and post-crisis stability with a much steeper yield curve since mid-2009.

Thus just as the steep yield curve for the New Deal years corresponds precisely with the so-called Second New Deal, when Roosevelt and his leading subordinates and advisers went on the warpath against investors as a class, the recent transition corresponds to the volatility associated with the period of frenetic government action and financial market fluctuations between September 2008 and the middle of 2009,[3] leaving in its wake a much steeper yield curve.

I view these financial data as consistent with the hypothesis of recently heightened regime uncertainty. Of course, they do not "prove" that it is true,

---

3. Robert Higgs, "Cumulating Policy Consequences, Frightened Overreactions, and the Current Surge of Government's Size, Scope, and Power," *Harvard Journal of Law & Public Policy* 33 (Spring 2010): 531–56.

just as the striking data I found for the 1930s do not "prove" the hypothesis as applied to that episode. But in economic history, one looks above all for the *correspondence of various forms of evidence* with the interpretation one places on the observations. In the current episode, as during that of the latter 1930s, we find that (1) a great deal of direct testimony by businessmen and investors, (2) an account of the government's ideological character and the historical narrative of what the government has done, and (3) the bond-market evidence (as well as the movements of the stock market, although they are more difficult to interpret) all conform with a hypothesis that places significant weight on regime uncertainty.

In any event, these preliminary explorations certainly show that the hypothesis should not be dismissed out of hand because it is not "scientific" or because it is not part of the mainstream macroeconomist's customary style of mathematical modeling. If mainstream analysts continue to disregard the role of regime uncertainty in the major depressions of the modern era, especially in accounting for their extraordinary duration, they will only demonstrate the poverty of their own mode of analysis.

54

Do the Post-Panic Changes in Corporate Bond Yield Curves Indicate Regime Uncertainty or Only Expectations of Increased Inflation?

ON AUGUST 24, I posted some data and analysis on yield curves for high-grade corporate bonds since the beginning of 2008, seeking to determine whether changes in these curves are consistent with the hypothesis that the current economic crisis has given rise to regime uncertainty.[1] If it has done so, the yield curves should display increased spreads between the period immediately before the financial panic in the latter part of 2008 and the period since mid-2009, when the extraordinary volatility of the bond markets had ceased.

A reader of this post, Chris Lemens, commented: "I would imagine that, if the yield curves for both private and federal bonds moved similarly, that would mainly tell us about inflationary expectations, not regime uncertainty. (Well, inflation is a kind of regime uncertainty, but you know what I mean.)"

Here I respond to Lemens's comment, which raises an important issue, inasmuch as economists commonly interpret a steepening of the yield curve as indicative of increased inflationary expectations and nothing else. First, one should appreciate, as Lemens does, that changes in expectations about future inflation may themselves reflect changes in regime uncertainty. If, for example, bond traders came to expect a transformation of government policies that would entail a substantial further attenuation of private property rights, they would also be likely to expect that in the future the rulers who preside over the new economic (dis)order will find themselves in serious economic trouble. (Economies without fairly firm private property rights do not work

---

1. "Regime Uncertainty: Are Interest Rate Movements Consistent with the Hypothesis?" The Beacon, August 24, 2010, at http://blog.independent.org/2010/08/24/regime-uncertainty-are-interest-rate-movements-consistent-with-the-hypothesis-2/.

well.) Perhaps the most time-honored of all government actions to escape from such difficulties is the issuance of more and more new money, to be used sooner or later to pay the government's bills; and the virtually inevitable consequence of such large-scale monetary effusion is a rising rate of general price inflation for newly produced goods and services, along with a diminished rate of real economic growth, perhaps even economic contraction.

So, increased regime uncertainty may give rise to increased inflationary expectations. But increased inflationary expectations may also occur in a context of substantial certainty with regard to the persistence of the existing economic order. Traders may expect that the government's actions will lead to a greater rate of price inflation simply because the government (that is, its central bank) is adopting an easier-money policy, not because the government will pose a substantially greater threat to private property rights across the board in the future than it does now. In light of these realities, we must be careful about how we try to tease from the yield-curve data a distinction between increased inflationary expectations per se and increased regime uncertainty.

To pursue this inquiry, I have constructed bond yield curves (again using the data and the graphing tools available at Bondsonline.com[2]) for U.S. Treasury securities, creating the same comparisons by term to maturity that I examined for corporate bonds in my previous post. The Treasury spreads show a number of important differences with the corporate spreads.

First, most notably, the Treasury yields have neither the extreme volatility nor the yield curve inversions that the corporate yields display between September 2008, when the financial panic developed, and mid-2009, when it subsided. All of the Treasury bonds examined here (2 years, 5 years, 10 years, and 20 years to maturity) show substantial drops in effective yield in the final months of 2008, as traders scrambled for the imagined security and liquidity of U.S. government securities during the crisis, bidding up their prices and hence depressing their yields. From the beginning of 2009 onward, however, Treasury yields returned more or less to their previous levels, although at the shortest maturities, the Treasuries continued to yield much less than they had before the panic. The 2-year bond has yielded a steady 1 percent since the end of 2008, even less in recent months. The yield on the 5-year bond has also tailed off substantially in the past six months or so.

---

2. *Bondsonline.com*, http://www.bondsonline.com/Chart_Center.php.

On the Treasuries with longer terms to maturity, the post-crisis persistence of approximately the same yield as before the crisis suggests that traders now expect no greater inflation than they did before the panic. Data for Treasury Inflation-Protected Securities (TIPS)—bonds that pay interest and principal adjusted for changes in the price level—show increased yields for a few months beginning with the crisis in September 2008. But after January 2009, these yields returned to more or less the level they had maintained before the crisis. The fact that the nominal yields on longer-term Treasuries, relative to the yield on TIPS of corresponding maturities, were no higher after the crisis had subsided also suggests that traders have not adjusted their inflationary expectations upward in the wake of the crisis.

Unlike the corporate bond spreads, the spreads for Treasuries did not become uniformly greater from mid-2009 onward. The yield curve steepened at the lower end, but this change reflects almost entirely the reduction in the 2-year bond's yield, inasmuch as the longer-term bonds examined here all returned to approximately the yield they had established before the panic. Spreads on longer-term bonds against the 5-year bond and against the 10-year bond have not widened noticeably since the end of 2008. At the longer end of the yield curve, spreads have remained approximately constant; indeed, they have remained about the same as they were immediately before the panic.

In sum, the widening of corporate yield spreads after mid-2009, which I documented in my previous post, has no counterpart in the Treasury yield spreads. The Treasuries also show no indication that expected inflation was substantially greater after the crisis than it was before the crisis. Whatever has caused the corporate yield spreads to widen during the past 15 months or so, it probably was not an increase in expected future inflation.

In my judgment, a very plausible reason for this widening is heightened regime uncertainty, which expresses itself in the traders' insistence on a risk premium (reflecting the diminished expected security of future private property rights) that increases with a corporate bond's term to maturity. The fact that other forms of evidence, including a great deal of direct testimony[3] by business leaders and others, also point in the same direction only strengthens my confidence in this hypothesis.

---

3. Thomas F. Siems, "Government and the Uncertainty Trap," *Wall Street Journal* online, http://online.wsj.com/article/NA_WSJ_PUB:SB10001424052748704271804575405302 726656506.html.

55

The Great Divergence

*Private Investment and Government Power
in the Present Crisis*

PRIVATE SAVING AND investment are the heart and soul of
the dynamic market process. Together they provide and allocate the resources
used to augment the economy's productive capacity, generate sustained long-
run economic growth, and thereby make possible a rising level of living. Economic crises interrupt this process by discouraging investors and causing them
to consume their resources or to employ them in relatively safe, low-yielding
ways. Without entrepreneurs willing to take the great risks that characterize
investments in important technological and organizational innovations, the
growth process fades into economic stagnation or even decline.

The present recession starkly displays this characteristic crisis-related
abatement of the economy's investment process. Indeed, the decline of private
investment during recent years has been much greater than most observers
realize. Consider the following data, taken or derived from the most recently
revised National Economic Accounts prepared by the Commerce Department's Bureau of Economic Analysis (Tables 1.1.5, 1.1.6, and 5.2.6).

In 2006, gross private domestic investment reached its most recent peak, at
$2.33 trillion (in constant 2005 dollars), or 17.4 percent of GDP. After remain-
ing almost at this level in 2007, this measure of investment fell substantially
during each of the next two years, reaching $1.59 trillion, or 11.3 percent of
GDP, in 2009. This decline is severe enough, but it does not give us all the
information we need to gauge the extent of the investment bust.

The greater part of gross investment consists of what the statisticians call
the capital consumption allowance, an estimate of the amount of money that
must be spent simply to offset wear and tear and obsolescence of the existing
capital stock. In a country such as the United States, with an enormous fixed

capital stock built up over the centuries, a great amount of funds must be allocated simply to maintain that stock. In recent years, the private capital consumption allowance has ranged from $1.29 trillion in 2005 to $1.46 trillion (in constant 2005 dollars) in 2009. Thus, even in the boom year 2006, about 60 percent of gross private domestic investment was required merely to maintain the economy's productive capacity, leaving just 40 percent, or $889 billion in net private domestic investment, to augment that capacity.

From that level, net private domestic investment plunged during each of the following three years, taking the greatest dive between 2008 and 2009, when it fell to only $54 billion (in constant 2005 dollars), having declined altogether by 94 percent from its 2006 peak! Last year only 3.5 percent of all private investment spending went toward building up the capital stock. Thus net private investment did not simply fall during the recession; it virtually disappeared.

Unless this drastic decline is reversed soon, the future will be bleak for the U.S. economy. Without substantial net private investment, brisk economic growth is unthinkable beyond the very short run. Although private investment spending has recovered somewhat since it reached its trough in the third quarter of 2009, gross private domestic investment in the most recent quarter (April to June) of 2010 remained 21 percent below its peak in the first quarter of 2006, and net private domestic investment remained about 64 percent below its previous peak.

While this private-sector disaster was occurring, however, the government sector of the economy was booming. The ratio of all federal government spending—purchases of goods and services plus transfer payments—to GDP increased from 20.6 percent in the fourth (October to December) quarter of 2007 to 25.4 percent in the most recent (April to June) quarter of 2010.

Of this increase, about 73 percent represents an increase in transfer payments. According to the National Economic Accounts (Table 3.2), federal transfer payments for social benefits to persons—old-age pensions, unemployment-insurance benefits, disability-insurance benefits, Medicare benefits, and so forth in great variety—increased from a seasonally adjusted annual rate of $1.28 trillion in the fourth quarter of 2007 to $1.72 trillion in the second quarter of 2010, a leap of more than one-third in only two and a half years. During the same period, government grants-in-aid to state and local governments rose from a seasonally adjusted annual rate of $382 billion to $525 billion, an increase of more than 37 percent.

Data compiled by the Bureau of Labor Statistics show that the number of private nonfarm employees fell from 114.1 million in 2006 to 108.4 in 2009, and even further this year, reaching 107.9 million in August 2010. At the same time, the number of government employees at all levels increased from 22.0 million in 2006 to 22.5 million in 2009, although a slight reduction has occurred recently, putting the number at 22.4 million in August 2010.

The Federal Reserve System has played a major role during the current recession, acting in unprecedented ways to inject funds into the financial system in general and into selected failing firms in particular, especially AIG, Fannie Mae, and Freddie Mac, which have been effectively taken over by the government, giving rise to a situation in which the government supplies or insures about nine-tenths of all new residential mortgage loans. Before the recession, the Fed's financial assets consisted overwhelmingly of U.S. Treasury securities. It now holds a variety of securities, including mortgage-backed securities valued on the Fed's books at approximately $1.1 trillion. In this way, the Fed has become the major direct source of funds for the government-sponsored enterprises that provided an inviting secondary market for the commercial banks and other primary lenders that inflated the housing bubble.

Through the TARP (Troubled Asset Relief Program) scheme, created late in 2008, the U.S. Treasury acquired ownership stakes in hundreds of commercial banks.

Of course, the government also took over General Motors and Chrysler, bypassing existing bankruptcy laws and ramming into place restructuring arrangements that served the Obama administration's political goals, especially its support for members (active and retired) of the United Auto Workers.

The foregoing measures constitute only a small fraction of the many significant actions the federal government has taken to augment its size, scope, and power during the current recession. Thus, while the market system's driving force—private investment—was being brought to its knees, the government's crisis-driven surge only added an additional discouraging feature to those operating though market channels, such as the reluctance of commercial banks to make new loans and investments and the desire of households to repay debts and increase their holdings of cash balances. A government growing in so many different directions at once, with many additional initiatives—such as higher tax rates, new taxes on energy use, and new restrictions on financial service providers—still awaiting enactment or regulatory specification, creates tremendous uncertainty for anyone contemplating a long-term investment: who knows what the contours of future government exactions, restrictions, and requirements will be, and hence whether a particular investment will prove to be profitable or not?

Therefore, a major consequence of the Great Divergence—the starvation of private investment and the feasting of government—is what I call regime uncertainty. This form of uncertainty is a pervasive incalculable apprehension about the future security of private property rights in capital and the income it yields to investors; indeed, a pervasive apprehension that extends beyond investors to include nearly all private participants in the economy—consumers, workers, and managers, as well as investors—in regard to the future economic order. The Great Divergence in itself is very bad news. Its effects in enhancing regime uncertainty only make it more unfortunate for everyone outside the privileged precincts of government.

56

Private Business Net Investment Remains in a Deep Ditch

IF ANY ONE THING estimated in the Commerce Department's National Income and Product Accounts may be described as the engine of economic growth, *private domestic business net investment* is that thing. This variable has such tremendous importance because, if accurately gauged, it tells us better than any other measure how many resources are being devoted to building up the private business capital stock and improving it by innovation. An economy that has anemic private business net investment almost certainly will falter soon, if it is not doing so already.

Notice that every aspect of this awkwardly named variable is critical.

- First, it has to do with *private* investment, not so-called government investment. The latter, which looms fairly large in the official accounts, ought never to have been labeled as investment, because it comes about not as a result of wealth-seeking motives and rational economic calculation, but as a result of political motives, calculations, and actions that often clash with the creation of real wealth, rather than contributing to it.

- Second, we are looking here at *business* investment, excluding what the Bureau of Economic Analysis calls private "household and institutions" investment, which has somewhat murky underlying objectives, determinants, and consequences.

- Third, we are examining *net*, rather than gross, investment. The latter includes a large element of expenditure aimed merely at compensating for the wear and tear and obsolescence of the existing stock of private business capital. For example, even at its most recent peak, in the third quarter of 2007, gross private domestic business investment was running at $1,661 billion (annual rate), whereas net private domestic business investment was only $463 billion (annual rate), or about 28 percent of the total. (The investment data cited here are taken from Table 5.1, Saving and Investment by Sector,[1] in the National Income and Product Accounts, accessed 02/16/11.)

It is obviously important that businesses compensate for ongoing depreciation of their existing stock of capital goods, which includes structures, tools and equipment, software, and inventories. But unless firms do more than make up for depreciation, they do not expand their productive capacity except to the extent that they can embed improved technology in their replacements for worn-out or obsolete capital goods. In general, economic growth requires net investment, and more rapid economic growth requires a greater rate of net investment.

With that essential idea in mind, let us examine what has happened recently to private domestic business net investment, which I will henceforth call simply net private investment. Such investment reached its recent cyclical peak in the third quarter of 2007, at $463 billion (annual rate). It then fell steadily for the next four quarters, reaching $336 billion in the third quarter of 2008. At that point, it plunged steeply, falling to only $159 billion, or by 53 percent, in the fourth quarter of 2008.

Although the financial-market panic that had flared up in late September 2008 began to subside early in 2009, net private investment continued to fall, becoming negative (–$53 billion, annual rate) in the first quarter of 2009 and even more negative (–$119 billion) in the second quarter. Although some improvement began in the third quarter of 2009, net private investment remained negative during the third and fourth quarters. For the entire year 2009, the amount of net private investment amounted to a large negative amount (–$69 billion). So, in other words, the value of the private business capital stock fell

---

1. U.S. Department of Commerce, Bureau of Economic Analysis, http://www.bea.gov/ National/nipaweb/TableView.asp?SelectedTable=137&ViewSeries=NO&Java=no&Request 3Place=N&3Place=N&FromView=YES&Freq=Qtr&FirstYear=2005&LastYear=2010&3 Place=N&Update=Update&JavaBox=no.

by that amount. Hardly by coincidence, real GDP also fell substantially in 2009, by 2.6 percent.[2]

In 2010, net private investment increased smartly for three quarters, reaching an annual rate of $270 billion in the third quarter, then contracted sharply—by almost 47 percent—to $144 billion in the fourth quarter. For the entire year, the amount of private net investment was $177 billion. Whether the collapse in the final quarter of 2010 will turn out to have been a fluke or the beginning of a longer-term decline, we shall have to wait to see.

According to the National Bureau of Economic Research,[3] the most recent business-cycle peak occurred in December 2007, and the trough was reached in June 2009. As we have seen, net private investment peaked slightly sooner, in the third quarter of 2007. So, we are now more than three years past the economy's overall peak and some 20 months past its trough, yet net private investment in the most recent quarter was running at only 31 percent of the annual rate at its previous peak.

Net private investment is currently running far below the rate required to sustain a rapid rate of economic growth. Real consumer spending, in contrast, peaked in the fourth quarter of 2007, fell only slightly (about 2.5 percent) to the second quarter of 2009, and by the fourth quarter of 2010 exceeded its previous quarterly peak (by almost 1 percent). Despite the wailing and gnashing of teeth among Keynesian economists and politicians with regard to allegedly inadequate consumption, a collapse of consumption is not to blame for the economy's anemic recovery to date. However, looking elsewhere for the cause, we find that the economy's true engine of growth—private business net investment—continues to sputter, running in the most recent quarter at less than a third of its previous peak rate and, for the entire year 2010, at only 40 percent of its rate for the entire year 2007.

Unless net private investment recovers more rapidly, the overall economy's recovery is sure to remain slow at best, certainly too slow to bring down

---

2. U.S. Department of Commerce, Bureau of Economic Analysis, http://www.bea.gov/National/nipaweb/TableView.asp?SelectedTable=1&ViewSeries=NO&Java=no&Request 3Place=N&3Place=N&FromView=YES&Freq=Year&FirstYear=2005&LastYear=2010&3 Place=N&Update=Update&JavaBox=no.

3. National Bureau of Economic Research, "US Business Cycle Expansions and Contractions," Sept. 20, 2010, http://www.nber.org/cycles.html.

significantly the high unemployment rate that has been stuck for a long time between 9 percent and 10 percent (and would be substantially greater if we took into account the millions who have left the labor force recently because they did not believe they could find a job even if they searched for one). As matters now stand, real stagnation is a likely prospect and, given the Fed's massive ongoing purchases of Treasury debt and the stupendous amount of excess reserves in the commercial banks' accounts at the Fed, stagflation also seems to be a credible expectation.

Investors continue to view the future with major misgivings, owing to the unsettled condition of the government's future actions with regard to health care, financial regulations, energy regulations, taxation, and other matters that have serious implications for business costs and the security of private property rights in business capital and its returns. Although Obamacare and the Dodd-Frank bill have already been enacted, these massive statutes leave scores of important details awaiting determination by administrative agencies and courts whose actions will be fiercely contested at every step. Future tax rates also remain up for grabs in Congress.

Nor are the investment-paralyzing uncertainties confined to the United States. Europe in particular continues to wrestle with the aftermath of the malinvestments and other distortions wrought in its asset markets and financial institutions during the boom of 2002–2006, and several countries teeter on the brink of sovereign default. Given the close linkages of national markets in today's world, U.S. companies will feel a great impact from any new crises in Europe—something else to worry about as they contemplate the desirability of increasing their investment spending.

Of course, the major trading countries and their governments may ultimately find a way to muddle through. They have eventually weathered major storms in the past. Yet, however the world's economy moves in the longer term, the immediate prospect for investors in the U.S. economy remains troubled, at best. A substantial, rapid recovery of private business net investment must await the clearing of these clouds. Until such a recovery does occur, however, overall economic prospects must remain rather gloomy for the near and medium terms.

57

The Confidence Fairy
versus the Animal Spirits

Not Really a Fair Fight

THE HUMOR COLUMNIST for the *New York Times*, Paul Krugman, has recently taken to defending his vulgar Keynesianism[1] against its critics by accusing them of making arguments that rely on the existence of a "confidence fairy." By this mockery, Krugman seeks to dismiss the critics as unscientific blockheads, in contrast to his own supreme status as a Nobel Prize–winning economic scientist.

The irony in this dismissal, as others, including my friend Donald Boudreaux, have already pointed out,[2] is that Krugman's own vulgar Keynesianism relies on a much more ethereal explanatory force for its own account of macroeconomic fluctuations—namely, the so-called animal spirits. The master himself wrote in *The General Theory*: "Thus if the animal spirits are dimmed and the spontaneous optimism falters, leaving us to depend on nothing but a mathematical expectation, enterprise will fade and die. . . . [I]ndividual initiative will only be adequate when reasonable calculation is supplemented and supported by animal spirits."[3] Because Keynes conceived of his "animal spirits" as "a spontaneous urge to action rather than inaction," he of course had no way to explain their coming and going or to measure or evaluate them in any way. They are as surreal as a ghost—when and why they come and go,

---

1. Robert Higgs, "Recession and Recovery: Six Fundamental Errors of the Current Orthodoxy," *The Independent Review*, 14: 3 (Winter 2010) 465–472.

2. Don Boudreaux, "The Fairies Have It," *Café Hayek* online, Aug. 2, 2011, http://cafehayek.com/2011/08/the-fairies-have-it.html.

3. John Maynard Keynes, *The General Theory of Employment, Interest and Money* (New York: Harcourt, Brace and World, 1936), 161–62.

no one knows or can know. Such is the force that drives the ups and downs of private investment in Keynesian economic theory, and such theory unfailingly drives Krugman's commentaries on the recession and on the possibility and effective means of recovery from it.

Regime uncertainty, however, rests on a much firmer foundation. In my own research on the topic,[4] I have presented evidence derived from (1) a mass of testimony by investors, businessmen, and other contemporaries, (2) voluminous historical facts on the character of government actions that reasonable people had every reason to interpret as threatening the security of their private property rights, (3) variations in the structure of investment, especially as between short-term and longer-term projects, and (4) specific twists in the term-structure of returns on private corporate bonds, as well as other relevant evidence on the behavior of financial markets.

As against this varied and substantial evidence, what does the proponent of animal spirits have to offer? Well, to be perfectly honest, nothing at all. The idea is purely fanciful, the product of Lord Keynes's fertile imagination.

However, we would do well to note that in the section of his book where Keynes introduces the idea of animal spirits, he also discusses it in a way that makes their effects somewhat similar to those of regime uncertainty as described in my own writings.

> This [operation of varying animal spirits] means, unfortunately, not only that slumps and depressions are exaggerated in degree, but that *economic prosperity is excessively dependent on a political and social atmosphere which is congenial to the average business man.* If the fear of a Labour Government or a New Deal depresses enterprise, this need not be the result either of a reasonable calculation or of a plot with political intent;—it is the mere consequence of upsetting the delicate balance of spontaneous optimism. In estimating the prospects of investment, we must have regard, therefore, to the nerves and hysteria and even the digestions and reactions to the weather of those upon whose spontaneous activity it largely depends. (p. 162, emphasis added)

---

4. Robert Higgs, "Regime Uncertainty: Why the Great Depression Lasted So Long and Why Prosperity Resumed after the War," *The Independent Review* 1 (Spring 1997): 561–90.

Although Keynes greatly underestimated the degree to which investors' expectations about the security of their property rights rest on perfectly rational grounds for fearing what a Roosevelt administration or an Obama administration might do, he recognizes that, whatever the basis for variations in the flow of animal spirits, business confidence plays an essential part of driving private investment. Paul Krugman, please reread your master's magnum opus.

58

Important New Evidence
on Regime Uncertainty

WHEN I INTRODUCED the concept of regime uncertainty[1] in 1997, attempting to improve our understanding of the Great Depression's extraordinary duration, I anticipated that many people—especially my fellow economists—would not welcome this contribution. Their primary objection, I ventured, would be that the concept remained too vague and, most of all, that it had not been reduced to a quantitative index of the sort that modern mainstream economists customarily work with, especially in their empirical macroeconomic analyses.

My argument did not lack evidence, however, and I regarded the agreement of *several different forms of evidence* as an important element of the argument's force. The evidence I adduced with regard to changes in the yield spreads for high-grade corporate bonds of differing terms to maturity seemed to me both systematic and especially compelling, though not decisive because alternative explanations of those changes might be offered. (I considered several such explanations and rejected them as unpersuasive in one way or another.) Recently, in my application of the concept of regime uncertainty to help us understand better the persistent economic troubles since 2007, I again advanced several different kinds of evidence, including as before an analysis of changes in the yield curves for high-grade corporate bonds. This time, too, the evidence[2] is consistent with the underlying argument.

---

1. Robert Higgs, "Regime Uncertainty: Why the Great Depression Lasted So Long and Why Prosperity Resumed after the War," *The Independent Review* 1 (Spring 1997): 561–90.

2. Robert Higgs, "Regime Uncertainty: Are Interest-Rate Movements Consistent with the Hypothesis?" *The Beacon*, Aug. 24, 2010, http://blog.independent.org/2010/08/24/regime-uncertainty-are-interest-rate-movements-consistent-with-the-hypothesis-2/.

Nevertheless, the argument scarcely gained widespread assent, and most analysts either ignored it completely or, like Paul Krugman, dismissed it as a fairy tale[3]—in his view, the sort of wholly fictitious notion that would be peddled only by think-tank whores in the pay of Republican plutocrats. (I trust that everyone who knows me will see how poorly I fit this template.)

Now, however, more respectable analysts than I have accepted the challenge of showing that regime uncertainty can be measured systematically and that the resulting index "shows U.S. policy uncertainty [is currently] at historically high levels." This research has been carried out by three analysts at two of the world's preeminent research universities: Scott R. Baker and Nicholas Bloom at Stanford University and Steven J. Davis at the University of Chicago. I highly recommend that anyone interested in this matter read the October 5 summary of these analysts' research published online by Bloomberg News.[4]

Some highlights:

- A major factor behind the weak recovery and gloomy outlook is a climate of policy-induced economic uncertainty. An index we devised . . . shows U.S. policy uncertainty at historically high levels.

- We constructed our index by combining three types of information: the frequency of newspaper articles that refer to economic uncertainty and the role of policy, the number of federal tax code provisions set to expire in coming years, and the extent of disagreement among forecasters about future inflation and government spending.

- Our index shows prominent surges in policy uncertainty around the time of major elections, the outbreak of wars and after the Sept. 11 attacks. It shows another surge after the bankruptcy of Lehman Brothers Holding Inc. in September 2008. Policy uncertainty has remained at high levels ever since.

---

3. Robert Higgs, "The Confidence Fairy versus the Animal Spirits—Not Really a Fair Fight," *The Beacon*, Aug. 3, 2011, http://blog.independent.org/2011/08/03/the-confidence-fairy -versus-the-animal-spirits-not-really-a-fair-fight/.

4. Scott R. Baker, Nicholas Bloom, and Steven J. Davis, "Policy Uncertainty Is Choking Recovery: Baker, Bloom and Davis," *BloombergView.com*, Oct. 5, 2011, http://www.bloomberg .com/news/2011-10-06/policy-uncertainty-is-choking-recovery-baker-bloom-and-davis.html.

- [T]he data refute the view that economic uncertainty necessarily breeds policy uncertainty. In the last decade, however, policy became a larger source of movements in overall economic uncertainty and an increasingly important concern for businesses and households. . . . [T]he persistence of policy uncertainty . . . reflects deliberate policy decisions, harmful rhetorical attacks on business and "millionaires," failure to tackle entitlement reforms and fiscal imbalances, and political brinkmanship.

- To identify the drivers of policy uncertainty, we drilled into the Google News listings and quantified the factors at work. Several factors account for the high levels of policy uncertainty in 2010 and 2011, but monetary and tax issues predominate. Uncertainties related to health-care policy, labor regulations, national security and sovereign-debt concerns play contributing roles.

- Negative economic effects of uncertainty operate through multiple, reinforcing channels. When households are fearful about job loss, wages, taxes and retirement funds, they cut back on expenditures. The drop in consumer spending means weak sales for businesses and lower sales-tax collections for governments.

- When businesses are uncertain about taxes, health-care costs and regulatory initiatives, they adopt a cautious stance. Because it is costly to make a hiring or investment mistake, many companies will wait for calmer times to expand. If too many businesses wait, the recovery never takes off. Weak investments in capital goods, product development and worker training also undermine longer-run growth.

- So how much near-term improvement could we gain from a stable, certainty-enhancing policy regime? We estimate that restoring 2006 levels of policy uncertainty would yield an additional 2.5 million jobs over 18 months. Not a full solution to the jobs shortfall, but a big step in the right direction.

See the authors' report for more detail.

The index constructed and analyzed by Baker, Bloom, and Davis, like any such index, may be faulted in various ways. Working with such data and the indexes constructed from them is a never-ending task of correction and refinement for empirical researchers. Nevertheless, these analysts have met the challenge of producing a systematically measured quantitative index of regime uncertainty (they call it policy uncertainty) over a long period, and they have presented reasonable arguments that tie the index's movements to specific policy measures and future possibilities. Their evidence certainly deserves as much respect as the standard National Income and Product Accounts (NIPA) estimates prepared by the Commerce Department's Bureau of Economic Analysis, much of which derives from highly questionable definitions and assumptions and from underlying data subject to a variety of errors—yet economists swallow the NIPA estimates all the time without choking.

The idea of regime uncertainty had sound economic theory and substantial empirical evidence to support it from the beginning, and a great deal of additional evidence has accumulated over the past three years. Yet critics have continued to dismiss it either as Republican bunk bought and paid for by Obama-hating billionaires or as a sort of "just so" story concocted by flaky think-tank nobodies, such as yours truly. Now, however, the research reported by Baker, Bloom, and Davis knocks the ball firmly back into the critics' court. Don't be surprised if they take a whack at it. Whether their attempt will succeed intellectually is another matter.

59

The Sluggish Recovery
of Real Net Domestic
Private Business Investment

MAKING SENSE OF economic fluctuations can be a daunting task. The economy comprises a gigantic set of interrelated assets, inputs, processes, transactions, and outputs, and its dimensions can be and have been measured in countless ways. If we are to speak sensibly about the economy as a whole—recognizing that almost anything we say about the whole may not apply to various subsets of it—we must carefully choose the variables that hold the most promise for helping us to understand its broad movements.

Economists largely agree that net private investment is a key variable. Such investment adds to the private capital stock (with its embodied technologies), which makes inputs of labor increasingly productive over time—that is, net private investment (with the technological improvements it embodies) drives economic growth in the long run. And because private investment spending varies much more than consumption outlays (either private or governmental) in the short and medium terms, such investment also drives aggregate fluctuations in output and employment. When investment collapses, recessions ensue; when investment expands, so do output and employment. Economists do not agree, however, about *why* private investment varies disproportionately in the short and medium runs. Keynesians and Austrians, for example, disagree completely about the explanation of this disproportion and about its consequences.

My own view is broadly Austrian, which leads me to concentrate my analysis on net private investment as the key variable in explaining aggregate booms and busts. Of course, the Austrian view is not an "overinvestment" theory of the boom, but rather a "malinvestment" theory derived from recognition that rapid expansion of artificial, bank-created credit pushes interest rates below market levels and thereby encourages an unsustainable volume of investment in longer-term investments. So, when the bust occurs, as it ultimately must in these circumstances, the crucial requirement for a return to prosperity is a reconfiguration of the distorted *structure* of assets, employment, and outputs that the malinvestment-driven boom has created.

Nevertheless, it is also essential for recovery that the overall volume of net private business investment recover from its collapse during the bust—a collapse that sometimes, as in 2009, drives net private business investment into the negative range, where the volume of new investment falls short of the amount required merely to keep the capital stock intact.

The Bureau of Economic Analysis prepares the National Income and Product Accounts, which consist of hundreds of separate but interrelated data series, including many that relate to saving and investment. Of these, I find it most instructive to emphasize one in particular: *net domestic private business investment* (NIPA Table 5.1, line 52[1]). Unfortunately, so far as I have been able to determine, this particular variable is reported only in current dollars, not in real (price-level-adjusted) dollars. To deflate it, I have used the Producer Price Index for Final Goods, Capital Equipment (designated PPICPE[2]), averaging the monthly values for June and July to approximate the index value for the entire year. This short-cut method suffices for my purposes here because the rate of increase in the PPICPE has been quite low in recent years.

From the foregoing data, I have constructed an index of real net domestic private business investment from 2005 to 2012, where the 2007 value = 100 (see Table 59.1).

As the figures show, real net domestic private business investment reached its recent peak in 2007 (only slightly above the level for 2006), then plunged in 2008 and dropped even more precipitously in 2009. Although it recovered somewhat during the past three years, it remains extremely depressed relative to its previous peak. Five years after its bust and partial recovery, real net private business investment, in 2012, remained 41 percent below its previous peak. The weakness of this investment recovery—a greater weakness than

---

1. U.S. Department of Commerce, Bureau of Economic Analysis, "National Income and Product Accounts Tables," http://www.bea.gov/iTable/iTable.cfm?ReqID=9&step=1#reqid =9&step=1&isuri=1&904=2000&903=137&906=a&905=2012&910=x&911=0.

2. Federal Reserve Bank of St. Louis, "Producer Price Index: Finished Goods: Capital Equipment," updated Nov. 18, 2014, http://research.stlouisfed.org/fred2/series/PPICPE?cid=31.

Table 59.1. Index of Real Net Domestic Private Business Investment, 2005 to 2012 (2007 = 100)

2005	81
2006	98
2007	100
2008	68
2009	−26
2010	20
2011	36
2012	59

in previous postwar recoveries and a weakness reminiscent of the investment malaise of the post-1933 years of the Great Depression—surely plays a key role in explaining why output recovery has been so slow and employment recovery even slower in recent years.

One might concede this weakness in the recovery of net private business investment, yet argue that nevertheless a recovery has been occurring, and it is only a matter of time until full recovery is attained and new heights are reached. Quarterly data for recent years, however, cast doubt on such confidence. For example, after advancing smartly in the second and third quarters of 2010, net private business investment fell during the following two quarters before resuming its advance in the second quarter of 2011. In 2012 it fluctuated around a slightly higher level but finished lower in the fourth quarter than it had been in any of the preceding four quarters. Such slow, erratic recovery does not inspire confidence that we will see continued investment recovery in 2013, much less a truly robust recovery.

Even if the recovery of net private business investment should continue, however, it is now at such a relatively low level that two years or more will be required to bring it back to the level it attained in 2006 and 2007. If that course should be followed, we will then stand at a level equal only to the level attained nine years earlier. Such performance still would not signify a full recovery, however, because in a normal, growing economy, net business investment also should grow. Had the economy performed well since 2007, it would by now be generating much more investment, not simply an equal amount, and in 2015 it ought to be generating still more investment. The trend line slopes upward, and any level of investment needs to be appraised relative to its trend value at that point, not merely relative to a previous peak.

The U.S. economy, in short, seems to be stuck in a decidedly subpar condition. Private investors are not making the volume of investments required to propel living standards upward at the same rate at which the economy achieved such improvements historically for almost two centuries. Moreover, this reluctance to invest prevails despite the enormous cash holdings that many nonfinancial corporations now possess. The current situation is not simply an artifact of wounded banks' reluctance to make new loans, because many businesses are in a position to invest in long-term projects by using low-cost internal financing, but they are not doing so. Something else must be invoked to account for the bloodlessness of investors and entrepreneurs during recent years. I have repeatedly suggested that regime uncertainty[3] deserves serious consideration in our attempts to understand the economy's present sluggishness. Nothing in the foregoing survey of real net private domestic business investment leads me to abandon this view of the matter at this time.

---

3. Robert Higgs, "Government Spending and Regime Uncertainty—A Clarification," *The Beacon*, Oct. 17, 2013, http://blog.independent.org/?s=%22regime+uncertainty%22& submit=go.

60

Government Spending and
Regime Uncertainty—A Clarification

IN VIEW OF my sixteen-year campaign to bring about an understanding of the idea of "regime uncertainty," one might think that I would be gratified by the growing recognition of the importance of the closely related (but narrower) idea of "policy uncertainty" in relation to the unusually slow recovery from the bust of 2007–2009. However, I notice that many commentators (for example, Andy Sullivan, writing recently for Reuters[1]) are interpreting the ill effects of the current policy uncertainty as having something to do especially with the congressional squabbling about sequesters, shutdowns, and other imagined horrors connected with Congress's inability to write an annual budget and stick with it without ongoing emergency adjustments (e.g., increases in the statutory limit on public debt). These commentators suppose that such policy uncertainty harms the recovery because it impedes the public's reliance on relentless increases in government spending, which they regard along Keynesian lines as a positive contribution to economic growth.

In contrast, I consider regime uncertainty as a form of uncertainty related to the public's—especially the private investors'—confidence in the future security of private property rights, which can be impaired by future regulatory changes (e.g., Dodd-Frank and Obamacare regulations), court decisions, administrative twists and turns, tax increases in various forms (e.g., Obamacare penalties enforced through the income-tax system), monetary-policy changes that threaten the dollar's purchasing power and distort the allocation of credit,

---

1. Andy Sullivan, "Analysis: Washington becomes the biggest risk to the U.S. economy," *Reuters*, October 17, 2013. http://www.reuters.com/article/2013/10/17/us-usa-fiscal-economy-analysis-idUSBRE99G05T20131017.

and personnel changes in the government's corps of executives, judges, and assorted capos.

Unlike the commentators I mentioned in the first paragraph, I do not perceive cutbacks or interruptions in government spending as matters of critical concern except to the members of special interests, including government employees and contractors themselves. For the overwhelming majority of the people, reduced government spending is a godsend, even if many people do not know that it is, because it helps to reduce the scale and scope of the government's destructive involvement in economic life and because it reduces the crowding out of productive private activities, such as private provision of education and of assistance to the poor and others in economic distress. Shifting resources from the government to private individuals is always a beneficial development, given that the government not only wastes many resources, but actually employs resources in destructive ways that harm the welfare of the general public.

Mainstream commentators seem to get their knickers in a twist especially when government employees are furloughed or some sort of government handout is temporarily suspended. In anything but the shortest-term perspective, however, these developments are positive, not negative. It is good to get people off the dole, and if budgetary mismanagement brings about this result, so much the better for the mismanagement. Above all, people need to learn to assess such incidents without falling back into the misleading framework of Keynesian analysis. The inclusion of government purchases in GDP has worked much mischief over the years, and the current wailing and gnashing of teeth over the government's inability to produce its budgets responsibly and on schedule is only the latest occasion for such misinterpretation of the government's role in the economy. If only people could bring themselves to see the government for what, all in all, it is—a force for plunder, waste, and destruction—they might then have the wit to worry less about government spending cutbacks and to worry more about the manifold ways in which the government generates what I call regime uncertainty.

PART V

Boom, Bust, and Macroeconomic Policy

61

World War II

*Still Being Touted as the
Quintessential Keynesian Miracle*

SOMEONE MUST HAVE IMAGINED that my hopes for improved economic understanding might be excessively optimistic today and thus needed to be curbed to restore my normal emotional balance, because that person undertook to smash any such hopes to dust by emailing me a link to a *Huffington Post* article by Paul Abrams, "Economically, World War II Was Stimulus on Steroids."[1] This screed turns out to be an ostensible macro-economics lesson composed in equal measure of economic foolishness, historical ignorance, and ideological tendentiousness—the veritable epitome of a worse-than-worthless contribution to public enlightenment.

The opening paragraphs indicate the direction of Abrams's argument:

> The next time someone argues that the New Deal failed, and only the Second World War ended the Depression, as "proof" that government spending does not work, one can respond with the details of economic growth and unemployment reduction up to 1940, or one can ignore the claim and thank them for making your case for massive government spending in a deep, broad recession.
>
> Right wing politicians are loathe to credit the New Deal with any success in hoisting the United States out of the Great Depression, but credit World War II for that achievement, believing that that somehow disproves Keynesian economic theory.
>
> That claim, however, undermines their entire premise.

---

1. Paul Abrams, "Economically, World War II Was Stimulus on Steroids," *Huffington Post.com*, June 13, 2011, http://www.huffingtonpost.com/paul-abrams/economically-world -war-ii_b_875722.html?view=print.

Abrams concludes that "massive government spending at a time of severe economic downturn and dislocation can indeed get an economy humming again," as World War II shows; the New Deal was merely too timid. He seems unaware that his argument merely restates the fallacy-ridden hodge-podge of conventional wisdom about how World War II "got the economy out of the Depression" that has dominated the thinking of economists, historians, and the public ever since the war itself.

When I began to teach U.S. economic history at the University of Washington in the late 1960s, I quickly realized that this tale of the wartime "Keynesian miracle" could not withstand critical scrutiny once one went beyond the barest account of it in terms of the elementary Keynesian model and the standard government macro measures, such as GDP, the consumer price index, and the rate of civilian unemployment. Almost immediately I saw that unemployment had disappeared during the war not because of the ineluctable workings of a Keynesian multiplier, but entirely because about 20 percent of the labor force was forced, directly or indirectly, into the armed forces and a comparable number of employees set to work in factories, shipyards, and other facilities turning out war-related "goods" the government purchased only after forcing the public to pay for them sooner (via wartime taxes and inflation) or later (via repayment of wartime borrowing). Thus, the great wartime "boom" consisted entirely of (1) some people's mass engagement in wreaking death and destruction and (2) other people's employment in producing supplies for these warriors after the government's military labor drain, turning out "goods" never valued by consumers or private producers in voluntary transactions, but rather ordered by government functionaries and priced completely arbitrarily in a command-and-control economy. In no sense was the alleged "wartime prosperity" comparable to real, normal prosperity. The pervasive regimentation, rationing, price controls, direct government resource allocations, and forbidden forms of production (e.g., civilian automobiles) should have served as a tip-off.

After teaching my own students along these lines for many years, I eventually began to write articles and books pulling together my various studies. The most germane and coherent of these books is *Depression, War, and Cold War*, published originally by Oxford University Press in 2006. For all of the good I've done in correcting people's understanding of what happened to the U.S.

economy during World War II and what lessons one might justifiably draw from that experience about, say, the scientific validity of the Keynesian model or its related fiscal-policy implications, I might just as well have held my breath and turned blue. Here we are in June 2011, and millions of Americans are being presented with the purest potion of economic misinformation one can imagine, an account in no way superior to those the young Keynesians were peddling so confidently in 1944, the year in which I was born. Perhaps my mother ought to have strangled me in my crib, thereby sparing me the bitter disappointment of seeing the research and writing I've carried out over more than forty years prove to have been completely in vain.

For the Paul Abrams of this world, of course, none of this makes the slightest difference. They are at pains not to understand how the economy actually works or to endorse policies that promote its greater productivity, but only to concoct a plausible rationale for the government's taxing "the rich" more heavily and spending oodles of money on a laundry list of leftist idols—government "infrastructure," green energy-conservation programs, high-speed rail, and the rest of the wasteful and economically foolish projects that progressive politicians espouse to feather their own nests and enrich their cronies and political dependents at public expense. If they haven't learned any sound economics by this time, chances are slim to none that they will ever learn any, but in any event I cannot believe that they care about such learning. Politics is the name; plunder is the game.

There's a lesson here, besides the obvious one that public discourse consists overwhelmingly of ideological sound and fury, signifying nothing solidly connected to reality. For me, the main lesson is this: mommas, don't let your babies grow up to become economic historians. If you do, you only put them in line to have their hearts broken.

62

One More Time

Consumption Spending Has Already *Recovered*

COMMENTATORS AND PUNDITS, some of whom ought to know better, continue to harp on the idea that the recession persists because consumers are not spending. Every Keynesian seems to believe that because consumers are in a dreadful funk, only government stimulus spending can rescue the moribund economy, given (to them, at least) that investors will not spend more because the Fed, having already driven interest rates to extraordinarily low levels, cannot use conventional policies to drive them any lower and thereby elicit more investment spending.

People, please look at the data. They are conveniently available to one and all at the website[1] maintained by the Commerce Department's Bureau of Economic Analysis, the outfit that generates the national income and product accounts for the United States.

According to these data, real personal consumption expenditure recovered from its recession decline by the fourth quarter of 2010. Continuing to grow, it now stands (as of the most recent data, for the second quarter of 2011) even farther above its pre-recession peak.

Real government expenditure for consumption and investment (this concept does not include the government's transfer spending, such as unemployment insurance benefits and social security benefits) is also running higher than its pre-recession level. In the second quarter of 2011, it was running more than 2 percent higher (recall that this is "real," or inflation-adjusted spending; nominal spending has grown substantially more).

---

1. U.S. Department of Commerce, Bureau of Economic Analysis, National Income and Product Account Tables, http://www.bea.gov/iTable/iTable.cfm?ReqID=9&step=1#reqid=9&step=1&isuri=1.

The economy remains moribund not because consumption spending has failed to recover and not because government spending has failed to increase, but because the true driver of economic growth—private investment—remains deeply depressed. Gross private domestic fixed investment fell steeply after the second quarter of 2007, and in the second quarter of 2011 it remained 19 percent below its pre-recession peak. This figure fails to show how bad the investment situation really is, however, because the bulk of the investment spending now taking place is for what the accountants call the "capital consumption allowance," the amount estimated as necessary to compensate for the wear and tear and obsolescence of the existing capital stock.

The key variable is net private domestic fixed investment—the investment that builds the productive private capital stock. Quarterly data through this year are not currently available at the BEA website, but the annual data show that an index of its real amount peaked in 2006, fell substantially in each of the following three years, and recovered only slightly in 2010, when the index showed net private domestic fixed investment was running about 78 percent below its level in 2005 and 2006. Here is the true reason for the recession's persistence.

Private investors, despite the full recovery of real consumer spending and the increase of real government spending for final goods and services, remain apprehensive about the future of new investments, especially new long-term investments. I have argued repeatedly during the past three years that an important reason for this apprehension and the consequent reluctance to make new capital commitments is regime uncertainty—in this case, a widespread, serious fear that the government's major policies in regard to taxation, Obamacare, financial reform, environmental regulation, and other areas will have the effect of depriving investors of control over their capital or diminishing their ability to appropriate the income that the capital generates. President Obama's harping on the desirability of making "the rich" pay their "fair share" (that is, more) of the government's ever-rising costs only exacerbates regime uncertainty. Business leaders have spoken again and again of how the present political environment is discouraging risk-taking and entrepreneurship.

In any event, it should be crystal clear that the problem is not the failure of consumer spending to recover. Let us please have more respect for the facts than to continue singing that old, thoroughly worn-out tune.

63

U.S. Economic Recovery Remains Anemic, at Best

HOW GOES THE RECOVERY? Not well, it seems. Indeed, according to the most recent official estimates, it is anemic, at best.

As Figure 63.1 shows, real GDP has recovered its losses during the recent contraction and is now running at about the same rate as it was at its pre-recession peak in late 2007. So the rate at which the U.S. economy produces total output has gained nothing during the past four years, and its present rate of growth, even if it continues, is too slow to bring back into employment many of the potential workers now without work, including a disturbing number who have been without employment for years.

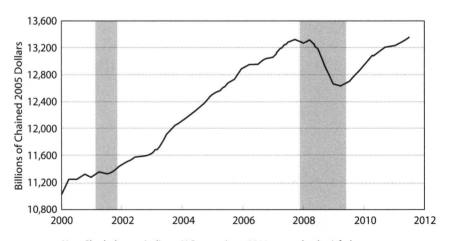

Note: Shaded areas indicate U.S. recessions. 2011 research.stlouisfed.org

Source: U.S. Department of Commerce: Bureau of Economic Analysis

Figure 63.1. Real Gross Domestic Product, 1 Decimal (GDPC1)

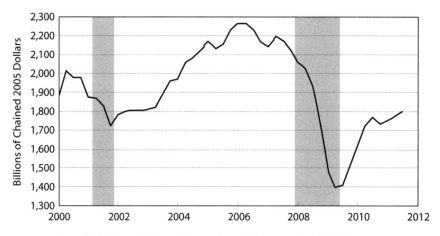

Note: Shaded areas indicate U.S. recessions. 2011 research.stlouisfed.org

Source: U.S. Department of Commerce: Bureau of Economic Analysis

Figure 63.2. Real Gross Private Domestic Investment, 1 Decimal (GPDIC1)

As I have discussed previously,[1] consumption spending has recovered fully, and government spending has reached new highs. Investment spending, however, remains depressed despite some recent pickup. Real gross private domestic investment has increased from its recession trough of about $1.4 trillion per annum to a current annual rate of about $1.8 trillion, as Figure 63.2 shows. However, it remains far below its prerecession peak of almost $2.3 trillion. Moreover, about $1.5 trillion of the current gross spending rate does nothing but compensate for depreciation—obsolescence and wear-and-tear—of the current capital stock, leaving only about $0.3 trillion per annum as real *net* private domestic investment.

We all understand, of course, that the housing boom and bust have left the country with a great deal of residential housing that cannot be sold without much greater reductions in the already-greatly-reduced asking prices. Therefore, little incentive exists for new investment in residential housing, and so this type of investment is currently running at only about 40 percent of its

---

1. Robert Higgs, "One More Time—Consumption Spending HAS Already Recovered," *The Beacon*, Sept. 9, 2011, http://blog.independent.org/2011/09/09/one-more-time-consumption -spending-has-already-recovered/.

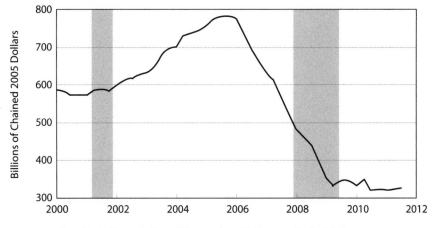

Note: Shaded areas indicate U.S. recessions. 2011 research.stlouisfed.org
Source: U.S. Department of Commerce: Bureau of Economic Analysis

Figure 63.3. Real Private Residential Fixed Investment, 1 Decimal (PRFIC1)

pre-recession peak rate, as Figure 63.3 shows, and it has shown no substantial sign whatever of recovery.

However, the residential housing bust is scarcely the whole story of the presently depressed investment spending. As Figure 63.4 shows, real private *non*residential fixed investment (a much larger component of total investment,

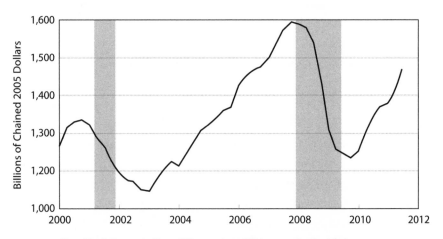

Note: Shaded areas indicate U.S. recessions. 2011 research.stlouisfed.org
Source: U.S. Department of Commerce: Bureau of Economic Analysis

Figure 63.4. Real Private Nonresidential Fixed Investment, 1 Decimal (PNFIC1)

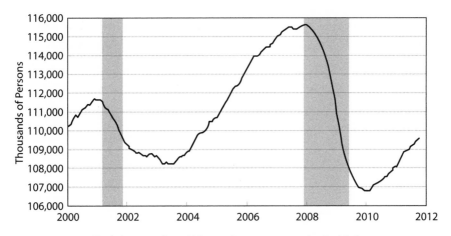

Note: Shaded areas indicate U.S. recessions. 2011 research.stlouisfed.org

Source: U.S. Department of Labor: Bureau of Labor Statistics

Figure 63.5. All Employees: Total Private Industries (USPRIV)

even during the housing boom), despite rapid recovery from its recent trough in late 2009, remains well below—about 7 percent below—its prerecession peak rate.

The rate of unemployment of labor (U-3) has remained stuck in the 9–10 percent range for roughly two and a half years. Given the difficulties of interpretation associated with the labor department's measures of unemployment, we can see with more assurance what has been happening in the labor market by looking instead at employment. Here we see, as Figure 63.5 shows, that although almost 3 million persons have been added to the employment rolls during the past two years, approximately six million fewer persons are employed in private industries now than were employed at the prerecession peak. Moreover, fewer persons are privately employed now than were employed in 2000—eleven years ago, when the population was substantially smaller.

In sum, although we see some indications that recovery has occurred, the labor market remains far from a full recovery, as does the volume of net private investment.[2] The former is unlikely to recover fully until the latter begins to grow rapidly. However, given the present clouded prospects for the security

---

2. Robert Higgs, "What's Holding Back the Recovery?" *The Beacon*, Feb. 21, 2011,http://blog.independent.org/2011/02/21/whats-holding-back-the-recovery/.

of investors' private property rights, with regime uncertainty[3] hovering over public policy in many critical regards, the likelihood of a strong investment boom must be considered extremely slight.

3. Robert Higgs, "Important New Evidence on Regime Uncertainty," http://blog.independent .org/2011/10/08/important-new-evidence-on-regime-uncertainty/.

64

Likely Fiscal and Monetary Legacies of the Current Crisis

I AM NOT A PROPHET, nor do I play one on TV. Neverthe-less, I will hazard some conjectures here about certain likely legacies of the current crisis. I focus on fiscal and monetary matters. In a future post, I will deal with regulatory and ideological matters. I will try to avoid mere guesses or hunches about what the future will bring. Instead, I will try to proceed in the spirit that Joseph Schumpeter expressed seventy years ago:

> What counts in any attempt at social prognosis is not the Yes or No that sums up the facts and arguments which lead up to it but those facts and arguments themselves. . . . Analysis, whether economic or other, never yields more than a statement about the tendencies present in an observable pattern. And these never tell us what *will* happen to the pattern but only what *would* happen if they continued to act as they have been acting in the time interval covered by our observation and if no other factors intruded.[1]

My speculations rest in part on my past analyses of national-emergency crises and the ratchet effects they produced in various dimensions of eco-nomic, social, political, legal, institutional, and ideological life in the United States. We have no assurance that past patterns will continue to prevail in the aftermath of the current crisis, but several broad similarities to this point suggest that we may not be entirely misled if we look to the past as a rough guide to the future.

---

1. Joseph A. Schumpeter, *Capitalism, Socialism and Democracy*, 3rd ed. (New York: Harper & Brothers, 1950), 61.

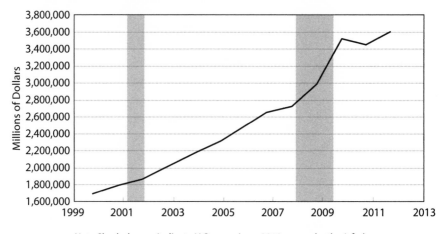

Note: Shaded areas indicate U.S. recessions. 2012 research.stlouisfed.org
Source: The White House: Office of Management and Budget

Figure 64.1. Federal Net Outlays (FYONET)

Certainly one of the most important features of the present crisis is the large increase in federal spending (see Figure 64.1). Between fiscal years 2008 and 2009, net federal outlays increased by almost 18 percent. Outlays dipped slightly in fiscal 2010, but rose again in 2011, reaching a level almost 21 percent greater than the level in 2008. Viewed in the context of the growth of outlays in the decade before the onset of the full-blown crisis in the fall of 2008, outlays since that time appear to have ratcheted up to a higher trajectory, about $300 billion or more above the amount they would have reached if the pre-recession trend had prevailed since 2008. Of course, outlays might eventually converge to their pre-recession trend line, but if so, they would be departing from the pattern followed in previous crises since World War I.

While federal outlays were increasing rapidly, federal revenues were falling equally rapidly. Between fiscal years 2008 and 2009, federal receipts declined by almost 17 percent because of the decline in income and employment. The upshot was that the federal budget deficit exploded, rising from slightly more than 3 percent of GDP in 2008 to about 10 percent of GDP in 2009. Therefore, the government had to borrow about $1.4 trillion in fiscal year 2009. Continued deficits of more than a trillion dollars in each of the following years have sent the public debt skyward almost like an ICBM taking off. As Figure 64.2 shows, the debt has increased by about 100 percent in less than five years

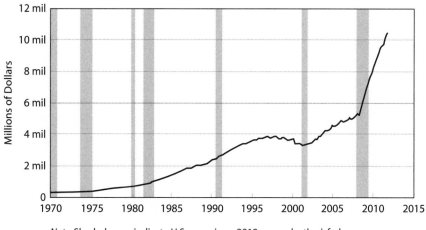

Note: Shaded areas indicate U.S. recessions. 2012 research.stlouisfed.org

Source: U.S. Department of the Treasury, Financial Management Service

Figure 64.2. Federal Debt Held by the Public (FYGFDPUN)

(between January 2007 and July 2011). Projections indicate that federal debt will certainly continue to increase rapidly in the near term, notwithstanding frequent political promises to bring down the annual budget deficits.

The government's rapid run-up of debt has proved possible notwithstanding the extraordinarily low yields on its securities for two main reasons. The first is that foreigners, who in many countries had to contend with monetary and fiscal policies just as bad as or even worse than those in the United States, fled the uncertainties of their own situations for the relatively safe haven of U.S. government securities as a means of protecting at least the bulk of the capital value invested. As Figure 64.3 shows, federal debt held by foreign and international investors increased from about $2.2 trillion at the beginning of 2007 to more than $5 trillion in October 2011—an increase of 127 percent in less than five years. As a result, such investors now hold almost half of the federal debt in the hands of the public.

In view of the currently negative real yields on most U.S. Treasury securities, foreign holders may well desire to terminate their purchases as fear subsides and government policies are improved in their home countries and as prospects dim for the dollar's exchange value—that is, the accumulations occasioned by the foreign holders' "flight to safety" may be drawn down. If the Treasury loses its usual horde of foreign buyers, it may find itself hard

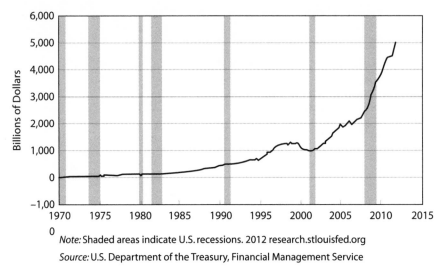

Note: Shaded areas indicate U.S. recessions. 2012 research.stlouisfed.org

Source: U.S. Department of the Treasury, Financial Management Service

Figure 64.3. Federal Debt Held by Foreign & International Investors (FDHBFIN)

pressed to finance its huge annual deficit without substantial increases in the yields of its bonds.

Pressed between the rock of unwilling bond buyers and the hard place of paying higher rates of interest, the government may well turn to the bottomless pit known as the Federal Reserve System. Indeed, it has already done so in recent years in a big way. As Figure 64.4 shows, the Fed first drew down its holdings of Treasuries at the onset of the crisis in swaps and other arrangements aimed at bailing out banks and other institutions that found themselves holding private and agency (GSE) securities with shrunken and in many cases extremely uncertain values. In 2009, however, the Fed increased its holdings of U.S. government securities from $492 billion in the first quarter to $769 in the third quarter. In the latter part of 2010, the Fed began another rapid buildup of its Treasury holdings, and by the third quarter of 2011, it held about $1,665 billion, or an amount equal to roughly 17 percent of the amount in the hands of the public. These two surges pushed the Fed's portfolio of Treasuries to more than twice the amount it held before the onset of the crisis.

When the government sells bonds and the Fed acquires government bonds, the effect is the same as printing money and handing it to the Treasury. If

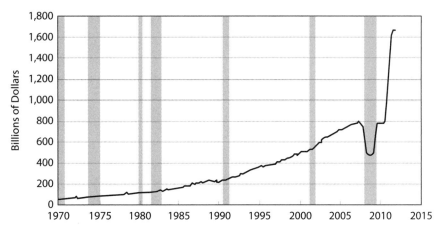

Note: Shaded areas indicate U.S. recessions. 2012 research.stlouisfed.org

Source: U.S. Department of the Treasury, Financial Management Service

Figure 64.4. Federal Debt Held by Federal Reserve Banks (FDHBFRBN)

we view the Fed as a part of the government, which for many purposes is the most appropriate way to view it, the operation is tantamount to the government's issuance of "greenbacks" (U.S. Treasury notes) during the War Between the States. This sort of action has great potential for general price inflation, and even if significant price inflation does not occur, as it has not during the present crisis so far, the partial (or "other things being equal") effect of such increases in the monetary base is to diminish the value of previously existing dollars. Figure 64.5 shows that the monetary base—roughly the amount of currency plus commercial bank reserves in the Federal Reserve Banks—has ballooned since late 2008, increasing by 211 percent between September 10, 2008, and March 7, 2012.

As Figure 64.5 also shows, the monetary base had changed slowly and steadily before the current crisis, and the Fed's actions that caused its explosion during the past three years have no precedents in nature or magnitude. Indeed, if a monetary economist had been given (by divine miracle) a preview of Figure 64.5 in, say, 2007, he would probably have concluded that the Fed's managers were destined to go mad in the near future. I daresay no economist expected such an action (or set of actions). Now that it has occurred, however, it places the Fed in an unprecedented—and extremely dangerous—situation.

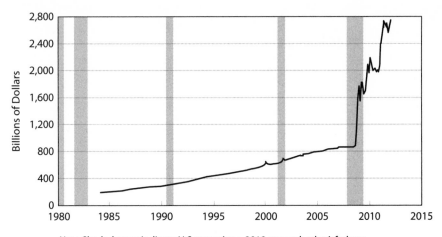

Note: Shaded areas indicate U.S. recessions. 2012 research.stlouisfed.org
Source: Federal Reserve Bank of St. Louis

Figure 64.5. St. Louis Adjusted Monetary Base (BASE)

So far the potential hyperinflation that this explosion of the monetary base might normally have been expected to produce has not occurred because the banks have simply absorbed almost all of it in the form of increases in their reserve balances at the Fed. As Figure 64.6 shows, commercial banks historically held their excess (that is, not legally required) reserves close to zero, because such reserves had no yield and hence entailed an opportunity cost equal to the yield the banks could realize by using those funds to make loans and investments. With the onset of the crisis, however, the demand for bank loans has fallen greatly and the banks' fears about the safety of loans and their worries about their balance sheets have grown, with the result that as the Fed has pumped money into the financial system by purchasing securities, the sellers have deposited the proceeds of those sales in their bank accounts and the banks have parked the money at the Fed, which sweetened the deal slightly, beginning in late 2008, by paying a small rate of interest (which soon settled at 0.25 percent). Thus more than $1.5 trillion now sits in excess reserves at the Fed.

Because the banks have acted so bizarrely during the past three years, the money stock has not grown very much. As Figure 64.7 shows, M2 increased substantially during the macroeconomic contraction, then leveled off in late 2009 and early 2010 before resuming a more rapid rate of increase in late 2010.

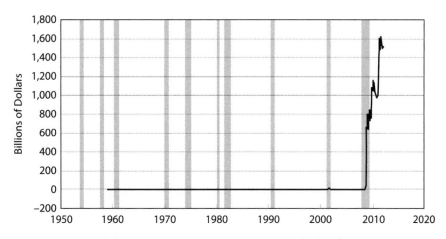

Note: Shaded areas indicate U.S. recessions. 2012 research.stlouisfed.org
Source: Board of Governors of the Federal Reserve System

Figure 64.6. Excess Reserves of Depository Institutions (EXCRESNS)

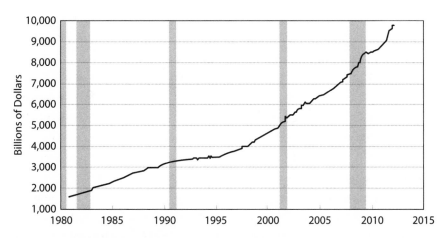

Note: Shaded areas indicate U.S. recessions. 2012 research.stlouisfed.org
Source: Board of Governors of the Federal Reserve System

Figure 64.7. M2 Money Stock (M2)

Between September 29, 2008, and February 20, 2012, M2 increased by 22.6 percent. This increase in just 41 months is not negligible, but it is only a tiny fraction of the increase that would have occurred if the banks had acted in a normal way during this interval.

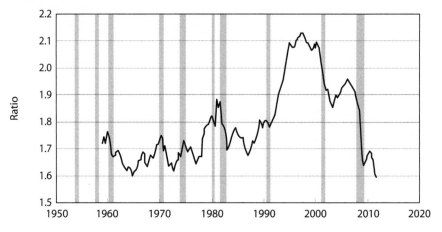

Note: Shaded areas indicate U.S. recessions. 2012 research.stlouisfed.org

Source: Federal Reserve Bank of St. Louis

Figure 64.8. Velocity of M2 Money Stock (M2V)

The increase in M2 that has occurred since the onset of the recession has had little effect on the general price level because the public's demand for money to hold has increased substantially. Equivalently, we may say that the velocity of monetary circulation—the ratio of GDP to money stock—has fallen substantially. As Figure 64.8 shows, M2 velocity has fallen by about 16 percent since the recession began, and it now stands at the lowest value it has attained since the 1950s. We live in unusual times, indeed. An increase in the public's demand for money to hold also occurred in previous postwar recessions, but not to the extent that it has occurred recently.

In view of the foregoing evidence, what should we conclude about the likely fiscal and monetary legacies of the current crisis? First, the federal government is unlikely to reduce the budget deficit very much as long as it can continue to sell its bonds at anything near their current high prices (and consequently low yields). Even if foreigners grow skittish about the dollar's exchange value or regain their courage enough to make more investments in their home countries rather than parking their money in Treasuries, the government will continue to run extraordinarily large budget deficits—and therefore to sell extraordinarily large amounts of bonds—as long as it can sell its debt to the Fed; that is, as long as it can effectively monetize the debt.

The Fed shows complete willingness to continue bankrolling the Treasury. The Fed's gigantic accumulation of Treasuries—more than $1 trillion in the past three years—speaks much louder than anything Ben Bernanke might say about an "exit strategy." Indeed, the Fed seems to have painted itself into a corner. If the public begins to wind down its current extraordinary demand for money to hold and pushes the velocity of monetary circulation back toward its pre-recession levels, the Fed will face accelerating general price inflation. To slow this inflation, it will need to sap money from the financial system. But how can it simultaneously withdraw money (to slow inflation) and inject money (via purchase of new federal debt)? Moreover, as the commercial banks begin to feel more comfortable about their balance sheets, they may dive into their mountain of excess reserves at the Fed and increase the volume of their loans and investments, which will add additional fuel to the fire breaking out because of increasing monetary velocity. How the Fed will resolve this dilemma I do not know. At present, the Fed's managers talk as if the problem either does not exist or will be easy to deal with when the need arises, but such talk amounts to whistling past the cemetery.

The ratchet in the government's outlays probably will not be eliminated in the near or intermediate term. The president, Congress, and the leadership of both major parties are firmly wedded to the government's spending as much as it can get away with. Political leaders talk about reining the government's profligacy, but their actions belie their words. Every cow in the budget turns out to be sacred when someone tries to wield an ax.

The prospect in the aftermath of the crisis—which, to be sure, is not yet over and may take a nasty second-dip before it ultimately passes—is for significantly bigger government in fiscal terms (and, as I shall argue elsewhere shortly, in regulatory, statutory, and ideological terms as well). Federal taxes may return to their postwar average of 18 percent of GDP, but with the federal government's outlays stuck at 23 or 24 percent of GDP, we will have to endure deficits of 5–6 percent of GDP for a long time.

We will also have to endure a huge, ever growing amount of federal debt and, sooner or later, a grave threat that the Fed, in monetizing additions to the debt, will be unable to keep the lid on accelerating general price inflation. Therefore, probably the best we can hope for is stagnation: slow or no real economic growth, probably accompanied by chronically large numbers of unemployed and underemployed persons sustained partly or entirely at taxpayer expense. The worst outcome would be hyperinflation, which would be utterly ruinous. The most likely outcome in my view is for a long period of stagflation: little or no real economic growth, accompanied by troublesome (and probably quite variable) rates of general price inflation—something like the 1970s, though with less real growth. How this scenario fits into the currently more globalized economy is anyone's guess. Much depends on how irresponsible foreign leaders will be in their policy actions—and we may count on most of them to be as horrible as possible. In these circumstances, Americans will have to put up not only with unsatisfactory performance of the economy, but also with great uncertainty about what the next quarter or the next year may bring. All in all, our most likely prospect seems fairly ugly, but with luck we may escape complete ruin.

65

Counsel of Despair?

OVER THE YEARS, I have heard many people say that the government's adoption of a laissez-faire stance during a business recession or depression amounts to "do-nothing government"—the unstated assumption always being that it is better for the government to "do something" than to do nothing. Recommending such a hands-off stance is often described as a "counsel of despair." Moreover, it is frequently added, in a democratic polity, the electorate will not tolerate such a policy.

Implicit in such criticism is the assumption that the government knows how to improve the situation and has an incentive to do so. If only it will take the known remedial action, people's suffering will be relieved, and the economy will return more quickly to full employment and rapid economic growth. All that blocks such remedial action, it would seem, are outdated ideas about the proper role of government and, perhaps, the opposition of certain selfish special interests. Government need only step on the gas pedal, by means of expansionary fiscal and monetary policies, and the economic engine will accelerate. If the government is already taking such actions, it need only press down harder on the gas pedal.

Adherents of the Austrian school of economics are sometimes singled out as moss-backed exponents of the "liquidationist" position said to have been taken by Treasury Secretary Andrew Mellon after the onset of the Great Depression in the United States. According to Herbert Hoover, Mellon urged him to refrain from involving the government in the situation, in order to "liquidate labor, liquidate stocks, liquidate farmers, liquidate real estate.... [I]t will purge the rottenness out of the system. High costs of living and high living will come down. People will work harder, live a more moral life. Values will be adjusted, and enterprising people will pick up from less competent people."[1]

Although not so colorful in their policy advice, Austrian economists do recommend that the government stand aside when a business bust occurs. (They also explain how government action, especially its monetary policy, has brought about the preceding, unsustainable boom.) By so doing, the policy-induced structural distortions whose unsustainability brought on the bust in the first place will be corrected. Resources will be reallocated away from enterprises that are losing money and capital value because consumers are unwilling to support their profitable operation, and they will be put to work in other lines, where prospects of successfully satisfying present and future consumer preferences are brighter. Business bankruptcies, unemployed labor and capital, and other dire developments only attest that mistakes have been made. In order to restore sustainable prosperity, these mistakes must be corrected, not papered over.

If the government props up unprofitable firms with bailouts and cheap loans and subsidizes unemployed workers with extended unemployment-insurance benefits and other income supports, it only obstructs and delays the necessary restructuring of the economy's resource allocation. Although it may appear to be relieving people's pain—and, indeed, it is doing so for those fortunate enough to receive booty at the public's expense—it is only ensuring that by falsifying the price and profit signals that tell economic actors how to act most rationally in the society's long-term benefit, it is preserving an economically irrational allocation of resources and thereby planting a time bomb that will explode later in the form of an even worse bust.

Thus what seems to be governmental "compassion" is scarcely true compassion, but only a spurious assistance to some at the present expense of others and, ultimately, to the detriment of almost everyone. The true counselors of despair are those who insist that the government act even though the government cannot act constructively and its actions will, at best, only produce short-term improvement in the patient's symptoms while ensuring that in the

---

1. "Andrew W. Mellon," *Wikipedia*, http://en.wikipedia.org/wiki/Andrew_W._Mellon.

long term, he will fall victim to an even more painful malady. If the patient is bleeding, it is scarcely compassionate to attach government leeches so that he loses blood even more rapidly. The true counselors of despair are those who hope against hope—and historical experience—that the government can and will act constructively. Such wishful thinking cries out for deeper study of Austrian economics and economic history, not to mention a more thorough understanding of the sort of people who run governments and of their reasons for exercising government power.

66

Unprecedented Household Deleveraging since 2007

FOR DECADES, AMERICAN families espoused the not-quite-Cartesian ontology: I go into debt; therefore I am. Household debt climbed ever higher through good times and bad. Since the onset of the current recession, however, household debt has contracted substantially for the first time in more than half a century.

After reaching a peak at $13.82 trillion in the first quarter of 2008, household debt outstanding fell to $12.87 trillion in the third quarter of 2012, down by about $1.0 trillion, or almost 7 percent (see Figure 66.1).

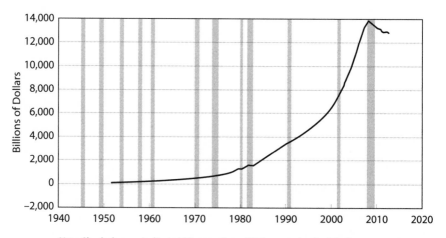

Note: Shaded areas indicate U.S. recessions. 2012 research.stlouisfed.org
Source: Board of Governors of the Federal Reserve System

Figure 66.1. Household Sector: Liabilities: Household Credit Market Debt Outstanding (CMDEBT)

During the past year, the rate of decline has slowed considerably, so the outstanding debt may be converging on a minimum. But should the economy's sputtering recovery falter even further or a new downturn occur, households appear primed to continue their deleveraging.

The unprecedented decline in household debt outstanding during the past five years joins many other variables in attesting that the economic expansion between 2002 and 2007 consisted in large part of an artificial boom—a credit bubble—fueled by the Fed's easy-money policies, which spilled from the mortgage-financed housing bubble and the stock-market run-up, to rising commodity markets and bloated housing-related sectors, and ultimately to the entire economy's unsustainable expansion.

The sloughing off of household debt in recent years also signals, for the first time since World War II, a change in people's long-term outlook. As long as people had faith in the continuation of economic progress in the long term, they did not hasten to pay down debts when recessions occurred. This time, however, they seem to have lost their faith in the economy's long-term performance. This change at the household level goes hand in hand with the regime uncertainty that has brought about extraordinary reluctance to make long-term investments among investors and entrepreneurs.

It is a common failing for pundits and others to overreact to short-term economic changes, mistaking them for watersheds that alter the character of the economy's long-run dynamics. The evidence in regard to the household deleveraging and the still-depressed net private investment in recent years, however, may be seen as consistent with an interpretation that the post-2007 economy may indeed have changed in a more fundamental way. If so, we may rightly trace its enduring sickness to the extraordinary government and Federal Reserve actions of the past five years. In the immortal words of Leonard Cohen's song "Everybody Knows,"

Everybody knows that the boat is leaking
Everybody knows that the captain lied

The policymakers, sad to say, appear to have operated in this period according to the rule, no economic event is so bad that we cannot make it worse if we try hard enough.

67

An Overview of Recent Changes in Federal Finances

EVERYONE WHO PAYS any attention to public affairs knows that after the onset of the current recession, the federal government's finances took a very bad turn for the worse. As taxable income fell, federal tax receipts also fell, especially between 2008 and 2009 (see Figure 67.1; here as elsewhere in this post, unless otherwise noted, references to years are to federal fiscal years, which end on September 30).

Even if nothing else had changed, this precipitous drop in revenues would have created a huge increase in the budget deficit, which was already very large—$459 billion in 2008. However, as the government's receipts were fall-

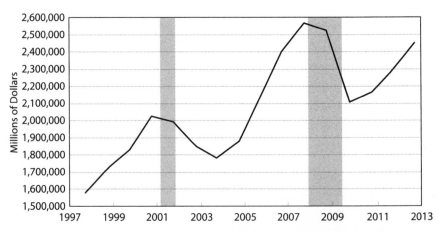

Note: Shaded areas indicate U.S. recessions. 2012 research.stlouisfed.org

Source: The White House: Office of Management and Budget

Figure 67.1. Federal Receipts (FYFR)

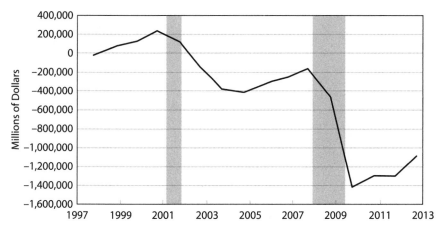

Note: Shaded areas indicate U.S. recessions. 2012 research.stlouisfed.org
Source: The White House: Office of Management and Budget

Figure 67.2. Federal Surplus or Deficit [–] (FYFSD)

ing sharply, fiscal decision makers took a number of measures ostensibly to "stimulate" the economy and thereby cushion its contraction by increasing federal spending. This action made the increase in the budget deficit even greater than it otherwise would have been.

Between 2008 and 2009, the deficit increased by nearly $1 trillion, an amount equivalent to roughly 7 percent of GDP at the time (see Figure 67.2). Although the economy's decline hit bottom in mid-2009 (calendar year) and began a slow recovery, the deficit did not decline much during the next three years. After reaching the astonishing amount of $1.4 trillion in 2009, it was $1.3 trillion in 2010 and 2011, and $1.1 trillion in 2012.

The deficit did not decline faster because federal outlays, which had leaped up by an amazing 11 percent in 2009, have remained lodged at their elevated level of about $3.5–3.6 trillion during the recovery (see Figure 67.3). What was represented as an emergency level of spending in late 2008 and 2009 has subsequently turned into the normal level of spending, even though four years have passed since the perceived crisis occurred in the final third of 2008 (calendar year).

After a gigantic jump in 2009, however, federal net outlays did not increase further. One upshot of this stability was that the rate of increase in federal outlays between 2007 and 2012 (5.3 percent per year on average) was

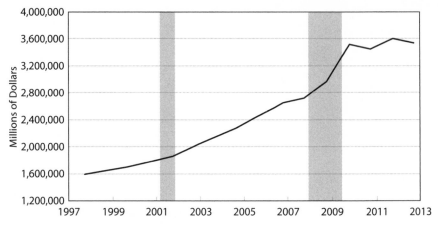

Note: Shaded areas indicate U.S. recessions. 2012 research.stlouisfed.org
Source: The White House: Office of Management and Budget

Figure 67.3. Federal Net Outlays (FYONET)

actually less than it had been between 1998 and 2007 (5.7 percent per year on average). Thus, whereas the George W. Bush administration had increased its spending rapidly year after year, the Barack Obama administration crammed its spending increase into one huge jump in 2009. Unless the government resumes substantial increases in its spending fairly soon, the apparent ratchet in spending created in 2008 and 2009 will disappear as the trend line converges with the current outlays.

Meanwhile, the state of the federal finances is sufficiently desperate, especially if we view it in the perspective of the increases in entitlement payments the government has promised to recipients of benefits under the Social Security, Medicare, and Medicaid programs, among others, for decades to come. These prospective long-run fiscal difficulties were crying out for rectification even before the recession began. However, the government's fiscal management since 2008, which has been dominated by short-run concerns, has made these long-run difficulties even greater and the need for a serious response to them more pressing than ever before. The day is coming—and coming quite soon—when the federal fiscal authorities will no longer be able to employ their traditional subterfuge of kicking the can a little farther down the road.

PART VI

Labor Markets

68

Will the Real Rate of Unemployment Please Stand Up?

AS THE RECESSION has deepened and the rate of unemployment has risen, a number of commentators have sought, for various reasons, to portray the situation as far graver than the "official" rate of unemployment indicates. Some of these commentators charge that the government is deliberately misrepresenting the amount of unemployment and that the "real" rate of unemployment is much greater than the official rate that the government announces and the news media report each month.

I have no desire to claim that the government never hides bad news—indeed, the extent of its blatant lies and outrageous propaganda[1] ought to have provoked public outrage a long time ago—but in the present instance, I believe the critics are the ones who are misrepresenting the situation. If the government is hiding the bad news about unemployment that the critics are courageously "revealing," it is hiding that bad news in plain sight. Since 1940, the Bureau of Labor Statistics (BLS) has provided a variety of information on the population's employment status derived from the Current Population Survey, a rather complicated, stratified random sample of approximately 60,000 households conducted each month. A BLS website explains how the data are collected.[2] From these data, various measures of the rate of unemployment may be, and routinely are, computed. Again, a BLS website lays out these measures[3] for all

---

1. Robert Higgs, *Resurgence of the Warfare State: The Crisis since 9/11* (Oakland, CA: Independent Institute, 2005).

2. U.S. Department of Labor, Bureau of Labor Statistics, "BLS Handbook of Methods," http://www.bls.gov/opub/hom/homch1_f.htm.

3. U.S. Department of Labor, Bureau of Labor Statistics, "Economic News Release: Unemployed Persons by Duration of Unemployment," http://www.bls.gov/news.release/empsit .t12.htm.

the world to see, and it makes available the component figures for anyone who wishes to compute a differently defined rate.

Thus, in October 2009, the most recently reported month, the rate designated U-3, which is defined as "total unemployed, as a percent of the civilian labor force (official unemployment rate)," stood at 10.2 percent. The persons classified as unemployed in this measure, the most commonly reported one, are basically those who are not currently working but who have made an attempt to find a job in the past four weeks. By adding other categories of persons to those regarded as unemployed in the U-3 measure, one may arrive at greater rates.

The broadest such measure, designated U-6, is defined as "total unemployed, plus all marginally attached workers, plus total employed part time for economic reasons, as a percent of the civilian labor force plus all marginally attached workers." This rate stood at 17.5 percent in October 2009. A note attached to the BLS table of unemployment rates explains: "Marginally attached workers are persons who currently are neither working nor looking for work but indicate that they want and are available for a job and have looked for work sometime in the recent past. Discouraged workers, a subset of the marginally attached, have given a job-market related reason for not looking currently for a job. Persons employed part time for economic reasons are those who want and are available for full-time work but have had to settle for a part-time schedule."

One does not need to devote a lifetime to studying how these statistics are defined and measured to realize that in many ways they tend to *over*state how dire the unemployment situation really is. For example, the persons classified as in the labor force but currently unemployed must have actively sought a job during the past four weeks, but a wide variety of actions qualifies as evidence that they have actively sought a job, including: (1) "contacting: an employer directly or having a job interview; a public or private employment agency; friends or relatives; a school or university employment center"; (2) "sending out resumes or filling out applications"; (3) "placing or answering advertisements"; (4) "checking union or professional registers"; and (5) "some other means of active job search." So, if you are out of work and tell the CPS data collector that three weeks ago you asked Uncle Charlie whether he knew of any job openings, then you qualify as officially unemployed, even though you made no other effort to find employment. Many of those classified as "marginally attached workers" and included in the U-6 measure are even more questionable. After all, they admit that they are neither working nor doing anything to find work. Merely *saying* that "they want and are available for a job and have looked for work sometime in the recent past," though not in the past four weeks, does not evince much genuine interest in employment.

Strange to say, many commentators have insisted from the very onset of the current recession that we are plunging into a second Great Depression. Perhaps we are, but the evidence to date does not confirm such a plunge. Yes, by taking an extremely loose view of what constitutes unemployment, we can say that perhaps one worker in six is now out of work. But in 1933, the official rate of unemployment was nearly 25 percent, and perhaps another 25 percent of the labor force comprised persons working part-time who wanted to work full-time, so the U-6 rate at that time (long before the requisite data for such an estimate were routinely collected) was in the neighborhood of 50 percent—and that at a time when workers' earnings and assets were much less than they are now and hence long spells without work were correspondingly more frightening. Small wonder if a typical scene from the early 1930s shows dejected workers standing on the sidewalk in a soup line, whereas the typical queue nowadays is more likely to show cheerful customers waiting to be seated in an upscale restaurant. The year 2009 may not be the best of years, but it is miles away from 1933.

69

Short-Term Employment Changes in Longer-Term Perspective

MANY COMMENTATORS HAVE noted in recent years that Americans have been leaving the labor force. Their departure has made interpretation of unemployment statistics more difficult, and because the Bureau of Labor Statistics (BLS) publishes six variants of the unemployment rate, considerable debate has occurred about the "real" rate of unemployment. Much of this confusion can be avoided by examining not data on unemployment, however measured, but data on employment, which are substantially less ambiguous.

When we examine the ratio of employment to population (reported by the BLS for the civilian noninstitutional population age 16 and over[1]), we find that indeed the overall employment ratio has fallen considerably since the onset of the current recession. In 2007, the ratio for both sexes combined was about 63 percent. In 2008, it fell steadily, and by December it had reached 61 percent. In 2009, it continued to fall steadily, and by December it had reached 58.2 percent. At that point, it more or less stabilized at its recession low point, and during the past two years it has remained in the range 58–59 percent. The most recently reported ratio, for January 2012, was 58.5 percent.

As Figure 69.1 shows, however, this ratio had been even lower between the late 1940s and the late 1970s. Starting in the mid-1970s, the employment–population ratio trended upward, increasing from about 57 percent to more than 64 percent by 2000. Note, too, that the ratio is pro-cyclical, rising during macroeconomic expansions and falling during macroeconomic recessions.

---

1. U.S. Department of Labor, Bureau of Labor Statistics, "Data Retrieval: Labor Force Statistics (CPS),"http://www.bls.gov/webapps/legacy/cpsatab1.htm.

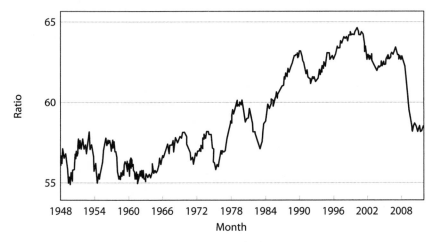

Source: U.S. Department of Labor: Bureau of Labor Statistics

Figure 69.1. Employment-Population Ratio, Both Sexes, Age 16 and Over, Civilian Noninstitutional Population

The cyclical drop during the present recession has been larger than preceding ones, however, and it has also stuck at the bottom, whereas preceding declines were followed by quick rebounds.

The tendency of the employment–population ratio to rise during the last quarter of the twentieth century was driven entirely by an increase in the ratio for females. As Figure 69.2 shows, the employment–population ratio for women increased steadily from the late 1940s to 2000, rising from about 31 percent in 1948 to more than 57 percent in 2000. It remained at a high level until the onset of the current recession, and between December 2007 and January 2012, it declined only from 56.5 percent to 52.9 percent.

The historical path of the employment–population ratio for men looks quite different. As Figure 69.3 shows, this ratio has been trending downward since the early 1950s—for roughly sixty years—although the downward trend was hardly noticeable during the quarter-century before the onset of the current recession. During this macroeconomic bust, however, the ratio for men has dropped precipitously, declining from almost 70 percent in 2006 to a low of only 63.3 percent in December 2009. Since then it has rebounded only slightly; in January 2012, it was 64.5 percent.

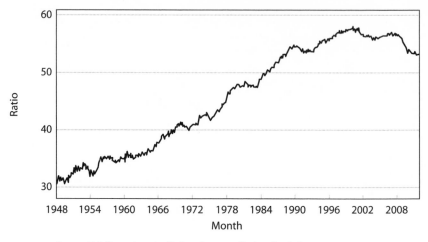

Source: U.S. Department of Labor: Bureau of Labor Statistics

Figure 69.2. Employment-Population Ratio, Women Only, Age 16 and Over, Civilian Noninstitutional Population

Source: U.S. Department of Labor: Bureau of Labor Statistics

Figure 69.3. Employment-Population Ratio, Men Only, Age 16 and Over, Civilian Noninstitutional Population

Thus we see that the current recession has brought about an exceptionally steep drop in the ratio of employment to population for the entire civilian noninstitutional population age 16 and over, and that the decline has been roughly twice as great for men as for women. Both of these changes, however, should be viewed in a longer-term perspective, which shows that the employment ratio for men moved downward for a long time, whereas the ratio for women increased for a long time. Women have constituted a growing share of the total labor force for more than half a century, and during the present recession, that change has only surged further.

The changes described and depicted here have a variety of demographic, social, and economic causes, and labor economists and others have made great efforts to explain them. Such analysis lies outside the scope of this brief commentary. I hope, however, that the data alone contribute something toward the reader's appreciation of recent and longer-term changes in U.S. employment.

70

Cessation of Labor Force
Growth since 2008

THE UNITED STATES has a long history of population growth
and concomitant labor force growth. As Figure 70.1 shows, the number of
men in the civilian labor force (men either working in paid employment or
actively seeking work) increased fairly steadily over the past half-century—at
least, until the onset of the current recession.

For the past five years, however, the number of men in the labor force has
fluctuated around a fairly level trend line at approximately 82 million (see
Figure 70.2). This cessation of growth came on the heels of a 6-million-man
increase during the previous seven years.

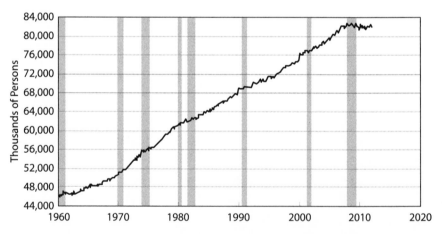

Note: Shaded areas indicate U.S. recessions. 2012 research.stlouisfed.org

Source: U.S. Department of Labor: Bureau of Statistics

Figure 70.1. Civilian Labor Force Level—Men (LNS11000001)

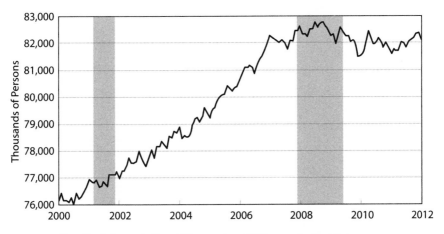

Figure 70.2. Civilian Labor Force Level—Men (LNS11000001)

In the post–World War II era, the number of women in the labor force grew even faster than the number of men, and also tended to grow fairly steadily. When the current recession began, the female labor force continued to grow, increasing by about a million women between the officially designated beginning and end of the recession (December 2007–June 2009). In the second half of 2009, however, this growth stopped, and a slight reversal occurred, putting the total on a lower, fairly level trend line throughout 2010 and 2011, albeit still at a higher level than the female labor force had reached before the recession began (see Figure 70.3).

Labor economists and others have been puzzling over what has happened. Although labor force growth tended to slow or even to halt momentarily during past recessions of the postwar era, the current cessation of growth has no precedent in that era, and hence analysts have found its explanation to be a challenge.

Whatever the answer(s), one thing is clear: unless the labor force resumes something like its historically normal growth, we cannot expect a resumption of historically normal economic growth. Labor inputs are major contributors to the production of goods and services. Increases in labor productivity are only a partial substitute unless the rate of productivity growth can be made much greater than observed historically over long periods.

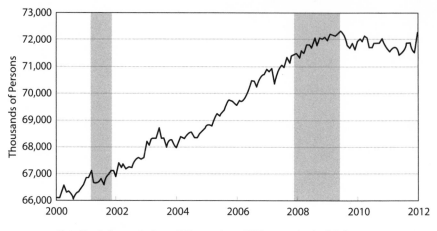

Note: Shaded areas indicate U.S. recessions. 2012 research.stlouisfed.org

Source: U.S. Department of Labor: Bureau of Labor Statistics

Figure 70.3. Civilian Labor Force Level—Women (LNS11000002)

One also wonders: how are the millions of people who normally would have been in the labor force occupying themselves? Who is supporting them? What are their expectations and plans? Their extended stay outside the labor force joins a number of other puzzling features of the present recession, during which the patterns of economic changes and policy responses have differed significantly from those observed during previous macroeconomic busts. We are living, as the cliché has it, in interesting times. Unfortunately, many of the developments that make these times interesting also make them worrisome.

71

Labor Markets Are Still in Bad Shape

THE RECENT REPORT that the standard (U-3) rate of unemployment fell to 7.7 percent last month seems to have stirred considerable joy in Mudville. But before we spend a lot of time shouting huzzahs, we might well bear in mind a few other data and, of course, recall that not so long ago, a 7.7 percent unemployment rate would have been a cause for lament, rather than celebration.

Because the data on which the various official rates of unemployment rest are so problematic, we often do better to examine not unemployment, but employment, which is subject to fewer difficulties of measurement and interpretation. On this front, the news—especially when put in historical perspective—does not look so good.

As Figure 71.1 shows, total civilian employment, though it has tended to increase during the past three years, still stands about three million jobs below its level at the end of 2007. So, after five years, the job total still has a long way to go merely to get back to where it was before the bust began.

Meanwhile, however, the population has continued to grow, and therefore the ratio of civilian employment to civilian noninstitutional population aged 16 and older is in much worse shape than total employment.

This ratio plummeted during the contraction, and since the overall economy hit bottom in mid-2009 and began to rebound, albeit slowly, the ratio of employment to population has scarcely budged, remaining stuck at 58–59 percent. To find a time with a comparable ratio, we must go back thirty years to the recession of the early 1980s (see Figure 71.2).

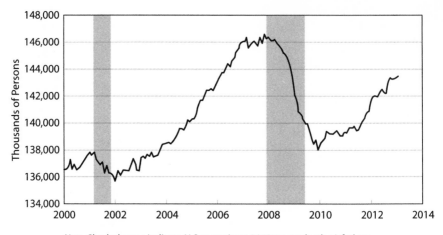

Shaded areas indicate U.S. recessions. 2013 research.stlouisfed.org

Source: U.S. Department of Labor: Bureau of Labor Statistics

Figure 71.1. Civilian Employment (CE16OV)

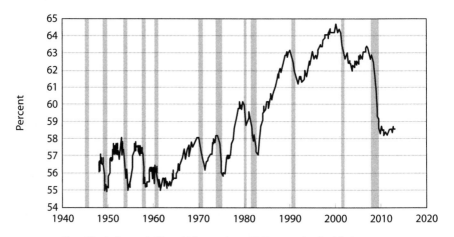

Note: Shaded areas indicate U.S. recessions. 2013 research.stlouisfed.org

Source: U.S. Department of Labor: Bureau of Labor Statistics

Figure 71.2. Civilian Employment-Population Ratio (EMRATIO)

Clearly the labor markets remain in a funk. Although they have improved during the past three years in some regards, they have failed to improve in other regards. However we measure their condition, it is clear that the situation remains poor by historical standards and, in some ways, by the standards of only a few years ago. The collapse of the employment/population ratio in particular indicates that something may have occurred since 2008 or 2009—perhaps the many additional or increased government subsidies of unemployment and of absence from the labor market—to keep the job market stuck in a distinctly subpar position.

PART VII

Libertarianism

72

Are Questions of War and Peace Merely One Issue among Many for Libertarians?

MOST AMERICANS EXPRESS support for private enterprise. Outright socialists are rare in this country, except on university campuses, and even progressives, who favor pervasive regulation and heavy taxation, often declare that they support a free-enterprise economy—they simply oppose "unbridled capitalism." For many sincere friends of the free market, however, free enterprise shines as only one star among a host of others in their ideological firmament, and with regard to one critically important service—protection from foreign threats—they favor a government-monopoly supplier with an established reputation for recklessness and unnecessary ferocity. Thus notable free enterprisers include both hawks (for example, Thomas Sowell, George Shultz, and Walter Williams) and doves (for example, Thomas Gale Moore, David Henderson, and Donald Boudreaux) in their views about U.S. foreign and military policy.

Among libertarians in particular, the U.S. invasion of Iraq brought this difference to the fore more visibly than any previous event. Some professed libertarians supported the U.S. attack and the ensuing occupation; others opposed these actions; and still others hedged, positioning themselves somewhere in between. On October 22, 2004, for example, a well-publicized and well-attended libertarian conference at the Cato Institute, "Lessons from the Iraq War: Reconciling Liberty and Security," gave the podium to advocates of each of these positions. (I was one of the invited speakers.) Supporters of "big-tent" libertarianism counseled that libertarians ought to steer clear of fratricidal conflict over this issue. After all, they say, we still agree on many other issues, and we should not allow ourselves to be divided by a difference over a single issue.

Although I generally eschew quarrels with fellow libertarians over doctrinal matters—my crucial dispute is with the government, not with other libertarians—I draw the line at the question of war and peace. In my judgment, this issue is fundamental; it well nigh defines a genuine libertarian ideology. Professed libertarians who support an aggressive warfare state are in effect giving up the ship of liberty without a fight. They are making the same mistake that has long condemned conservatives to serving as de facto buttresses of Leviathan, no matter how much they might complain about high taxes and excessive regulation.

My claim is that those who give a free hand to the government in its foreign and defense policymaking will ultimately discover that they have handed their rulers the key that opens all doors, including the doors that might otherwise obstruct the government's invasion of our most cherished rights to life, liberty, and property. The war-making key is, so to speak, any government's master key because when critical trade-offs must be made, war will override all other concerns, and as an ancient maxim aptly warns us, *inter arma silent leges*. Anyone who has looked into the U.S. Supreme Court's history, for example, knows that during wartime the justices have placed themselves on the casualty list by effectively rolling over and playing dead. Without at least a semblance of the rule of law and an independent judiciary, all hopes for the maintenance of a free society are in vain.

I have been researching and documenting the preceding claims for thirty years, and my books *Crisis and Leviathan* (1987), *Against Leviathan* (2004), and *Depression, War, and Cold War* (2006), among many other published works, present a great deal of evidence and analysis that support the "master key" thesis. My book *Resurgence of the Warfare State* (2005) demonstrates that the characteristic relationships operative during the world wars and the Cold War are now operating in the so-called war on terrorism. The main conclusion of all this research is that when a nation-state goes to war or makes great efforts to prepare for war, all bets are off for the preservation of the people's liberties. As political scientist Bruce Porter concluded in *War and the Rise of the State*,[1] a study of the past five centuries in the West, "A government at war

---

1. Bruce Porter, *War and the Rise of the State* (New York, NY: Free Press, 1994).

is a juggernaut of centralization determined to crush any internal opposition that impedes the mobilization of militarily vital resources. This centralizing tendency of war has made the rise of the state throughout much of history a disaster for human liberty and rights" (1994, xv). Hawkish libertarians would do well to ponder these conclusions. Not for nothing have dovish libertarians made a veritable mantra of Randolph Bourne's declaration that "war is the health of the state."[2]

An obvious response by hawkish libertarians appeals to an axiom of classical liberalism: we need the state to protect us from genuine foreign threats; moreover, provision of such protection is the state's most basic responsibility. Unfortunately, this reply, which rests more on wishful thinking than on a hardheaded understanding of the state, raises more questions than it answers (and incidentally reveals a fatal flaw in the doctrine of classical liberalism).

First, what makes anybody think that the state will protect *us*, as distinct from the state's leaders and its apparatus of rule? For more than a century, nearly all of the U.S. government's military activities have been devoted to protecting someone or something other than you and me (or our forebears). Spain did not threaten Americans in 1898, and the Filipinos did not threaten them between 1899 and 1902. Germany did not seriously threaten any genuine American right in 1917—the right to travel unmolested in a war zone on munitions-laden British or French ships does not qualify, notwithstanding Woodrow Wilson's tortured logic—and the Kaiser's government repeatedly made conciliatory efforts to maintain peaceful relations with the United States from 1914 until 1917. Germany did not seek war with the United States in 1940 and 1941 (until its alliance with Japan tipped it into a declaration of war on December 11, 1941); indeed, Hitler's regime, hoping to keep the United States at bay, displayed remarkable forbearance in the face of Franklin D. Roosevelt's attempts to provoke a war-justifying naval incident in the North Atlantic. In more recent decades, North Korea, North Vietnam, Panama, Serbia, Iraq, and Libya, among others, did not threaten American rights before the U.S. government launched wars against them. If in making war the government

---

2. Randolph Bourne, "War Is the Health of the State," 1917–18, unpublished, at http://www.antiwar.com/bourne.php.

has intended only to protect Americans from foreigners who threaten our lives, liberties, and property here on our own territory, then we must conclude that the government has displayed astonishingly bad judgment in choosing its targets. Why would anyone want to rely on a protector who manifestly cannot shoot straight?

Second, even if we do need the government's protection from foreign attack, can the government deliver the goods? Did it prevent the Japanese attack on Pearl Harbor? Did it prevent the terrorist attacks of September 11, 2001? Of course, state officials constantly tell us that they are protecting us, but talk is cheap and in their case often untrue, especially when it pertains to matters outside our common experience and therefore beyond our power to verify easily.

Consider the government's highly publicized announcement in 2006 that it had arrested the members of "a homegrown terrorist cell" in Miami, thereby preventing them from blowing up the Sears Tower in Chicago.[3] Even before the government had completed its high-profile press conference, peals of laughter were ringing out across the land: the seven "terrorists" lacked explosives, training, contacts with any real terrorist group, and, most of all, the wit to blow up a skyscraper. Deputy Director John Pistole of the Federal Bureau of Investigation (FBI), describing the alleged plot as "aspirational rather than operational," had to suppress his giggles. These men deserved perhaps a week in jail for the crime of flakiness, whereas the government agents, including the sting man who planted seeds in the men's receptive but pathetically puerile minds, might justly have been sentenced to ten years behind bars for abusing their authority. One has to wonder: if real terrorists threaten the American people, why are government agents wasting their highly paid time and other resources in this fashion? Aside from the few pathetic men the government has entrapped in such schemes, the FBI and other ostensible antiterrorist protectors have very little to show for themselves over the past decade, aside from engorging massive amounts of taxpayer money and unreasonably violating the public's privacy and other rights on a massive scale.

We should pose an even more fundamental question regarding the instances in which other countries or political entities have attacked us: Why? We

---

3. "'Homegrown Terrorists' Arraigned in Court," MSNBC, June 23, 2006, at http://www.msnbc.msn.com/id/13497335/ns/us_news-security/.

might ask, for example: Why did the Japanese attack Pearl Harbor in the first place? The U.S. government had initiated economic warfare to put the Japanese economy into a stranglehold from which, given the U.S. ultimatum regarding the Sino-Japanese war, the Japanese government could extricate itself only by making a humiliating withdrawal from Japan's hard-won gains on the Asian mainland or by breaking free of the U.S.-British-Dutch economic embargo by taking extremely risky military countermeasures. These facts surely have a causal bearing on the Japanese decision to attack Pearl Harbor, as intercepted Japanese diplomatic cables attest. For more recent events in general and for the 9/11 attacks in particular, we might ask: What had the U.S. government done in the Middle East to make so many Muslims willing to die for the sake of taking revenge against the United States? Anyone who has followed the news or dipped into the historical literature understands that for more than half a century the U.S. government has been vigorously meddling in the Middle East, making enemies right and left in the process (see, for example, Richman 1991[4] and Leebaert 2010[5]).

U.S. government officials always tell us, of course, that they are as pure as driven snow in their dealings with people abroad, that we Americans are invariably minding our own business and dispensing nothing but sweetness and light to everybody on earth regardless of race, color, and creed when crazed foreigners attack us for no reason at all except an insane hatred of our way of life. Even a superficial exposure to the pertinent facts exposes the government's official line as the sheerest fairy tale. Far from protecting us, the government has now spent more than a century busily making enemies for Americans around the globe. Some protection! If the government were a private security guard, we would have fired him in 1898 and never purchased his trigger-happy services again. Americans desperately need to clarify a basic distinction: protecting the just rights of Americans here in America and exercising a globe-girdling hegemony over other people are two different things.

---

4. Sheldon Richman, "'Ancient History': U.S. Conduct in the Middle East since World War II and the Folly of Intervention," *Cato Institute Policy Analysis No. 159* (Washington, DC: Cato Institute, August 16, 1991).

5. Derek Leebaert, *Magic and Mayhem: The Delusions of American Foreign Policy from Korea to Afghanistan* (New York: Simon and Schuster, 2010).

These observations lead to an even more fundamental question: What makes anyone think that government officials are even *trying* to protect us? A government is not analogous to a hired security guard. Governments do not come into existence as social service organizations or as private firms seeking to please consumers in a competitive market. Instead, they are born in conquest and nourished by plunder. They are, in short, well-armed gangs intent on organized crime. Yes, rulers have sometimes come to recognize the prudence of protecting the herd they are milking and even of improving its "infrastructure" until the day they decide to slaughter the young bulls, but the idea that government officials seek to promote my interests or yours is little more than propaganda—unless, of course, you happen to belong to the class of privileged tax eaters who give significant support to the government and therefore receive in return a share of the loot. For libertarians to have lost sight of the fundamental nature of the state and therefore to expect its kingpins selflessly to protect them from genuine foreign threats, much as a hen protects her chicks, challenges comprehension. Imagine: people who recognize full well that they cannot rely on the government to do something as simple as fixing the potholes nevertheless believe that they can rely on that same government to protect their lives, liberties, and property. One is tempted to conclude that by making this colossal mistake, they have demonstrated that they were never really libertarians in the first place.

In sum, the issue of war and peace does serve as a litmus test for libertarians. Warmongering libertarians are ipso facto not libertarians. Real libertarians do not expect pigs to fly: they do not believe the government's lies about the multitude of foreign fiends poised to pounce on us; they do not credit the government's promise to protect us from any real monsters that may exist beyond our borders; they do not even take seriously the government's declaration that its primary objective is to secure our rights against foreign invasion or other harm originating abroad.

During wartime, governments invariably trample on the people's just rights, disseminating so much propaganda to the abused citizens that they believe they are trading liberty for security. Yet time and again after the dust has settled, the U.S. government's wars have yielded the net result that Americans enjoy fewer liberties in the postbellum era than they enjoyed in the antebellum era. This ratchet effect must be expected to accompany every major military undertaking the U.S. government carries out. In every war with a decisive outcome, the people on both sides lose, the government on the losing side loses, and the government on the winning side wins. In light of these realities, what sort of libertarian wants to support the warfare state?

73

Freedom

Because It Works or because It's Right?

LIBERTARIANS DIVIDE INTO two broad classes: those who espouse a free society because it gives better results than an unfree society, and those who espouse a free society because they believe that it is wrong to deny or suppress a person's right to be free (unless, of course, that person is suppressing the equal right of others to be free). "Consequentialists versus deontologists" is the oft-encountered labeling of this difference. It is unfortunate that so much energy has been devoted to infighting between these two groups.

I first embraced libertarianism on utilitarian or consequentialist grounds related to my training as an economist. I was convinced that a free society—certainly in the long run, if not at every moment—would be healthier, wealthier, and happier than an unfree society. From economic theory and economic history, I came to understand the horrendous failures of the centrally planned economies in the USSR, China, and other countries. This understanding struck me as an adequate basis for anyone's embrace of libertarianism.

Lacking a solid background in philosophy, I did not spend much time thinking about the moral case for libertarianism, at least in the early stages of my journey. Yet no one really needed to persuade me that people by nature deserve to be free, that each person possesses a natural right to control his own life insofar as the exercise of that right does not conflict with other people's exercise of the same right. So, when I was first asked—more than twenty years ago as a panelist at a libertarian conference—whether I was a consequentialist or a deontologist in my libertarianism, I answered that I was both: I believed that people ought to respect other people's right to be free of aggression (the initiation of violence or the threat of violence) *and* that if everyone behaved in this way, people would attain the best possible social and economic outcomes for the whole society.

Over time, I found myself making moral arguments for libertarianism more and more frequently. In some ways, I was simply expressing the grounds for my outrage against one coercive evil after another of which I became aware. Yet I never surrendered my belief that a free society works better than an unfree society along many social and economic dimensions. I was also persuaded by the great rule-utilitarian Leland Yeager[1] that in the deepest possible sense, we must all be consequentialists. No one of good will can cling to the rule "fiat justitia ruat caelum" (let justice be done though the heavens fall) all the way down. If the most committed libertarian deontologist knew for certain that adherence to every critical element of libertarianism would entail, say, the utter destruction of the human race, even he would have to relent and to rest his decision on the consequences of a no-exceptions adherence to a normally binding moral rule.

Fortunately, this dilemma is one we do not face in reality. Indeed, almost always, if not always, we can follow the rule of perfect freedom and rest assured that not only will doing so not cause destructive outcomes, but it will actually conduce to the realization of the most constructive feasible outcomes.

In any event, after the more recent decades of my libertarian journey, I am now struck by a different aspect of this longstanding debate, which has to do with our *strategy* for winning people over to libertarianism. Strategy 1 is to persuade them that freedom works, that a free society will be richer and otherwise better off than an unfree society; that a free market will, as it were, cause the trains to run on time better than a government bureaucracy will do so. Strategy 2 is to persuade people that no one, not even a government functionary, has a just right to interfere with innocent people's freedom of action; that none of us was born with a saddle on his back to accommodate someone else's riding him.

In our world, so many people have been confused or misled by faulty claims about morality and justice that most libertarians, especially in the think tanks

---

1. Leland Yeager, *Ethics as Social Science: The Moral Philosophy of Social Cooperation* (Northampton, MA: Edward Elgar Publishing, 2002).

and other organizations that carry much of the burden of education about libertarianism, concentrate their efforts on pursuing Strategy 1 as effectively as possible. Hence they produce policy studies galore, each showing how the government has fouled up a market or another situation by its ostensibly well-intentioned laws and regulations. Of course, the 98 percent or more of society (especially in its political aspect) that in one way or another opposes perfect freedom responds with policy studies of its own, each showing why an alleged "market failure," "social injustice," or other problem warrants the government's interference with people's freedom of action, and each promising to remedy the perceived evils. Anyone who pays attention to policy debates is familiar with the ensuing, never-ending war of the wonks. I myself have done a fair amount of such work, so I am not condemning it. As one continues to expose the defects of anti-freedom arguments and the failures of government efforts to "solve" a host of problems, one hopes that someone will be persuaded and become willing to give freedom a chance.

Nevertheless, precisely because the war of the wonks—not to mention the professors, pundits, columnists, political hacks, and intellectual hired guns—is never-ending, one can never rest assured that once a person has been persuaded that freedom works better, at least in regard to situation X, that person has been won over to libertarianism permanently. If a person has come over only because of evidence and argument adduced yesterday by a pro-freedom wonk, he may just as easily go back to his support for government intervention tomorrow on the basis of evidence and argument adduced by an anti-freedom wonk. As John Maynard Keynes once cleverly replied to someone who asked him about his fluctuating views, "When the facts change, I change my mind. What do you do, sir?" If libertarians choose to fight for freedom solely on consequentialist grounds, they will be at war forever. Although one may accept this prospect on the grounds that "eternal vigilance is the price of liberty," this kind of war is deeply discouraging, given that the anti-freedom forces with which libertarians must contend possess hundreds of times more troops and thousands of times more money for purchasing munitions.

In contrast, once the libertarian has persuaded someone that government interference is wrong, at least in a certain realm, if not across the board, there is a much smaller probability of that convert's backsliding into his former support for government's coercive measures against innocent people. Libertarianism grounded on the moral rock will prove much stronger and longer-lasting than libertarianism grounded on the shifting sands of consequentialist arguments, which of necessity are only as compelling as today's arguments and evidence make them. Hence, if we desire to enlarge the libertarian ranks, we are well advised to make moral arguments *at least* a part of our efforts. It will not hurt, of course, to show people that freedom really does work better than state control. But to confine our efforts to wonkism dooms them to transitory success, at best.

If we are ever to attain a free society, we must persuade a great many of our fellows that it is simply wrong for any individuals or groups, by violence or the threat thereof, to impose their demands on others who have committed no crime and violated no one's just rights, and that it is just as wrong for the persons who compose the state to do so as it is for you and me. In the past, the great victories for liberty flowed from precisely such an approach—for example, in the anti-slavery campaign, in the fight against the Corn Laws (which restricted the British people's free trade in grain), and in the struggle to abolish legal restrictions on women's rights to work, own property, and otherwise conduct themselves as freely as men. At the very least, libertarians should never concede the moral high ground to those who insist on coercively interfering with freedom: the burden of proof should always rest on those who seek to bring violence to bear against innocent people, not on those of us who want simply to be left alone to live our lives as we think best, always respecting the same right for others.

74

The Salmon Trap

An Analogy for People's Entrapment by the State

A SALMON TRAP (also known as a pound net) is a setup for
catching salmon as they return to their spawning places in the gravel beds of
shallow inland streams. Such traps were used in Washington and Oregon until
they were outlawed[1]—by Oregon in 1926 and by Washington in 1934—and
in Alaska until they were banned in 1959. They were highly efficient arrangements for harvesting salmon, outlawed only because the operators of competing types of gear and sportsmen's groups ultimately had more political clout.

The traps can be constructed in various ways, but a common type was a
carefully shaped arrangement of netting or wire mesh secured to driven piles,
usually placed not far from shore along observed migration paths of returning salmon (see Figure 74.1). The "lead" was a straight fence of netting, often
several hundred feet long, extending from the bottom to the high-water level
and running in a direction approximately perpendicular to the shoreline.
After encountering the lead, the salmon swam along it toward the shore into
the "outer heart," a V-shaped semi-enclosed arrangement of netting; proceed-
ing through the outer heart toward the shore, they squeezed into the "inner
heart," another V-shaped enclosure from which the only avenue of escape
was the narrow passage through which they had entered. (Some traps had no
inner heart.) From the inner heart, the determined salmon, whose instinctual
reluctance to turn in their own wake made the traps so effective, proceeded
through a narrowing tunnel into the "pot," a shallow holding area from which
almost no fish could escape. Some traps had a "spiller" adjacent to the pot,

1. Robert Higgs, "Legally Induced Technical Regress in the Washington Salmon Fishery," *Research in Economic History* 7 (1982): 55–86.

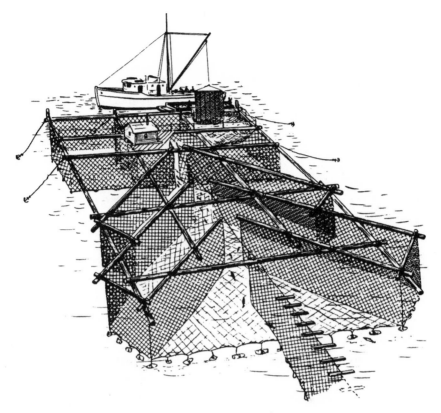

Figure 74.1. A salmon trap, also known as a pound net.

and connected with it by another tunnel, to facilitate emptying the captured fish into a scow. A few traps, so-called double-enders, had hearts and pots at both ends of the lead.

I have often pondered the analogy between the salmon's being caught in a trap and a human population's being caught in the institutional arrangement we call big government. Just as the salmon trap's lead intercepts the fish in the course of their normal life cycle and directs them into captivity, so various political devices and entreaties intercept people in the course of their normal life and direct them toward dependence on the state. Salmon instinctively strive to return to their spawning places. Human beings strive to get wealth and security, and if they can get something seemingly for nothing, they may deviate from a normal, self-supporting life and support political appeals for plundering their fellows via the state. Only when it is too late, if ever, do people realize that the plunder-masters who have enticed them into supporting the expansion of government's size, scope, and power are, along with their chief cronies in the private sector, the only ones who truly gain. The masses of duped people find themselves caught in a trap, dependent on the state for everything from food, housing, and medical care to the education of their children and security in their old age.

Like the narrowing opening through which the salmon enter the "hearts" of the traps, the ways out of people's helplessness and dependence on the state are narrow and hard to locate. Moreover, going out as they came in flies in the face of their natural proclivity to live at others' expense and care. As the salmon's "mind" tells him not to turn back, so the human mind, especially when it has been bewitched by government propaganda and statist ideology, tells people not to turn back. Having lost the capacity for assuming individual responsibility, people are fearful of taking on such responsibilities as their forebears bore routinely.

Ultimately, people find themselves in something like the salmon trap's pot, an enclosure in which they can be disposed of as their captors decide. All imaginable avenues of escape have been eliminated by design, so that people can only mill about, dreaming perhaps of salvation, but unable to overcome the barriers the state and their own thinking place in the way of their true liberation.

People would do well to acquire a keener appreciation of institutional path dependency, especially of the irreversibilities inherent in political and institutional arrangements. It is very often much easier to get into something than it is to get out of it. To retain their liberty, self-reliance, and self-respect, people might well remember the poor salmon and skirt the leads that political plunderers construct to divert them from their normal, decent ways of life. Having entered the "heart" of the state, people have little chance of escape, even if they should seek to do so.

75

Libertarian Wishful Thinking

AS A RULE, libertarians incline toward wishful thinking. They constantly pluck little events, statements, and movie scenes from the flow of life and cry out, "Eureka! Libertarianism is on the march!" With some of my friends, this tendency is so marked that I have become amused by its recurrent expression—well, there he goes again!

Some of this tendency springs, I believe, from their immersion in abstract thought and writing. Many of them have read hundreds of books and articles on libertarianism itself or on closely related ideas and personalities. They love to point out that ideology controls everything and to remark that as soon as we can bring a substantial minority over to our way of thinking, the whole social and political apparatus will tip from tyranny into liberty—rather as the old Eastern European satellites of the USSR (seemingly) abandoned their Communist regimes and substituted much less oppressive regimes almost overnight, in most cases with little bloodshed.

Although I agree that ultimately ideology controls many other elements in social and political affairs, I do not agree that ideology in the Western welfare-warfare states is nearly as fragile as Communist ideology was in the old Soviet satellites. Libertarians rarely invest much time in the detailed study of how the dominant ideology is generated and maintained in the contemporary West. Even fewer of them dig into the detailed composition and operation of the many economic, social, and political institutions that are tied in countless ways into reliance on and support of the politico-economic status quo. Hundreds of thousands of such organized efforts go on every day all over the country at every level. One has only to thumb through the telephone directory for the Washington, D.C., area to gain an impression of the amazing array of well-organized, well-funded special-interest groups now working ceaselessly, in effect, to keep all attempts to restore liberty at bay and if possible to bind individuals down by additional legal restraints and obligations. Participatory fascism in the contemporary United States and other advanced Western countries is an arrangement so vast and far-reaching that it defies the grasp of any single researcher. Specialists can easily work full-time in simply trying to understand the workings of one tentacle among the thousands that the beast possesses.

To suppose that an overnight ideological conversion or "tipping" can remove all of these organizations from the scene or lead them to alter their objectives and modus operandi is fanciful beyond imagination. To borrow from the vernacular, it just ain't gonna happen. For it to do so would amount to the most preposterous instance of the tail wagging the dog in human history. Communist regimes could be (seemingly) tipped because Communism was widely recognized as a failure, a recipe for societal backwardness and a low level of living. After its initial revolutionary surge of support, its ideological underpinnings grew weaker and weaker with each passing year and, by the 1980s, not many true believers remained.

Such is not at all the case in the West today. Here nearly everybody is held tightly in the system by countless seemly beneficial ties that few people can imagine doing without: Who'll send grandma a monthly check to keep her in groceries? Who'll provide medical care for the scores of millions of lower-income people whose care now comes via Medicaid? Who'll cover the huge medical bills the elderly now expect Medicare to pay? Who'll subsidize the college loans on which millions of students rely? And so on and on. One has only to wade through the Code of Federal Regulations and ask on each page: if this particular regulation were scrapped today, how would its corporate and union beneficiaries react? Can one really imagine that the people who control these powerful institutions would simply shrug their shoulders if liberty should break out, after having fought for more than a century to forge the fetters that now bind the populace in the service of almost innumerable special interests?

One who maintains, as I do, that the existing system may crumble little by little, having heedlessly sowed thousands of poisonous seeds of its own destruction, but almost certainly will never just roll over and admit defeat, may seem to be a defeatist. But nothing is gained by entertaining an unrealistic view of what liberty lovers are up against. Even if one believes, as I do, that the existing system is not viable in the very long run, it may last in episodically patched-up forms for a long, long time. There are no magic bullets, such as abolishing the Fed. The state can use other means in the highly unlikely event that it should no longer have the Fed in its arsenal. The same can be said about most of the system's other key elements.

In truth, the time for liberty lovers to make a stand that had a fighting chance of success was a century ago. But that chance was squandered, if indeed it packed much punch even then. Powerful economic, institutional, and ideological currents were working against it then, and by now those currents, swelled by the self-interested efforts of several generations of statists in positions of great power and influence, have grown into a mighty river. This fascistic Rome wasn't built in a day, and it wasn't built by accident, either. It is not so flimsy that it will collapse because someone gives a libertarian-sounding speech in the Senate, because thousands of powerless college students turn out to hear Ron Paul speak, or because a writer embeds a libertarian sentiment in a film script. These things, however much they may cheer the libertarian heart, are the equivalent of the proverbial sparrow pecking at a pyramid. Wishful thinking about the impending triumph of liberty may be uplifting for libertarians, but it avails neither them nor the world anything of real importance.

76

"There Were Giants
in the Earth in Those Days"

Genesis 6:4

THERE ARE NOW many more libertarians in the world than there were fifty years ago. Libertarian writing has increased greatly, and the readership of libertarian literature has increased substantially, especially since the development and widespread adoption of the Internet and the World Wide Web. Yet, it seems to me, we no longer have libertarians of the same stature as the giants of the past two or three generations. Where today are the libertarians comparable to Ludwig von Mises, F. A. Hayek, Milton Friedman, Murray Rothbard, James Buchanan, and Thomas Szasz?

I am not saying that today's leading libertarians are chopped liver; not at all. Indeed, some are very impressive in their scholarship, public expression of libertarian ideas and policy proposals, and recruitment of young people to the movement. To avoid seeming to make invidious comparisons, I refrain here from naming names, but rest assured that I have the greatest respect for a number of currently active men and women.

Still, I do not consider any of them to be in the same league with the six I've identified. Mises's scholarship was truly fundamental, especially in regard to the socialist calculation problem and the analysis of the boom–bust cycle, and his efforts in keeping classical liberalism and Austrian economics alive during their darkest hours were genuinely heroic. Hayek's scholarship was similarly impressive, and he did much to combat immensely popular yet pernicious developments in economics, social and political theory, and other areas. Friedman, besides producing tremendously influential scholarship in monetary theory and history, played an important role in the termination of military conscription in the United States. Rothbard was indefatigable in research, writing, and rabble-rousing, and he was the clear leader in regenerating the libertarian movement when it was on its last legs. Buchanan compelled the mainstream of the economics profession to recognize that in the study of public affairs, government cannot be treated as a miracle-working alternative to "imperfect" markets; and during his long, amazingly prolific career, he created a flourishing new subfield of economic analysis—public choice—to analyze and in effect to debunk what he called the "romantic" view dominant among contemporary welfare economists and political scientists. Szasz wrote (probably) thousands of articles and dozens of books in which he contributed at every level of analysis and discussion to exposing the unholy alliance between the psychiatric profession (and its main ideas) and the state. He did more than anyone to create and energize the movement to release innocent people from imprisonment in so-called psychiatric hospitals.

Who among today's leading libertarians has so much to his or her credit? I am aware, of course, that Ron Paul has recruited many young people to the libertarian cause during the past few years, and he certainly deserves our gratitude for having done so. But Paul (until very recently) was a politician leading a political campaign, not a fundamental thinker in his own right. His contribution to libertarianism is therefore bound to be transitory. Other contemporary libertarians have cut much smaller figures. Most have only a tiny following among subject specialists or die-hard libertarians in a little sect. One or two, such as John Stossel, are known more widely, but Stossel is only a mouthpiece for ideas others have developed—an effective mouthpiece, to be sure, but, again, someone whose effect on the world certainly must have a very short half-life.

Of course, each libertarian has his present-day favorites. Some of them are obviously penetrating thinkers and powerful writers and speakers. Yet, unless I have greatly misperceived the recent history of libertarianism, none of them comes close to the giants of the immediately preceding generations.

77

The Rodney Dangerfields
of the Ideological Universe

LIBERTARIAN ANARCHISTS ARE the Rodney Dangerfields
of the ideological universe. Born and reared in a world pervaded by the state
and statism, we must fight our way through a dense jungle of clinging, collectivist vines, obscured by murky, mendacious propaganda, and populated
by brainwashed lizards, political opportunists, and a multitude of wormy
moochers. If we are hardy and continue to hack our way toward the light
of truth, we ultimately grasp an understanding of the state in all its violent,
unscrupulous, and shameless glory. Our reward for these arduous efforts,
however, is being seen as kooks and weirdos, at best, and all too often as un-
washed, bomb-throwing vandals bent on senseless acts of destruction. I tell
ya, we don't get no respect at all.

Anyone who defends any form of freedom from the state, much less someone who espouses the state's abolition, quickly encounters a standard set of
baseless comebacks. The first, of course, is the progressive knee jerk, the claim
that we are nothing but shills for soulless corporations that are raping the
world for the exclusive benefit of a handful of corporate plutocrats who already
possess almost all of the world's wealth and will not rest until they have
snatched the remainder and despoiled the environment in the process. It's a
life's work merely to explain some basic economics to these nincompoops, to
enlighten them to the startling news—well known at least since Adam Smith
discussed it clearly in the latter half of the eighteenth century—that business
people are typically the free market's greatest enemies, and to clarify that
libertarians endorse the free market, not the corporate privileges, subsidies,
and legal protections from competition that now masquerade in the guise of
"capitalism."

Next, if not indeed first in the litany of statist reactions, comes the personal attack on our sincerity. If we really do not believe in the state's various involvements in social and economic life, why do we ourselves drive on public streets, attend public schools, drink water purified in public water-treatment plants, and so forth—a list whose limits are defined only by the endurance of our critics in enumerating the countless elements of contemporary life run or regulated by the state. In view of the nature of the world in which we live—the world into which we had the temerity to be born, blameless for its accumulated sins—the indictment is basically that we libertarian anarchists are hypocrites for continuing to live at all, given the manifold "benefits" that we enjoy owing to the state's provisions, requirements, and prohibitions. How dare we live in this world! As the yahoos like to say, "Why don't you filthy anarchists go back where you came from?"

I tell ya, it taxes our patience that we must explain again and again that simply because we happened to be born into this twisted, hyper-politicized world, we bear no responsibility for its current configuration. We have been taxed, fined, charged, bullied, and tricked into providing our pro rata share of the resources with which it sustains its ugly self, yet, if our critics be credited, we have no right whatever to enjoy any of its benefits. I don't want to be unkind to people of limited intellectual capacity, but I must say, I'm getting a bit tired of their idiocy in this regard. Do they really think that after having been taxed to support the Social Security system throughout my working lifetime, I would be a hypocrite to draw a miserable pension from it? I didn't create this damned Ponzi scheme. If I had been asked—which I was not in regard to this or any of the state's other criminal enterprises—I would have said, don't create this monstrosity. Had I been asked whether road building should be left to private enterprise, I would have said yes, it should be. Had I been asked whether the state should be involved in education, I would have said that it absolutely should not be; and so forth, right down the line from A to Z of the alphabet of state interventions. But, again, I was not consulted. Statists and their supporters created this world. My fate was to be tossed into it, only to realize, in the fullness of time, how utterly fouled up it is owing to the state's pervasive involvement in it.

Punishment is unpleasant even when one has sinned and has it coming, but punishment—and even relentless, ignorant criticism—is even worse when one's only crime is that one has, after long and difficult effort, pried open his eyes to see the state and its actions for what they are: the emperor that has no clothes, the falsest of false gods, the fairy tale that nearly everybody believes even though it consists of little more than fantastic counter-factual claims and dreamy wishful thinking.

78

Classical Liberalism's Impossible Dream

I CAN UNDERSTAND why someone might embrace classical liberalism. I did so myself more than forty years ago. People become classical liberals for two main reasons, which are interrelated: first, because they come to understand that free markets "work" better than government-controlled economic systems in providing prosperity and domestic peace; second, because people come to believe that they may justifiably claim (along more or less Lockean lines) rights to life, liberty, and property. These two reasons are interrelated because the Lockean rights provide the foundation required for free markets to exist and operate properly.

Like Locke, classical liberals recognize that some persons may violate others' rights to life, liberty, and property and that some means of defending these rights adequately must be employed. On this basis they accept government (as we know it), but only with the proviso that the government must be limited to protecting people against force and fraud that would unjustly deprive them of life, liberty, and property. They believe that government (as we know it) can perform these functions, whereas private individuals without such government would be at the mercy of predators and hence that their lives would be, as Hobbes supposed, solitary, poor, nasty, brutish, and short. Nobody wants that.

So, to repeat, I can understand why someone might become a classical liberal. However, as the years have passed, I have had increasing difficulty in understanding why someone would remain a classical liberal, rather than making the further move to embrace genuine self-government in place of the classical liberal's objective, "limited government." My difficulty arises not so much from a dissatisfaction with government's being charged with protecting the citizens from force and fraud, but from a growing conviction that government (as we know it) does not, on balance, actually carry out these tasks and, worse, that it does not even try to carry them out except in a desultory and insincere way—indeed, as a ruse.

Truth be told, government as we know it never did and never will confine itself to protecting citizens from force and fraud. In fact, such government is itself the worst violator of people's just rights to life, liberty, and property.[1] For every murder or assault the government prevents, it commits a hundred. For every private property right it protects, it violates a thousand. Although it purports to suppress and punish fraud, the government itself is a fraud writ large—an enormous engine of plunder, abuse, and mayhem, all sanctified by its own "laws" that redefine its crimes as mere government activities—a racket protected from true justice by its own judges and its legions of hired killers and thugs.

Confronted with these horrors, the classical liberal takes a deep breath and resolves to seek "reforms" of government's "misguided" and "counter-productive" actions and policies. However, the dedicated classical liberal steadfastly refuses to recognize that such government's actions are anything but misguided; indeed, the government acts to attain its true objectives ever so directly, and it quickly discontinues anything that fails to enrich and empower its own leaders and their key cronies in the so-called private sector (which is something of a myth, given the government's pervasive interference in it). The government's actions and programs are not at all "counter-productive," once we recognize that its declared objective of serving the general public interest was never meant to do anything but serve as a smokescreen for its robbing and bullying the general public. What economists and others call "government failure"[2] is nothing of the sort, but only a failure to do what in reality the government's movers and shakers never had the slightest intention of doing in the first place.

In sum, the classical liberal who, in the face of these realities, clings to the myth of Lockean limited government would seem to be a person irrationally devoted to sheer wishful thinking. Dreams have their place in human life, no

---

1. Robert Higgs, *Against Leviathan: Government Power and a Free Society* (Oakland, CA: Independent Institute, 2004).

2. Robert Higgs, "The Myth of 'Failed' Policies," *The Free Market*, 13, no.6 (1995).

doubt, but the dream of a government (as we know it) that confines itself to its Lockean functions and stays so confined is a dream that never was and never can be realized. At some point, people must open their eyes to this emperor's nakedness—and, indeed, to the emperor's viciousness, brutality, and utter, systematic injustice. Otherwise, classical liberals do little more than provide objects of amusement for the cynical men and woman who control the government and employ its powers in the service of their own aggrandizement and aggressive caprice.

Addendum: When I speak of "government (as we know it)," I mean government as it now exists virtually everywhere and as it has existed in many places for thousands of years—a government that claims a monopoly of legitimate force in a certain territory and does not rest on the explicit, individual, voluntary consent of every adult subject to its authority. I contrast this type of government with "genuine self-government," which does have the explicit, individual, voluntary consent of every adult subject to its authority.

79

Why the Precautionary Principle
Counsels Us to Renounce Statism

I PROPOSE THAT the state be replaced by genuine self-government and immediately people come forth with a litany of objections—your
proposal is a pipe dream; it is untried; it would never work; it fails to solve
problem R and problem S; and so forth. So the objectors, however much they
may concede that the state conducts itself atrociously, always conclude that
they prefer it to any proposed alternative.

What none of the objectors ever recognizes, in my experience, is that
retention of the state as it now exists and conducts itself is practically a guarantee of humanity's ultimate destruction. Why? Because state leaders, especially in the so-called "great powers," are drawn to destructive weapons
more instinctively than moths are drawn to a fire. Indeed, not only do they
clamor to obtain the currently most destructive weapons, but they invest
huge amounts of resources in the search for even more destructive weapons
(see, for example, the painstaking study[1] of the U.S. nuclear weapons arsenal
by Stephen I. Schwartz and his collaborators). The leading powers have built
up stupendous arsenals of weapons of mass destruction (WMDs), far more
than enough to destroy civilization on earth. A glance back through history
strongly suggests that state leaders who possess the most destructive weapons
will, sooner or later, use them. Therefore, as the mad scientists at work in
the military-industrial-congressional complex[2] continue to create ever more
horrifying weapons, we can be virtually certain that ultimately those weapons

---

1. Stephen I. Schwartz, *Atomic Audit: The Costs and Consequences of U.S. Nuclear Weapons Since 1940* (Washington D.C.: Brookings Institution Press, 1998).

2. *Arms, Politics, and the Economy: Historical and Contemporary Perspectives*, ed. Robert
Higgs (New York: Holmes & Meier, 1990).

will be used. Eventually a weapon with the capacity to destroy human life will be devised and used—indeed, an all-out nuclear war between the USA and the USSR, an event that was averted only by the narrowest of margins on several occasions,[3] might have been sufficient to destroy humanity, owing to its effects on global climate, especially its creation of "nuclear winter."

So, statists of all stripes (including classical liberals), by all means continue to reject genuine self-government and carry on with support of your blessed state. But know well that you are flirting with the most horrifyingly destructive institution ever devised, one that will almost certainly annihilate everyone in the end. Statist ideologies justify and support the state as a military/bureaucratic apparatus whose leaders are not held to the moral standards to which all other persons are commonly held. By making this wholly unwarranted moral distinction, the adherents of such ideologies place state leaders in a position to prepare for and to carry out actions that, if committed by anyone else, would be recognized immediately as the most egregious crimes against humanity. Statism, which leads people to tolerate the development, deployment, and use of WMDs, poses a grave threat to the survival of the human species.

Given that the state is a vicious institution even in the absence of this danger and that, contrary to statist ideologies, it is neither necessary nor desirable for the maintenance of peaceful and prosperous societies, the risk that the state poses on account of its WMDs is one that decent, rational people should not tolerate.

---

3. "Close Calls—Mishaps That Nearly Led to Nuclear War," MHN, March 12, 2014, http://militaryhistorynow.com/2014/03/12/close-calls-incidents-that-nearly-led-to-nuclear-war/

80

Modern Communications Technology— Savior or Soma?

IN RECENT YEARS, I have noticed that many—seemingly a great majority—of my libertarian friends express an optimistic outlook that sooner or later freedom will triumph against tyranny, even in the United States of America, because of technological developments, especially the development of the Internet and the World Wide Web, along with all the hardware and software that facilitate these means of communication and expand their reach. The idea seems to be, at bottom, that technology in general and these technologies in particular are intrinsically anti-state and pro-freedom. Some people regard them as decisive factors in the struggle for liberty. I have never been persuaded.

The Internet and the Web are obviously employed to some extent for anti-state and pro-freedom purposes. Probably their most important effect is to loosen the state's hold on information about its leaders, their motives, and their actions, and thereby to speed the spread of truth to greater numbers of people who might otherwise have been taken in by the rulers' habitual resort to distortions, evasions, cover-ups, and outright lies. Such fabrications have always proved most useful to the U.S. state in its foreign relations and imperial actions, where the matters at issue are out of sight of the great mass of Americans. Because the new technologies of communication are not only powerful—allowing the instant transmission of photos, audio recordings, and video recordings, as well as written texts—but also available worldwide, they have the power to prick the state's balloons of misrepresentation about events abroad in short order.

Despite these anti-state effects, one must recognize that the state itself has hardly remained mired in ancient technologies while the public embraced the new ones. Drive from Dulles International Airport to Washington, D.C., and peer out at the huge office buildings inhabited in many cases by information technology companies that have put themselves—for a handsome reward, of course—at the disposal of the U.S. government. The rulers have in the past decade added to their longstanding military-industrial-congressional complex (MICC) a comparably vast security-industrial-congressional complex[1] (SICC). Perhaps the individual and small-scale tech wizards working their magic in the non-state backwoods will always remain a step or two ahead of the CSCs, Microsofts, and Oracles; I don't know enough about technology to speculate on this "IT arms race" in an informed way. I do know, however, that the state is not standing helplessly in place while the pro-freedom people innovate so as to render it toothless.

Much more important, however, is that whereas the new information technologies can spread information in the raw, as it were, they cannot so readily alter the mental filters—essentially the ideological screening and focusing—that the public uses to interpret and evaluate the information it receives. Consider, for example, the public's reaction to the recent disclosures about the state's all-encompassing spying on the American people's electronic communications, whether by ordinary telephone calls, e-mails, or other means. At this point, the situation appears to be that the rulers have unashamedly excused their unconstitutional conduct and painted the bearer of the bad news, Edward Snowden, as a traitor for exposing their secret snooping on one and all without warrant or any plausible reason, aside from technological overkill in the alleged search for terrorists; and the public appears to be more approving than condemning. Revealing the state's crimes serves no purpose in preserving or reestablishing liberty if the public receives such revelations with a yawn or, worse, with enthusiastic approval.

---

1. Robert Higgs, "The Security-Industrial-Congressional Complex (SICC)," Independent Institute, October 19, 2006, http://www.independent.org/newsroom/article.asp?id=1835.

It is instructive to compare modern communications technologies and firearms as means of preserving liberty. The Founding Fathers expressed great faith in the power of an armed populace to resist tyrannical government. They went so far as to embed this conviction in the Bill of Rights. Yet, even though Americans have always been and remain today armed to the teeth, these guns have availed them nothing in the preservation of their liberties, which the state has steadily, and sometimes abruptly, stripped from them. Even if the armed populace had risen up, guns in hand, to resist these invasions of their rights, however, they would have been defeated by the state and its legions of more heavily armed police and troops. It is silly to suppose that today the people's being armed provides any protection of their rights whatsoever against the state's violations.

What decides the issue in the end is neither guns nor information technologies, but the people's ideologies. These belief systems, however foggy and ill-formulated they are for most people, determine how people "see" the world, how they evaluate what they "see" as good, bad, or neutral, what political actions or programs they embrace in response to their understandings and evaluations and, finally, what personal identities they adopt as members of political or ideological communities of like-minded comrades. If people's ideologies are friendly to a vast, invasive state, as they are to an overwhelming degree in today's United States, flooding them with information will avail nothing in the struggle against an overweening state. They will either dismiss anti-state information as worthless to them—the product of cranks and crazies—or, worse, they will perceive those who spread such information as acting in opposition to what they believe to be proper, protective, and productive for the state to do. Indeed, they may look upon those who spread anti-state information as they now look upon Edward Snowden, as traitors.

Of course, the new communications technologies can deliver not simply raw information, but also ideological argumentation. In this way, many libertarians seem to believe, the public can be detached from their statism and brought over to pro-liberty views. In some cases such conversions may occur. On the whole, however, this view of how people adopt or give up an ideology is highly oversimplified. Only for a relatively small group of people—those unusually given to rational thought and self-education and unusually immune to social and cultural pressures—will such conversion by education be possible. In general, people's ideologies reflect not only intellectual and informational factors, but also, and usually more significantly, the nature of their own experience.[2] If, for example, their lives are going swimmingly, they have good jobs, and they are not being personally bothered by police or other state functionaries, they will be disinclined to raise serious questions about the state's actions, however criminal those actions may seem to others. If life is good, electronic toys are abundant, and entertainment is nonstop, why should they concern themselves with the state's mayhem in places beyond their immediate milieu?

Indeed, by providing unlimited means of diverting the public with funny videos, full-length movies, photos of cute cats or of rabbits nursing piglets, porn galore, and all the rest of the "information" transmitted in overwhelming volume by the Internet and the Web, people need never take any interest whatsoever in politics and the state's shenanigans. What's it to them? As the saying goes, If they've done nothing wrong, they have nothing to worry about. Thus, although the new technologies have the capacity to awaken people—to be more precise, certain sorts of people in certain sorts of circumstances—they also have the capacity to lull billions of people worldwide into a virtual coma of apathy in regard to the state. In the dystopia of Aldous Huxley's Brave New World, people were lulled into contentment by popping a soma. Today's amazing communications technologies, notwithstanding their potential power to aid resistance to the state, may have an even more powerful capacity to serve as the modern state's soma.

---

2. Robert Higgs, *Neither Liberty Nor Safety: Fear, Ideology, and the Growth of Government* (Oakland, CA: Independent Institute, 2007), 65–80.

81

On My Libertarian Catholicity

SINCE THE LATE 1970s, I have been working in some capacity with think tanks and similar organizations that one might view as interested in education, research, and advocacy in the broad area of classical liberal, libertarian, and free-market thinking. One does not have to follow such organizations very long to discover that they differ in various ways, so much so that some of them—or, at least, some of their friends and supporters—look on others with a very jaundiced eye. A few might even appear to be sworn enemies.

My position, from which I have never deviated, despite strong temptations to do so on certain occasions, has been to steer clear of such intramural squabbling except in one regard—support for unnecessary war, which I consider so terribly misguided and destructive of life and liberty that I cannot tolerate it. In my mind, the great enemy of freedom, decency, and humanity is the state, not other classical liberals or libertarians. Much energy is wasted in intergroup mud slinging that could be expended better in efforts to expose the state's many evils and to bring the libertarian perspective to the fore among the many people who have yet to encounter, understand, or value it.

Over the years I have worked off and on with about three dozen different think tanks and similar groups as a compensated writer, editor, lecturer, and conference participant. With some of them I have worked steadily or frequently; with others I have worked only once or a few times. However, to my knowledge, none of these organizations has been so displeased with the work I have done for it that its managers have cast me officially into ideological outer darkness. So, I apparently remain on civilized speaking terms with all of them, and hence, with only two or three exceptions, I would, if the terms suited me, be willing to work for them again.

To satisfy my curiosity, I have combed through my resume to identify the various think tanks and similar organizations for which I have worked in the capacities noted previously over the past thirty-five years or so. Here is the list I've compiled, with the organizations listed in no particular order:

- Hoover Institution (Stanford University)
- Cato Institute
- Pacific Research Institute for Public Policy
- Reason Foundation
- Institute for Humane Studies
- Sequoia Institute
- Liberty Fund
- Ludwig von Mises Institute
- Intercollegiate Studies Institute
- Charles G. Koch Foundation
- Independent Institute
- Heritage Foundation
- Free Enterprise Institute
- Institute for Research on the Economics of Taxation
- Competitive Enterprise Institute
- Foundation for Economic Education
- Foundation for Teaching Economics
- American Enterprise Institute
- Future of Freedom Foundation
- Center for Study of Public Choice (George Mason University)
- Young America's Foundation
- Liberales Institut der Friedrich-Naumann-Stiftung (Germany)
- Liberální Institut (Czech Republic)
- Universidad Francisco Marroquín (Guatemala)

- Mont Pelerin Society
- Mercatus Center (George Mason University)
- Fundación Libertad Panamá (Panama)
- New York City Junto
- Property and Freedom Society (Turkey)
- Federalist Society
- Center for Creative Alternatives (Hillsdale College)
- Manhattan Institute
- National Center for Policy Analysis

Perhaps other people who do the same kind of work that I do have charted an equally catholic course in their relations with such organizations, but at the moment I cannot think of anyone who has done so.

For young economists and other professionals just getting involved in the world of classical liberal, libertarian, and free-market research, education, and advocacy, I recommend this course of action. Of course, those who follow it will find that they often disagree in some regard with what appears to be an organization's stance, but they ought to understand that finding an organization with which they invariably agree is well-nigh impossible if they are genuinely independent thinkers. At least, I have never found myself in universal agreement in any case, although some organizations have made me feel a great deal more comfortable than others.

Often people who are unfamiliar with how such organizations function assume that each of them has an official line that it seeks to promote and that therefore anyone who works with an organization must adhere to this line in every regard. I have never found such comprehensive agreement to be either demanded or supplied. No organization has ever told me what to say or how to say it. I have invariably spoken my mind as freely in doing this sort of work as I have in any other situation, such as university teaching. Moreover, it should be obvious to any but the most slipshod observer that the usual case in think tanks is that their researchers, writers, and affiliated scholars have some disagreements; that is, the organization in fact enforces no rigid official line. Of course, each has its boundaries. Free-market think tanks do not sponsor advocacy of socialist central planning or the nationalization of private property, for example. Yet, in most such organizations, a substantial amount of internal diversity exists within these broad boundaries. And such is hardly surprising: anyone who has lived among scholars and researchers knows that they are somewhat prickly about their ideas and harder to herd than cats.

Besides encouraging young economists and other professionals to adopt a catholic stance in regard to working with various groups, I encourage outsiders who encounter squabbling among the various groups' adherents to look askance on such free-market or libertarian in-fighting. Not that all sides are equally right; far from it. But spending a great deal of time and energy in such fraternal squabbling is a poor use of one's personal resources. And, most important, it does little or nothing to lead one any closer to the ultimate goal of exposing the state's destructive character more fully and spreading this knowledge to a wider audience.

PART VIII

Remembrances
of Parents, Teachers,
Colleagues, and Comrades

82

William Jess Higgs

(March 21, 1909–October 15, 1977)

I'M NOT OLD. If you think I am, just ask my wife, and she'll straighten you out pretty quickly. Nevertheless, there is no denying that my father was born exactly one hundred years ago, just seventeen days after William Howard Taft became president of the United States. Looking back now, most of us have trouble imagining the world of 1909, and as I ponder my direct link to it, I have a strange feeling of a time long, long ago, yet not so long. Although my father died in 1977, many other Americans born in 1909—more than 79,000 of them—are still alive today.

William Jess Higgs (always known as Jess) does not appear on anybody's list of great men. Good thing, too, given the truth of Lord Acton's declaration that "great men are almost always bad men." (A statement whose truth, by the way, hinges on the assumption that Acton's reference to "great men" pertains to men who occupy positions of great governmental power. Who can dispute that William Shakespeare or J. S. Bach was a great man?) Jess never cast a shadow in the halls of power, nor did he wish to do so. When I was growing up and got old enough to think I knew something about politics and to express opinions about politicians, he used to infuriate me by simply saying, "They're all crooks." I'd think, What does he know about it? Fifty years later, I am inclined to think that he knew practically everything he needed to know about politicians.

Born in the backwoods of Muskogee County, Oklahoma, unable to attend school after a brief attendance at grade school, thrust at a tender age into the position of the family farm's chief worker by the death of his father and later by the death of his stepfather, Jess lived in the world of work. And he was very good at working: when I was growing up, I never knew him to miss a day of work. I always supposed that he was happiest when he was at work. He was reputed to be an excellent farmer, among many other things.

The range of things he knew how to do—to grow, to build, to repair—never ceased to amaze me. I used to look over his shoulder as he worked on an automobile or tractor engine and marvel that whenever he needed a wrench, he simply reached into the tool box and took out the one that fit every time. (To this day, I try one, discover it's too big; try another; discover it's too small; and pray for an eventual convergence on the right one.) Even after I had earned my Ph.D., he used to look at me with a gleam in his eye and say, "The trouble with you is that you don't know nothin'." And I knew he was right.

I didn't need any commandment to honor my father and mother. It never occurred to me to do otherwise, in view of the examples they set. My father belonged to a generation in which a father generally did not play the role of pal to his kids. Although I never doubted that he loved me, he occupied a different, somewhat elevated stratum. So, as I matured, I automatically came to respect him, at the same time that I loved him. I appreciated that in his own understanding, his chief duty in life was to support his family, which he invariably did, even during the Great Depression, when finding work was a difficult task. He was not the kind of man to go on the dole. Indeed, I doubt that he ever gave any thought to that possibility, even when people all around him were eagerly accepting some sort of relief.

Although he had a wonderful, practical-joking sense of humor and loved to tell cock-and-bull stories at the dinner table, waiting for my mom to finally catch on that he was pulling her leg, Jess was a taciturn man. Yet hardly a standoffish man. Everybody loved him, especially the children. He obviously preferred the kids to the grownups, if given a choice. Everyone who worked for him, when he became a foreman and then the assistant superintendent on the big ranch in the San Joaquin Valley of California where I grew up between 1954 and 1961, was extremely loyal to him and spoke highly of him: "Jess" they'd say, "is a good man to work for." He expected every man to do what he was hired to do, but he posed no threat to jerk anyone around just because he was in a position to do so. Although he had been reared in a racially bigoted environment and some of his idioms would not pass muster with today's guardians of political correctness, he treated everyone the same, regardless of race.

It's natural for a man to compare himself to his father. I've done so a million times, and not once did I measure up. After he died, so many people came to his funeral that the chapel overflowed, and some had to stand outside the doors during the service. I remember thinking, "When I die, I'll be lucky if a dozen people show up." To say that he had a greater, more fundamental effect than anyone else in making me the kind of man I became would be an understatement. I don't know for sure that they aren't making men like him anymore, but if they are, I'm not encountering them. Maybe the years that followed closely after 1909 produced a different kind of men, or maybe there was something in the water he drew from the family well on that backwoods farm in Muskogee County.

83

Work in Progress

A Boy and His Mom

ANYONE WHO KNOWS me well also knows that I revere my father. Two years ago, on the one-hundredth anniversary of his birth, I wrote a short remembrance[1] of him as a tribute to the most important man in my life, the kind of man who might well inspire others, as he inspired me. In view of how greatly I esteem my father, someone might infer that I do not have a great deal of appreciation for my mother (Doris Geraldine Higgs, née Leiby, May 14, 1917–May 25, 1980). Such an inference, however, would be a mistake. Although my mom was in many ways a different sort of person from my dad, she also had a great influence on her younger son (Bobby Larry, as she called me). As I have reflected on my relationship with her, I have come to believe that in an extremely important regard she influenced me in exactly the same way that my dad influenced me—which is to say, she gave me an appreciation of the joy of working, and of doing one's work readily and well, rather than grudgingly and carelessly.

Most important, perhaps, mom set a good example: she was a hard worker in her own daily life. Because the town in which she grew up had no high school and her father would not allow her to leave home to continue her education, she had no schooling beyond the eighth grade. When she was sixteen years old, she married my father (who was eight years older), and during the forty-four years of their marriage (ended by his death in 1977), she kept house as if being a good wife and mother constituted a vital and worthy occupation.

---

1. Robert Higgs, "William Jess Higgs (March 21, 1908–October 15, 1977)," *The Beacon*, March 21, 2009, http://blog.independent.org/2009/03/21/william-jess-higgs-march-21-1909-october-15-1977/.

Even if she had other things to do, she prepared three full meals (each almost always from scratch) every day. Meal preparation might be a fully integrated production process, starting with killing a chicken, then plucking and gutting it, and cutting it into pieces for frying. I sometimes brought home fish or crawfish I had caught or a cottontail rabbit I had shot, and, with my help in cleaning, shelling, or skinning, as the raw material required, she cooked these provisions for supper. (I also raised rabbits for our table.) After each meal, she washed and dried the dishes (though after supper my dad often dried them) and swept the kitchen. She cleaned the entire house daily, keeping it neat and spotless even though we lived in a dusty rural area during most of the years when I was growing up. Monday was laundry day for her, which meant that she labored in the garage with her old-fashioned wringer washer, hanging the damp clothing and other items on the clothesline to dry, and later gathering and carefully folding them and, for items such as shirts, pants, sheets, and pillow cases, ironing them before putting everything away in its proper drawer.

Cooking, cleaning, and washing, however, hardly composed the whole of her work. As a young woman, she had "felt the call" to preach the Gospel of Jesus Christ, and by the time I was four or five years old, she had become the pastor of a backwoods Pentecostal church somewhere beyond McAlester, Oklahoma, the town near which we lived at the time. Later, after we moved to California in 1951, she was again a pastor at several different churches in succession. This ministry demanded a great deal of work from her: preparing sermons, conducting services several times each week (sometimes every night, when a "revival meeting" was going on), and attending to the spiritual and personal needs of her congregation in times of sickness, bereavement, and other troubles. Her natural compassion and sincere sympathy, as well as her religious faith, served her well in this calling.

Although being a full-time housewife, mother, and pastor might have been enough, or even too much, for most women, she found time for a great deal of additional activity—her secret was that no matter what task she tackled, she worked very fast. She crocheted and embroidered decorative items, especially doilies and pillowcases, for our home. Once each week, for several hours, she met with other ladies at the church to make quilts in a team effort to help support the church. (I still have some of these beautiful works of folk art.) She tended a large vegetable garden in the spring and summer, as well as her beloved roses and other flowers. At certain times of the year, she went out to the cotton fields, which in those days still required a great deal of hand labor, to work with gangs of laborers in "chopping" (weeding) and "picking" (harvesting) cotton.

Because as a young boy I went everywhere she went—I can't recall ever having a babysitter, as such, although I sometimes spent time at a neighbor's house with my friends—I accompanied her in her work outside the house. The earliest such experience had to do with picking cotton, when I was perhaps four or five years old. I was too little to have my own sack, so I would go ahead of her in the row, plucking out the fluffy lint and building up a little pile in the row. When she had picked her way up to my pile, she would deposit it in her sack, and I would move farther ahead of her to repeat the process, again and again. I loved this work. Besides enjoying the picking itself, in good-natured company with a group of other pickers, I had a fine time tossing unopened bolls at other kids, who naturally tossed bolls back at me. By the time I was six years old, I had persuaded mom to make me a sack of my own, which she did by using a potato sack, attaching a strap that I could place over one shoulder in the standard manner for cotton pickers. When my little sack was stuffed full, I would take it to the scales, have it weighed, collect my per-pound payment, dump the contents of my sack into the trailer (sometimes adding a swan dive into the cotton if it had piled up high enough in the trailer), and return to the field to fill it again. As I got older, my sacks got bigger. By the time I was ten or eleven years old, I had graduated to the standard 12-foot sack the adults used, and I was able to pick as much as 200 pounds or so in a day. By the late 1950s, however, picking machines had displaced hand pickers almost completely in our area of California, so my cotton picking with mom ended when I was about twelve or thirteen years old.

Mom also took me on a variety of ad hoc work outings. In the late summer, we would visit peach and apricot orchards at which the commercial harvesting had ended, notwithstanding that a great deal of fruit remained here and there on the trees. It was going to rot unless someone took the trouble to collect it, so the owners allowed anyone and everyone to come into the orchards to pick it without charge. We would bring home big boxes filled with fruit, which my mom would can for our consumption during the following year. We would also go along the banks of the San Joaquin River where wild blackberries grew profusely and pick great quantities of them. Again, the haul would be canned and—best of all—made into my mom's mouth-watering blackberry cobbler. Also along the river, in season, we found and picked wild mustard greens, a delicacy in my mom's taste, though intolerable in mine.

Mom taught me to drive a car. When I was ten years old, I began to drive on the country roads, and when I was fifteen, she took me to get a driver's license (six months before I had reached my sixteenth birthday, which in those days was permitted because I had taken a driver's education course in school). She cringed but did not prevent me from getting my first shotgun at age ten. With my little .410 single-shot gun and an endless expanse of game-rich fields, sloughs, and marshes as my hunting ground, I became a great hunter—in my own mind, at least. (I confess that I was considerably more careful with the gun than I was with the car, and the end result tested my dad's patience on more than one occasion.) Mom taught me how to dress, how to "behave," how to write a check, and how to carry out a thousand other tasks an adult must master. I learned how to cook by watching her and helping with simple jobs in the kitchen, such as cleaning fish and grinding cabbage with the hand-cranked grinder to make coleslaw. Sometimes I helped with the dish washing and drying after supper.

Starting when I was fourteen, during school vacations in the summer, I worked full time in regular jobs, alongside the men, first on the ranch where we lived and later at a local box factory. My parents did not demand or even suggest such employment—"you'll have plenty of time to work later," they said—but I had learned from their examples to value earning my own way. So, from my sophomore year in high school onward, I did not need to take any money from them, although I continued to receive my room and board from them as before.

When I was a kid, mom allowed me to roam far and wide across the countryside, and my boyhood was occupied not only with attending school and playing on school sports teams—and with working, as I've described—but also with exploring, fishing, hunting, and swimming in the canals. In the evening, when supper was ready, I was often still outside somewhere, and my mom's voice would ring out across the darkening fields to call me in: "Bobby Laaaaaaareeee." In my memory, I hear it still as clearly as I heard it then.

Any boy would be fortunate, as I most certainly was, to have such a mother: loving, kind, gentle, compassionate, good-humored, hardworking, dedicated to her family and loyal to her friends, at home in her world, and at peace with her place in it.

84

Murray N. Rothbard
In Memoriam

MURRAY ROTHBARD'S SCHOLARSHIP spanned an enormous range, including philosophy, methodology, economic theory, the history of economic and political thought, economic history, economic policy, law, and contemporary politics. I was well along in my career as an economist specializing in the economic history of the United States when I began to read his work. Once I had started, I never stopped.

The first thing I can recall reading, soon after its publication in 1978, was the revised edition of *For a New Liberty*.[1] Having already absorbed a good deal of the work of Milton Friedman, Friedrich Hayek, and other free-market economists, I found much of this manifesto congenial, although I balked at the possibility of dispensing with government even for the provision of national defense and courts of justice. I spent many hours over lunches with my friend Andy Rutten chewing on Murray's ideas about how and why anarcho-capitalism would work.

In the following years I read a great deal of Murray's work, although I am sure that even now I've only scratched the surface of his oeuvre. Among the works that I have found especially valuable in my own research are his two chapters, "War Collectivism in World War I" and "Herbert Hoover and the Myth of Laissez-Faire," in *A New History of Leviathan*,[2] published in 1972. My own book on the American leviathan contains several references to Murray's essays, but probably does not reveal my full debt to those seminal chapters.

---

1. Murray N. Rothbard, *For a New Liberty: The Libertarian Manifesto*, rev. ed. (New York: Collier Books, 1978).

2. Ronald Radosh and Murray N. Rothbard, eds., *A New History of Leviathan: Essays on the Rise of American Corporate State* (New York: E.P. Dutton, 1972).

My closest encounter with Rothbard the economic historian, however, came off the record. Early in 1985 I submitted to the Pacific Research Institute a manuscript that, after several more revisions and some additions, was eventually published as *Crisis and Leviathan* in 1987. Pacific asked several eminent scholars, including Murray, to review my manuscript. Murray's review went far beyond what one might have expected, taking the form of a letter to Pacific's Greg Christainsen, dated May 27, 1985. It runs 26 single-spaced pages, probably over 12,000 words. Over the years, I have seen a lot of reports by referees and reviewers, but never anything that came close to this remarkable epistle.

The letter began with two pages of praise for my manuscript. Murray liked my general approach. "Perhaps without realizing," he wrote, "Professor Higgs approaches history from the Misesian praxeological viewpoint, knowing and applying the truths and laws of economics, but also realizing that ideological and other factors are also of crucial importance." He appreciated what he described as my "critiques of Chicagoite cliometrics and public choice history—both of which try to sum up all of history with a few equations, or with a one-dimensional simplistic approach."

Murray lauded my work for its not being value-free. "We have suffered for too long," he wrote, "from a dichotomy in which essayists and pamphleteers, who are unscholarly, are hard-hitting and value-laden whereas scholars are evasive, garbled writers who hide behind a careful cloak of value-freedom." He delighted that I was "calling a spade a spade and not a 'triangular implement for digging.'"

He declared that "Higgs's values are my values," applauding my realization that war and militarism are "the major cause and embodiment of intervention" in the market and the suppression of liberty and free enterprise. My hostility to conscription and my natural-rights objection to it—as opposed to a neoclassical efficiency objection—pleased him mightily. My comments on the gold standard garnered his approval, too.

Had I stopped reading after the first two pages, I might have considered myself a certified damned fine scholar. Any such temptation, however, was decisively deflated by the next 24 pages. These contained a minutely detailed yet broad-ranging critique, along with scores of suggestions for what needed to be added to my text and what additional books, articles, and dissertations I needed to read to correct my misapprehensions and flesh out my knowledge.

At several points, Murray prefaced his criticism by noting, "Professor Higgs is nodding here."

I can still recall the disappointed feeling I had after finishing the letter. I knew that I did not have sufficient life expectancy to accomplish what Murray had indicated needed to be done. Sad to say, I couldn't read that much in a decade, even if I did nothing else, much less incorporate all of it into a coherent book. Never before had I been shown my inadequacies as a scholar in such a well-documented way—after all, even the pathetic manuscript Murray was flogging had taken me five years to draft and rested to some extent on twenty years of study and research.

We are not all destined for greatness. I made a number of revisions of my text and my footnotes along the lines suggested in Murray's letter. Needless to say, I was not able to follow up on the great majority of his suggestions, and I have no doubt that my book was the worse for that inability. All I can say in my own defense is that the book, such as it is, did get finished and published in my lifetime. And my luck held. When Murray reviewed the book for *Liberty* magazine in 1987, he praised it extravagantly, breathing not a word about the shortcomings he had spent 24 pages detailing in a private communication written mainly for my benefit.

Murray's letter included a number of magnificent epigrams. To readers who had the wonderful opportunity to listen to Murray's lectures on economic history, as I did at several of the Mises Institute's summer programs, these will have a familiar ring. Here are a few of them.

On the nature of the state:

The State has its own agenda, that is, . . . all States everywhere are run by a ruling class, the people running the State, and one of their interests is to extend as well as maintain the power and wealth arising from that rule.

On intellectuals as servants of power:

Since . . . the existence of any State regime rests on public opinion, it becomes important for the State to engineer that opinion with the aid of the professional opinion-moulding group: the intellectuals. This cozy coalition benefits the State rulers—kings, nobles, political parties, whatever—because the public is persuaded to obey the king or State; the intellectuals benefit from a share in the tax revenue, plus their "market" being guaranteed by the government.

On hope for the dissolution of statist regimes:

The situation is not irreversible. . . . [G]overnment intervention is beset by 'inner contradictions' . . . breakdowns are inevitable and are coming faster in response to the stimulus of intervention—here the rational expectations people have some good points. Progressive and synergistic breakdowns in domestic and foreign intervention might lead to crises and fairly rapid and even sudden reversions to freedom. Note, for example, the remarkable, even if gradual, shift from Stalinism to free markets in Yugoslavia, the developing shift out of Maoism in China, and at least the public sentiments if not the reality underlying conservative regimes in the U.S. and England, growth in free-market and libertarian views in Western Europe, etc. And remember that the public choicers are wrong that revolutions can never occur.

These characteristic sentiments exemplify Murray's unflagging optimism. More than once he observed that my prognosis was "too pessimistic." Well, temperament is tough to slough off. I doubt that I shall ever acquire Murray's optimism, which I believe goes far to explain how he was able to keep slugging away until the day he died, always convinced that eventually those who favor a free society will win the great struggle.

It is not likely that we shall ever have another scholar of Murray's breadth. In his letter he referred to well over a hundred sources, many by exact author, title, publication date and publisher, even though he apologized for "not having access to the bulk of my books here in Las Vegas, nor to any decent library, so I will have to wing the citations from time to time." The references include many obscure or exotic books and articles (e.g., Etienne de La Boetie, *Discourse on Voluntary Servitude*; Alfred De Grazia, ed., *The Velikovsky Affair*; Colin Simpson, *The Lusitania Affair*; Eugene N. Golob, *The Isms*; and R. Palme Dutt, *Fascism and Social Revolution*). Murray also had extensive knowledge of the religious history of the United States, on which he expounded with great gusto in his historical lectures, in which the diabolical doings of the postmillennial pietists figured prominently. Many of us may remember Murray most fondly for his fabulous sense of humor. He was a truly entertaining conversationalist and lecturer, and his letters contained priceless witticisms and hilarious descriptions. In the letter I've been quoting, he told the following "lovely—and true!—story about one of the great social philosophers of our century, W. C. Fields. Fields was asked, among other celebrities, by the *Saturday Evening Post*, during World War II, to write a plan about how to end the war. W. C. sat down, quite seriously, and proposed his plan, which was to get the leaders of the warring nations together, bring them to the Hollywood Bowl, and 'let them fight it out with sackfuls of dung.' Needless to say, the *SEP* did not publish the article."

I was honored to know Murray Rothbard and privileged to work with him in a number of conferences and programs organized by the Mises Institute. I hold him to have been one of our century's great intellectual figures, whose neglect by mainstream academicians is inexcusable. He stimulated my thinking and enlarged my knowledge. My personal association with him brought me much pleasure. I do not expect to encounter another like him, and his passing grieves me greatly.

85

Jürg Niehans

(November 8, 1919–April 23, 2007)

WHEN I ARRIVED at the Johns Hopkins University to continue my graduate study in the fall of 1966, Jürg Niehans arrived there from Switzerland for an eleven-year stint as a professor in the Department of Political Economy. Because I had already completed a year of graduate work at the University of California, Santa Barbara, I only audited the microeconomics course that he taught for the first-year graduate students. I enrolled for credit in his course in advanced macroeconomics.

In addition, in the weekly department seminar, which was attended by all graduate students and all faculty members (an institution that Fritz Machlup had previously established, modeling it on the famous Mises seminar in Vienna that he had attended), I learned from Niehans in the course of each week's discussion. This seminar always lasted two hours or, as we said, "until the canary dies" (it never did, although it came very close a few times). Because the Hopkins graduate program was so small, having only about 35 students altogether and 10 or 11 faculty members, everybody knew everybody. Even if a student never took a professor's courses, he still had an opportunity to learn from that professor by virtue of his participation in the weekly seminar.

So I had many opportunities to learn from Niehans, and I learned a great deal, even in the course that I audited. He was a magnificent teacher—well organized in his lectures, clear in his explanations, patient in bearing with ignorant students (including me), and tireless in his correction of homework assignments and grading of exams, writing extensive notes to show where the student had gone wrong.

He was very "old school" in his European manners and personal conduct. A back slapper he was not. I was in awe of him, yet at the same time I developed a great affection for him, mainly because of his manifest competence, his evident dedication to the field of economics and to good teaching, and, perhaps most of all, his long-suffering patience.

For me, attending Hopkins was a joy and an honor. (After all, whereas my fellow students had graduated from good foreign universities or from Ivy League and other upscale schools in the United States, I had graduated from lowly San Francisco State College, and I never doubted that I was playing in the big leagues when in justice I should have been somewhere much lower in the academic pecking order.)

For Niehans as for my other professors at Hopkins, economics was a technical subject. The students learned economic concepts and models—the contents of the economist's "tool box"—without any preaching one way or another about politics or ideology. Later on, after I had begun my academic career, I would lose my inclination to regard economics as simply a technical subject or as little more than a box of tools. I would discover the value of subjects we had not studied, including private property rights and transaction costs, and I would discover as well the ideas of economists who were never mentioned in my graduate training, including Ludwig von Mises and F. A. Hayek.

Nevertheless, I have never regretted that I completed my Ph.D. work at Hopkins, and I have always been glad to honor the memory of the professors who taught me there. Having apprenticed at Hopkins, I was able to begin my academic career at a well-respected university and thus to continue to develop my skills and understanding by working with top-notch colleagues during the fifteen years that I remained at the University of Washington.

Of all my teachers at Hopkins, Niehans will always stand out in my regard. His kindness and dedication were unforgettable. Indeed, when I remember his teaching, I often call to mind the look that would flit over his face when he realized in the midst of a lecture that something he was taking for granted, we students really did not understand at all. For an instant, his face would show ever so slightly a look of pain and disappointment. Then he would say something like, "Let's back up and make sure we all know what XYZ is and how it works." After this patient backtracking to help us overcome our own deficiencies, he would proceed as planned, always finishing what he had scheduled for that day's class.

Jürg Niehans was well respected in the economics profession, and late in his life he was recognized with honors.[1] All of them, and others, were well deserved. After his retirement from teaching in 1988, he lived in Palo Alto, California, near a son. He died at the age of 87.

May you rest in peace, dear teacher. I will never forget you. It was a privilege and a great good fortune to know you and to learn from you.

---

1. "Jürg Niehans," *Wikipedia,* http://de.wikipedia.org/wiki/J%C3%BCrg_Niehans.

86

R. Max Hartwell
(1921–2009)

MAX HARTWELL died at his home in England on March 14. He leaves a loving family and a legion of admirers and friends. I was blessed to know him—and to love him—for forty years.

A native of Australia, Max enjoyed a long, eventful life. Born and reared in the outback of New South Wales, he progressed to teacher training, school teaching, service in the army during the war, graduate training, and a life of productive scholarship in England and the United States. He was an outstanding economic historian and contributed greatly to the "Standard of Living Debate," defending the view that the Industrial Revolution, far from having been a Marxist nightmare for the working class, was the means by which workers were gradually lifted from the poverty that had been their lot from time immemorial. Max spent the heart of his career at Nuffield College, Oxford, where he trained a number of outstanding economic historians. Later, after his retirement from Oxford, he alternated between teaching at the University of Virginia and teaching at the University of Chicago. Others will write full-fledged obituaries for him, I am confident. Here I wish only to recall how much I admired and loved him. He was one of the most decent people I have ever known. To be around him was always a joy, because Max was the very embodiment of a positive outlook and sheer *joie de vivre*.

I met Max in 1969, when he came to Seattle during the summer, and he and I team-taught a graduate seminar in European economic history at the University of Washington, where I had joined the faculty the previous year. One of my first publications was a somewhat controversial review article that we wrote together for the *American Historical Review*. Later, he invited me to Nuffield as a visiting fellow, and the time I spent there during 1971–72 was a landmark of my life and career. He delighted in advising and encouraging me, and in protecting me. More than once, at tea time at Nuffield, Max would sit silently while his fellow dons huffed and puffed about something in their characteristically arrogant way. Then, suddenly, Max would explode: "Bullshit!" Which always moved the conversation in a more illuminating direction.

I cherish countless stories Max told me of his life, career, and travels, and the people he knew. He was the classical liberal's classical liberal—always level-headed, always recalling the pitfalls that await every species of single-mindedness. I eventually became more radical than he, but I never lost an ounce of respect for his opinions. In the early 1990s, I was glad to participate in a Festschrift conference for him at the University of Virginia, where the assembled celebrants included some of the world's leading figures in economics and economic history, each of whom held Max in the highest regard. Max would refer to me in public as his "co-author," and I was always honored by this recognition. A longtime member of the Mont Pelerin Society, Max served as its president and wrote an excellent history of this important classical–liberal association, which I reviewed[1] in an early issue of *The Independent Review*.

No one can replace Max; he was one of a kind. He was, in more ways than one, a brightly shining light in a world of darkness. He lived life to the full, and he was fortunate that his days were long and filled with the love of his family and friends. Rest in peace, old friend.

---

1. Robert Higgs, "Fifty Years of the Mont Pelerin Society," *The Independent Review* 1:4 (Spring 1997): 623–25.

87

Manuel F. Ayau

(1925–2010)

WITH GREAT SADNESS, I convey the news I have just received that Manuel F. Ayau died yesterday. Known to his friends as Muso, Ayau was one of the greatest persons I have had the privilege to know. I am not given to hero worship, but I do not hesitate to affirm that, to me, Muso was a hero.

Ayau was the principal founder of the Universidad Francisco Marroquín in Guatemala City. He was also a successful entrepreneur, an active participant in the public affairs of his country, and a dedicated champion of liberty there and throughout the wider world. The proud patriarch of a beautiful family, a warm friend to countless adherents of classical liberalism, and man of tremendous energy and striking courage, he exemplifies the realization of the finest potential that human beings can achieve.

The university that he founded and led to maturity is now a beacon to those who seek knowledge and wisdom; it stands without doubt as the finest institution of higher education in Guatemala, and in many respects it has no peer anywhere in the world. I have been honored to have played a small role in its affairs, and I am sure that it will ascend to even greater heights of accomplishment in the future, paying a fitting tribute to the man whose vision, dedication, and personal bravery brought it into being.

Muso is gone now, but his spirit will live forever in the hearts of the multitude who knew, admired, and loved him.

88

Joseph Sobran
(1946–2010)

WITH SADNESS, I report the death of an old and cherished friend, Joe Sobran. Joe wrote and edited for *National Review* until he and William F. Buckley, Jr., had a falling out; he had a long-running engagement with CBS Radio as a commentator; and he wrote a syndicated newspaper column.

For most of his life, Joe was one of those rare conservatives who actually had and lived by sincere conservative values, rather than merely mouthing the usual banal conservative views and readily throwing principles overboard whenever an opportunity to influence or wield state power presented itself. Late in life, he embraced philosophical anarchism, having given up all hope that the state would ever do anything decent.

I met Joe about twenty years ago, and I was privileged to spend considerable time with him over the years. A gentle, learned, witty, and courageous man, Joe was one of the most beautiful writers I have encountered among commentators on public affairs. I keep a collection of quotations that express important ideas in an especially pithy, penetrating, arresting, or graceful way. Joe's declarations are well represented in my collection. In virtually every column of his that I read, at least once I would stop, reread a sentence or a paragraph, and mutter to myself, "How I would love to be able to write such prose!"

When a man dies, it is common for friends and admirers to say that he will be missed, but usually, in truth, he really will not be missed except by a handful of close friends and relatives. In Joe's case, however, I believe that many people really will miss him. I certainly will. He wrote in a unique voice, in sentences crafted with simplicity, grace, and precision, expressing ideas that all of us might profitably ponder.

Joe was a devout Catholic. Let us hope that in this regard, too, he charted a course to a safe harbor, and that he now resides in a better place.

89

Morris David Morris

(February 10, 1921–March 12, 2011)

I WAS SADDENED to learn of the recent death of Morris David Morris, who was my colleague in the Department of Economics at the University of Washington for thirteen of the fifteen years I spent there. Morris was my closest personal friend on the faculty at the UW, notwithstanding our differences of age, background, experience, and education. In each of these areas, he was definitely the man, and I the boy. Yet he was not one to pull rank on an ignorant and narrowly focused junior colleague, and we enjoyed wonderful times together socially, as well as illuminating times (for me) at the university.

Although Morrie's research specialty was the economic history of India, a field to which he made seminal contributions and in which he was a recognized authority, he seemed to know about everything—European history, sociology, psychology and psychoanalysis, labor relations, you name it. His mind was constantly leaping from one area of knowledge to another and making connections that broadened one's understanding. When he lectured, he did not write equations or draw graphs carefully on the blackboard, as other economists did. Instead, he wrote terms and labels inside circles, with arrows running from one circled term to another and with wild swirls gobbling up the entire scenario, until the board ultimately depicted something like the debris left after a tornado has struck. He created all of this illustrative interconnection while lecturing in an animated, yet scholarly manner. Although his rocket-science colleagues in the economics department looked down on him—truly an inversion of a just order of intellects—the graduate students loved him, albeit they sometimes were at a loss to know what to make of his instruction.

Morrie was a good-natured man, a pleasure to spend time with. He had a wealth of fascinating stories to tell about his various experiences while living in India on several different occasions and about his service in the Army during World War II, among other things. He was, for example, a member of a small Strategic Bombing Survey team that made the first Allied contact with and extensively interviewed Albert Speer, the German minister of armaments and war production, after the German surrender in 1945. John Kenneth Galbraith was also a member of this team, so Morrie had a raft of stories about him, too.

My close friendship with Morrie was cemented early in my time at the UW. In 1968, I was approached by a group of students who were circulating an antiwar petition and wanted someone to take it around to the faculty to solicit their signatures. Being staunchly opposed to the war, I agreed to perform this task. Little did I know how my colleagues, some of whom I had yet to meet, would react to my approaching them in this capacity. Some appeared to think that I was a lunatic who had escaped from an asylum. Most regarded me as they would have regarded someone offering them a complimentary bottle of cholera germs. Morrie, however, was ever so glad to sign. In a department with thirty-six faculty members, he was the only one who signed besides me.

Morris David Morris was a sophisticated, widely learned, highly cultured, emotionally upbeat person, and I, let us merely note, was none of these things. Yet we became good friends. I had the greatest respect for him, and he was willing to overlook my many deficiencies. I learned a great deal from him over the years, and his friendship was a blessing to me.

He lived to see his 90th birthday, and so far as I was ever aware, he lived for the most part a good and happy life. He was one of the most decent human beings I have had the good fortune to know. May he rest in peace.

90

Siobhan Reynolds

A True American Heroine (1961–2011)

SIOBHAN REYNOLDS was killed on Saturday, December 24, in a plane crash. Not many people knew her, I'm sure, yet she was a true heroine. She had, however, nothing whatever in common with those who are commonly regarded as heroes, especially the soldiers who slaughter, maim, and bring grief to unoffending people all over the world at the behest of the vile creatures who command the U.S. empire.

Siobhan, to whose life and heroic deeds Radley Balko has paid fitting tribute,[1] sought not to cause pain, as the military "heroes" do, but to alleviate it. She was motivated in the beginning by her husband's chronic pain and by the entire setup by which the government has made it virtually impossible for millions of people to get the drugs that would relieve their pain. Siobhan formed an advocacy organization, the Pain Relief Network, dedicated to helping these victims of government cruelty and madness. She had some success, and in response the government fought back in the most vicious imaginable way, by abusing the very arrangements and officialdom it has the audacity to call the "justice system." These despicable actions caused Siobhan much grief and ultimately led her, at the end of 2010, to disband the organization she had set up. She explained:

> The Members of the Board of Directors and I have decided to shut down PRN as an activist organization because pressure from the US Department of Justice has made it impossible for us to function. I have

---

1. Radley Balko, "Siobhan Reynolds, RIP," *The Agitator.com*, Dec. 26, 2011, http://www.theagitator.com/2011/12/26/siobhan-reynolds-rip/.

fought back against the attack on me and PRN but have received no redress in the federal courts; so, the board and I have concluded that we simply cannot continue.

Terminating the PRN did not mean, however, that Siobhan had stopped her personal fight against the evil apparatus the government maintains:

It certainly appears that the legal deck is stacked against pain patients and doctors. Despite this, others will keep trying because so very much is at stake. A group of us may bring another action in the Western District of Washington in the near future; but exactly how that will be framed is not yet clear. In any event, the action will *not* be undertaken under the auspices of PRN.

People in pain are still being abused, neglected, and left to die by the entire system. Physicians brave enough to treat chronic pain continue to be intimidated and prosecuted. It breaks my heart that we have to stop, but there is simply no way forward for PRN.

So Siobhan continued to fight, in person and in cooperation with hearty collaborators. A gentle woman by nature, she was endowed with deeps springs of hope and an abiding outrage against the wickedness of the government system she opposed.

I never met Siobhan in person. I became acquainted with her through Facebook, where she would send me kind messages about what she was learning from my books and other reading materials I recommended to her. She had an active, inquiring mind and a gentle heart. And above all, perhaps, she had tremendous courage, the sort of courage so manifestly lacking among those of us who complain and bluster about the government's evils, but do nothing of any consequence to stop them.

As fate would have it, I sent Siobhan a message on Facebook, in reply to a kind message she had sent me about my work, just two days before she died. In my message, I said, in part:

You have had no way to have known, but you have been one of my heroes (and I have very few) ever since I learned, more or less by chance, about your efforts on behalf of people denied pain relief by the whole congeries of sadistic government laws, functionaries, and activities aimed at keeping them in pain. I have the greatest respect for you and the few others who have the courage to do something concrete to fight the power.

Please accept my very best wishes for a happy Christmas and for better days to come. And please know, too, of the great esteem in which I hold you.

Rest in peace, brave, loving, gentle lady. Oh, that the world had a million more like you.

91

Anna Jacobson Schwartz

(November 11, 1915–June 21, 2012)

ANNA SCHWARTZ was one of the best economic historians of the past century. With Milton Friedman, she wrote (among many other works) that century's most influential economic history book, *A Monetary History of the United States, 1867–1960.*[1] Although not an economic theorist of Friedman's caliber, she was a fine economist in her own right. Friedman's statement that "Anna did all of the work, and I got most of the recognition" was not a mere expression of false modesty, but an honest confession that the immense body of historical evidence meticulously collected, compiled, annotated, and displayed in their landmark books was overwhelmingly the product of Anna's efforts.

Although I never knew Anna personally, I felt as if I did because I knew so many people who knew her well and because she was always friendly and helpful when our professional paths intersected. She wrote positive reviews of several of my books, and when Oxford University Press published my book *Depression, War, and Cold War* in 2006 she wrote a laudatory blurb for the dust jacket. Previously, when David Theroux and I made plans to launch a new journal, *The Independent Review: A Journal of Political Economy*, in the mid-1990s, we invited Anna to become a member of the journal's board of advisors, and she graciously agreed to do so.

Over the years, as I moved away from monetarism and toward Austrian economics, I found myself in growing disagreement with Friedman and Schwartz in regard to monetary theory in general and the causes of the Great

---

1. Milton Friedman and Anna Jacobson Schwartz, *A Monetary History of the United States, 1867–1960* (Princeton, NJ: Princeton University Press, 1963).

Depression in particular. At no point, however, did I lose my great respect for Anna as a scholar and as a person. Anyone inclined to dismiss her work with an offhand quip about the wrongheadedness of monetarists has almost certainly never plowed through the painstakingly constructed footnotes and appendixes in Anna's books. I once taught a graduate seminar at the University of Washington in which *A Monetary History of the United States* served as the core text, to be read in its entirety, and I assure you that the able students in this seminar had their hands full to overflowing, as did their professor. In this book we find careful, intelligent historical research displayed at its very best. Stunningly impressive as the 859-page *Monetary History* may be, however, it certainly was not the only thing Anna produced, by a long shot.

Anna remained a productive researcher for decades longer than most of us ever will. Just three years ago, I was in the audience for a New York conference at which she, in her capacity as a discussant, leveled scathing criticism at the Fed's mismanagement of monetary policy before and after the 2008 financial debacle. Although she was physically frail and needed assistance in entering and leaving the conference room, her mind was definitely firing on all cylinders, and she injected real passion into some of her critical remarks. Even in her nineties, she continued to learn, to reconsider her views, and to remain engaged in the key economic debates of the day.

If ever an economist fought the good fight, Anna certainly did so. Although her work tended to be overshadowed because of her having worked so often jointly with the world-famous Milton Friedman, she more than pulled her share of the load in their joint work, and we may hope that in time her contribution to twentieth-century economics and especially to economic history will receive its just recognition.

92

Thomas S. Szasz

(1920–2012)

WITH GREAT SADNESS, I note the passing on September 8 of the man I have long described as the greatest living libertarian. Thomas Szasz was, among other things, a powerful influence on the movement to release people who were being held in prisons on "psychiatric" grounds, even though they had not been convicted of any crime. Virtually single-handedly, he waged a half-century fight against the use of psychiatric excuses to punish innocent people or to relieve people who had committed crimes of responsibility for their actions. He exposed in countless ways the unholy alliance of the state and the psychiatric profession, and he laid bare the bogus foundation on which this alliance rests. He was one of the greatest humanitarians of the twentieth century, a man of incisive mind, unflagging determination, and tremendous energy. He died at 92, only a year after the publication of the latest of his many books. His *curriculum vitae* is a stunning testament of his intellectual breadth and depth and of his unyielding devotion to human freedom.

I got to know Tom in my capacity as editor of *The Independent Review*, and over the years I was proud to have placed several of his articles in the journal. As a friend and as a supporter of his work, I would send him little notes or news items occasionally. He was always prompt and gracious in his replies. From time to time he would send me items he thought might interest me. In this way, I got to know him better and greatly enjoyed his private, frank expressions of opinion about events and persons.

When I sent him one of my little messages on August 31, 2012, he replied quickly, as usual, thanking me, asking about my personal situation after Hurricane Isaac, and adding some unexpected personal information about himself.

"Good to hear from you," he said. "I am ok. Have stopped writing. I have had my say. Enough is enough." I immediately wrote back to him: "You surprise me. I thought you would continue to write as long as you continued to breathe. But if ever a writer gave an account of himself, you are the one. Your lifetime's work is a monument that will instruct and inspire people forever."

To my statement that I had expected him to continue writing as long as he lived, he responded: "I thought so too, but I didn't expect to live this long (92.5). Writing was—is—very much a part of my being. I feel that I have lost a large part of myself, but so have I also parts of my body—strength, mobility, hearing, etc. But I have enough left to carry on: I live alone, drive, walk with a cane (not far or long), etc., and am blessed with two wonderful daughters, very independent (a dermatologist at the Mayo Clinic and a university librarian in Va.), fine sons-in-law, and great grandson (senior at Carleton College, linguistics + premed). So no one needs me. A good feeling in old age. (But dangerous earlier.)" I was glad to know that he was still getting along fairly well, notwithstanding his limitations. Eight days later, he died.

In 2006, I was extremely honored to receive from the Center for Independent Thought one of its Thomas S. Szasz Awards for Outstanding Contributions to the Cause of Civil Liberties. On the occasion of this award, Tom made his way to Oakland, where The Independent Institute hosted a presentation program at which he and I spoke to a full house. This unforgettable occasion was the first and only time I ever had the pleasure of Tom's company in person. As always, he was extremely gracious.

Tom was unique, and he is utterly irreplaceable. Throughout his long life, he did not simply fight the good fight; he fought a truly magnificent fight, nearly alone against the hostile ranks of his own profession and the world at large, notwithstanding the ridicule and dishonor he so often received from people more interested in pelf and self-deception than in the plain truth. Tom's arguments were not technical or difficult to follow; many required only the precise, correct use of language. Someday, one fervently hopes, the world will look back in astonishment that such a battle ever needed to be waged, and will honor Tom's memory as we now honor the memory of those who fought against the entrenched institution of slavery in the eighteenth and nineteenth centuries. Tom fought to free our minds from fundamental misunderstandings, warning us against the perils of submission to the superstition, deliberate deception, and fraud that prop up the therapeutic state and its countless self-interested operatives.

RIP, dear friend. It is one of my life's greatest honors to have known you and to have called you a friend, and I shall always esteem your memory.

93

James M. Buchanan

(October 3, 1919–January 9, 2013)

JAMES M. BUCHANAN, one of the past century's most distinguished economists and most compelling champions of free markets, died earlier today at age 93. His professional career spanned more than sixty years, during which he wrote extensively on public finance, economic philosophy, and other topics in related areas. With Gordon Tullock, he founded a new subfield of economics—public choice—that has become established as a flourishing area of research, writing, and teaching. A focus of this scholarship is the journal *Public Choice*, which was long edited by Tullock. On his own, Buchanan established another subfield—constitutional economics—which might also be considered a subfield of political philosophy. Although it has not caught fire to the extent that public choice has, it has also attracted a substantial amount of scholarly activity. The journal *Constitutional Political Economy* is one fruit of this effort.

Buchanan's output as a writer is the stuff of which young economists' dreams are made. His collected works, published by Liberty Fund, comprise twenty volumes. Over the years, he wrote probably hundreds of articles, many of which were published in the top journals of economics, philosophy, and other fields, as well as many books. Several foreign universities recognized his accomplishments by awarding him honorary degrees. In 1986, he received the Nobel Prize in economics.

I first encountered Jim when he came to Johns Hopkins to present a seminar paper while I was a graduate student there, in 1967, as I recall. He did not make a good impression on me then. His presentation, like all his work, was nontechnical, and Hopkins specialized in a much more formal, mathematical style of economic analysis. When Professor Bela Balassa asked him a technical question, Jim shrugged it off as if its answer didn't matter much one way or the other. In the grad students' minds, this attitude toward the very sorts of things we were agonizingly trying to master suggested that he was a lightweight. In this respect, we could scarcely have been more mistaken.

Indeed, the hallmark of Buchanan's work from beginning to end was a deep seriousness of purpose and procedure that not many economists have matched in the past century. Unlike the typical mainstream economist, Jim was never just fooling around, toying with a tweaked model or a trivial, throw-away idea. To a rare degree, he kept his eyes focused on the prize of true economic understanding. When I began to read and ponder his writings seriously in the 1980s, I developed a tremendous respect for his view of what markets are and how they work. A more formally inclined economist would have had great difficulty in achieving his depth of understanding; the math and the technicalities have a way of overwhelming the substance of an economic analysis, and often of obliterating it entirely. To my knowledge, Jim never committed this professional sin.

I became personally acquainted with Jim in the 1980s. I recall the first time I was invited to lecture at George Mason University's Public Choice Center, which Buchanan and Tullock headed. Jim sat in the center near the front of the audience, two or three rows back. I had not spoken for more than 10 or 15 minutes before I noticed that Jim seemed to have fallen asleep. Splendid, I thought! My talk is so awful that the great man has simply dozed off. However, after another 10 or 15 minutes had passed, Jim interrupted me to ask a question related to something I had just said. I thereby discovered, as many others did over the years, that this pseudo-sleep was simply something Jim did to relax. He definitely was not sleeping, but only closing his eyes while his ears remained fully operative.

After Buchanan received the Nobel Prize in 1986, I invited him to come to Lafayette College, where I was then a professor, to give some talks to students and faculty. He graciously came, which gave me my first opportunity to spend a substantial amount of time with him, getting to know him better and picking his brain. Later, over the years, I spent much time with him at Liberty Fund colloquiums, conferences, and other professional gatherings, each time gaining a new glimpse into his mind, outlook, and attitudes.

When we established *The Independent Review* in 1996, Jim agreed to serve on the board of advisers. Later he contributed two articles to the journal. His photograph graces the cover of the summer 2000 issue, to which he contributed an article.[1]

At the University of Chicago, where Buchanan earned his Ph.D. degree in 1948, he was a student of Frank Knight, who was clearly the greatest influence on his thinking from that time forward. Jim was not an Austrian economist, but he had many affinities with the Austrians, especially in his ideas on cost, which he developed in his little book *Cost and Choice.*[2] He respected Ludwig von Mises and F. A. Hayek, especially the latter. Other Austrians made a less favorable impression on him. In his political philosophy he was definitely not an anarchist, which put him at loggerheads with Austrians such as Murray Rothbard. In his work in constitutional political economy, Jim was striving to find a structural or institutional means of taming government power and making it truly answerable to the public. It never seemed to occur to him that this goal might be unattainable.

Jim's work deeply influenced many economists, including me. He gave me a deeper understanding of the market process than anyone else had given me. He raised many worthwhile questions that I continue to ponder. He offered me a shining example of the economist as a serious thinker, not simply an idiot savant fooling with models. My favorite works of his include *Cost and Choice* and his collection titled *What Should Economists Do?*,[3] which contains several articles that should be required reading for every graduate student in economics. Jim's autobiography *Better Than Plowing*[4] is a good source for gaining an understanding of the kind of man he was—which, in my experience, was unique. Perhaps another such deep, relentless, and sharply focused champion of the free market will come along to contribute to political economy, but I see no such person on the horizon at present.

---

1. James M. Buchanan, "The Soul of Classical Liberalism," *The Independent Review*, 5:2 (Summer 2000): 111–19.

2. James M. Buchanan, *Cost and Choice: An Inquiry in Economic Theory* (Chicago: University of Chicago Press, 1969).

3. James M. Buchanan, *What Should Economists Do?* (Indianapolis, IN: Liberty Fund, 1979).

4. James M. Buchanan, *Better Than Plowing and Other Personal Essays* (Chicago: University of Chicago Press, 1992).

94

Armen Alchian

(April 12, 1914–February 19, 2013)

ARLINE ALCHIAN HOEL reports that her father, Armen Alchian, "passed away peacefully in his sleep early this morning at his home in Los Angeles." He was 98 years old.

Alchian was a major figure in the economics profession for more than half a century. At UCLA, where he spent his academic career as a faculty member in the department of economics, he was a legend to generations of graduate students, who were required to take the price theory course he taught in the first year of the program. He used the Socratic method: he simply walked into the class each day and asked a student a question. From that point, the discussion went back and forth between teacher and students. Woe to any student who had arrived unprepared—and sometimes to those who had prepared. Public embarrassment was the price such students had to pay. But in the end, the students came away from the course with a healthy measure of their teacher's mastery of applied price theory.

And master he was. Besides having a knack for making sense of countless aspects of economic and social life by viewing them as relative-price or relative-cost problems, Alchian helped to blaze trails toward extremely valuable improvements in microeconomic analysis by bringing into the analysis careful treatments of information, uncertainty, transaction costs, and property rights. For him, little difference existed between micro and macro; both were to be understood by using the same basic economic analysis of individual choice.

Alchian's textbook, written with Bill Allen, differed from existing texts. It was, for one thing, not dumbed down. In addition, it included many questions at the end of each chapter, some of which were quite difficult. At the University of Washington in the late 1960s and 1970s, we used the Alchian and Allen book at every level: introductory, intermediate, and first-year graduate. The only difference came in the level of sophistication we expected in the answers to the questions. Although Alchian did not lack mathematical skills—from 1942 to 1946 he worked as a statistician for the Army Air Corps—his work did not display much mathematical formality. For the most part, he said what he meant in straightforward English prose, spiced with wit and sparkling asides.

Many of Alchian's students and friends believed that he well deserved a Nobel Prize in economics, but this recognition never came to him. Yet, aside from Ronald Coase, no one had a greater influence in creating and fostering what has come to be known as the New Institutional Economics, one of the most notable improvements in mainstream economics during the past half century. Armen was also a genial and friendly man who loved to play golf. He was always at ease among colleagues and affected none of the arrogance that lesser lights sometimes do. He leaves a rich legacy of grateful students and friends and a profession substantially advanced in no small part because of his creative efforts.

95

Robert William Fogel

(July 1, 1926–June 11, 2013)

ROBERT FOGEL[1] died a few days ago. He was a prominent figure in the academic economic history profession for five decades, virtually from the time he burst onto the scene with the publication of a polished-up version of his Johns Hopkins Ph.D. dissertation, *Railroads and American Economic Growth*, in 1964. This book was the most impressive accomplishment to date of the type of research espoused by those who participated in a research program known as the new economic history, econometric history, or cliometrics, which had begun to take shape in the late 1950s. The hallmark of this program was the systematic application of neoclassical economic theory and the methods of statistical inference in the study of economic history.

In his book, Fogel undertook to determine how important the railroads had been as contributors to U.S. economic growth by calculating what he called their "social saving," essentially the amount by which GDP would have been diminished if they had not existed and Americans had been compelled to use the next best means of transporting goods—by horse-drawn wagons on the land and by canal boats on a national system of canals. His conclusion that the social saving had been equal to less than 3 percent of the national product in 1890 cast great doubt on the beliefs historians had previously held about the railroad's great importance. Although many objections were raised subsequently to Fogel's approach, his specification of the no-railroads counterfactual, and his data, the book became an instant cliometric classic.

Having entered the economic history profession at the very top, Fogel then proceeded, along with his Johns Hopkins classmate Stanley Engerman,

---

1. "Robert Fogel," *Wikipedia*, http://en.wikipedia.org/wiki/Robert_Fogel.

to tackle the subject of slavery in the United States. This time the target was the widely accepted idea that prior to the War Between the States slavery had been on its economic last legs, and therefore had the war not led to slavery's destruction, this labor system would have died a natural death before long. In 1974, Fogel and Engerman brought their findings together in *Time on the Cross: The Economics of American Negro Slavery*, a book that probably made a bigger splash than any economic history book ever published in the United States. The main claims this time were that slavery had been economically thriving on the eve of the war, slave-plantation productivity had exceeded the productivity of comparable free-labor production, slaves had received much better treatment than generally believed, and the system had yielded handsome returns to the slave owners, in most cases at least as great as the returns that feasible alternative investments would have yielded them. The reaction to these findings bordered on academic violence as historians and fellow economists rushed to challenge Fogel and Engerman's methods, data, and conclusions, and to indict them for omissions and errors of various sorts.

Fogel, who believed that any research project that required less than a decade was scarcely worth undertaking, then spent much of the next decade and a half in accumulating additional evidence and carrying out additional analyses, often in collaboration with colleagues or graduate students, to support the initial findings. The fruits of these follow-up efforts appeared in a two-volume work, *Without Consent or Contract: The Rise and Fall of American Slavery*, published in 1989.

From the 1980s onward, however, Fogel devoted the lion's share of his research efforts to work that relates more closely to demographic changes in history than to economic history, although he always maintained that critical interrelations existed, for example, between improvements in nutrition and increases in labor productivity. I did not follow closely the mass of research that emerged from this project, much of it by other researchers in the United States, Europe, and elsewhere. I found that I could stand only a certain number of calculated height-by-age profiles and that I could not always accept the conclusions drawn on the basis of such data. In any event, many publications by Fogel and other economic historians grew out of this project.

Fogel taught mainly at the University of Chicago and, for a few years (1975–81) at Harvard. In 1993, he and Douglass C. North shared the Nobel

Prize in economics for their work as leaders of the new economic history. Fogel's work was also recognized by his election to prestigious scientific bodies and by the award of honorary degrees by leading universities in the United States and abroad. Yet he never rested on his laurels and remained engaged in research and writing until the end.

I got to know Bob in the early 1970s. At that time I was carrying out research on what had happened to the U.S. freedmen and their descendants during the half-century after the War Between the States, and I imagined that my book on this subject might be seen as a sequel to Fogel and Engerman's *Time on the Cross*. In 1977, Cambridge University Press published my book, titled *Competition and Coercion*.[2] Although it failed to receive anything like the gigantic recognition that Fogel and Engerman's blockbuster had received, Bob was gracious in his own reception. He rarely wrote book reviews, but he did review my book in 1978 for the *Business History Review* and gave it high marks. Shortly afterward, he invited me to Harvard to make a presentation at the economic history workshop (where I first met Robert Margo, then a graduate student and later a friend and coauthor of mine), and he and his wife Enid entertained me at their home for dinner with some colleagues from the Harvard Department of Economics. In the late 1970s Bob used to encourage me when I complained that my book had been largely neglected, assuring me that in fifty years, it would still stand up.

Bob never showed any indication that he understood Austrian economics or cared to understand it. He was a Chicago School economist, and he enjoyed immense professional success as such. At Chicago and Harvard he oversaw the training of many excellent graduate students, who are now among the leading economic historians in the world. He had no incentive to cut loose from his Chicago-School moorings, which in his mind were those of science, however much some of his work might now seem to me to be more scientistic than scientific.[3] At a symposium to honor my dear friend Max Hartwell, held at the University of Virginia in 1991, Bob became publicly angry with me for challenging, on Austrian grounds, his computation of "slave incomes." I left

---

2. Robert Higgs, *Competition and Coercion: Blacks in the American Economy, 1865–1914* (New York: Cambridge University Press, 2008 [1977]).

3. F. A. Hayek, *The Counter-Revolution of Science: Studies on the Abuse of Reason* (Indianapolis: Liberty Fund, 1979 [1952]).

academic employment in 1994 and never had any personal contact with him afterward. He must have got over his pique eventually, however, because in 2011, when I was honored with the Alexis de Tocqueville Award, he sent a very gracious video to be shown at the event in which he recalled my early days in the profession and praised my contributions to it.

It is difficult to imagine what academic economic history might have looked like during the past half-century without Bob Fogel. With the possible exception of only Doug North as a comparably influential figure, he did more than anyone to set the profession's standards, determine its leading topics and methods of research, and train its most highly regarded practitioners. Especially considering that he had become a Communist during his under-graduate years at Cornell and had worked afterward as a Party organizer for eight years before abandoning communism as an unscientific doctrine, one must say that he had a truly amazing career.

96

Donald S. Barnhart

(July 18, 1925–September 8, 2009)

IN THE FALL OF 1963, I transferred from Fresno State College, where I had recently completed my sophomore year, and enrolled in San Francisco State College, where I studied for two years and then was graduated in 1965. By the beginning of my senior year, I had already completed all of the requirements for graduation as an economics major except for having the total number of credit hours required for a bachelor's degree in any field. So, I resolved that during my final year, I would take only courses in which the professor was considered to be an excellent teacher, regardless of subject or department.

In so doing, I enrolled in a course in the Social Science Department called "Social Change in Modern Latin America," which was taught by a highly recommended professor, Donald S. Barnhart. I enjoyed the course immensely. The professor was indeed an outstanding teacher, intellectually provocative and masterful in getting and keeping the students' rapt attention, and I came away from the course having gained a lifelong interest in Latin America. Noting that Barnhart had a Ph.D. in history from the University of Chicago, I inferred, perhaps too hastily, that there must be something to the study of history—a subject about which I knew next to nothing—if it produced such fine, knowledgeable teachers as he.

Later, having completed my senior year, I visited Barnhart in his office to tell him that I knew very little about history but wanted to learn more, and to ask him to recommend a list of books for me to read in this quest. He did so, and I read all ten of the books he had recommended during the summer of 1965, before beginning graduate study in economics at the University of California, Santa Barbara, in the fall. Although I did not fully appreciate it at the time, I had been hooked on history. Two or three odd turns of fate later, when I was studying for my Ph.D. in economics at Johns Hopkins, I began to specialize in economic history, a field that, broadly construed, would occupy me to a greater or lesser extent for the rest of my life.

When I completed the work for my Ph.D. at Hopkins in the spring of 1968, I noted in the preface of my dissertation my gratitude to those who had trained me there, and I added words of appreciation for Amor Gosfield, one of my professors at Santa Barbara, and for Barnhart. Of the latter, I wrote: "It was he who first aroused my historical curiosity. His teaching was an inspiration, and his blending of history, economics, and other social sciences provided an example of the potential fruitfulness of interdisciplinary studies. Above all he encouraged me both explicitly and by his example to travel the scholarly path, and for that I am profoundly grateful."

A few years later, when I was teaching at the University of Washington, Barnhart wrote me to ask if I would write a letter of reference for him in connection with his application for a Fulbright Fellowship to support him during a sabbatical year in Peru. I was very glad to write the letter on his behalf, happy that I could, if only in small measure, do something to repay the man who had done so much to set me on my career path.

It is nothing out of the ordinary for a person's life to take unexpected turns—indeed, it would be stranger if one's life did not do so. I did not go to college to study history; I had little interest in this subject until I happened to encounter Barnhart and found his teaching to be an inspiration. He launched me as a sometime contributor to economic, demographic, and political history. Whatever I have done to make a mark in these areas can be traced back directly to him. I hope that the expressions of appreciation and gratitude I made to him many years ago truly conveyed how much I owed him.

Donald Stanford Barnhart,[1] after completing his graduate training at Chicago, taught history at the University of West Virginia and did graduate work at the Wharton School at Penn. He taught at San Francisco State from 1960 until his retirement in 1990. He died in 2009 at 84 years of age. He was a truly great teacher, and I will never forget him.

---

1. "Donald Stanford Barnhart," *The Daily Journal,* http://www.smdailyjournal.com /articles/obituaries/2009-09-24/donald-stanford-barnhart/117010.html

PART IX

Just for Fun

97

Mainstream Economists Will Have a Blast at This Year's Halloween Parties

THE LATEST DANCE CRAZE in mainstream economics is a reworking of a Halloween classic, updated to suit the ghosts and goblins haunting the profession today. (Chorus lines appear in **bold font**.)

The Econ Smash

I was working in the lab late one night
When my eyes beheld an eerie sight
A Keynesian from his slab began to rise
And suddenly to my surprise

He did the smash
He did the econ smash
The econ smash
It was a graveyard splash
He did the smash
It caught on in a flash
He did the smash
He did the econ smash

From my laboratory in academe east
To committee rooms where politicians feast
The ghouls all came from New Classical abodes
To get a jolt from outmoded electrodes

They did the smash
They did the econ smash
The econ smash
In the midst of the crash
They did the smash
It caught on in a flash
They did the smash
They did the econ smash

Zombie banks were having fun
The party had just begun
The guests included Greenspan
Geithner and Paulson

The scene was rockin', all were digging the noise
Bernanke broke his chains and freed the printing-press boys
The coffin-bangers were about to arrive
With their vocal group, "The Inflation Five"

They did the smash
They did the econ smash
The econ smash
In the midst of the crash
They did the smash
It caught on in a flash
They did the smash
They did the econ smash

Out from his coffin, Keynes's voice did ring
Seems he was troubled by just one thing
He opened the lid and started to yap
And said, "What has become of my Liquidity Trap?"

It's now the smash
It's now the econ smash
The econ smash
In the midst of the crash

They did the smash
It caught on in a flash
They did the smash
They did the econ smash

Now everything's cool, Keynes is leading the band
And the econ smash is the hit of the land
For you, the job seekers, this smash is meant too
To land a new job, tell them Krugman sent you

Then you can smash
Then you can econ smash
The econ smash
And do this graveyard splash
Then you can smash
You'll catch on in a flash
Then you can smash
Then you can econ smash

(With apologies to Bobby "Boris" Pickett)

98

"American Pie"

*Altered to Lament My Life and Times
as an Economist*

A LONG, LONG time ago . . .
I can still remember
Mainstream theory used to make me smile.
And I knew if I had my chance
That I could make equations dance
And, maybe, they'd be happy for a while.

But Joseph Stiglitz made me shiver
With every paper he'd deliver.
Bad news in the journals;
I flung them in the urinals.

I can't remember if I sighed
When I heard the link to gold decried,
But something touched me deep inside
The day the dollar died.

So bye-bye, Miss American Pie.
Drove my Chevy to the levee
But the levee was dry.
Them good old boys were drinkin' whiskey and rye
Singin', "this'll be the day that I die,
This'll be the day that I die."

Did you write the macro book,
And do you have faith in gobbledyegook,
If professors say it's true?

And do you believe in risk alone,
Does uncertainty chill you to the bone,
And can you teach investors what to do?

Well, I know that you're in love with math
'Cause I saw you dancin' down that path.
Your Hessians were well bordered
And your preferences well ordered.

I'd been a lonely teenage undergrad
With a K&E slide rule and a yellow pad,
But I knew I had just been had
The day the dollar died.

I started singin'
Bye-bye, Miss American Pie.
Drove my Chevy to the levee
But the levee was dry.
Them good old boys were drinkin' whiskey and rye
Singin', "this'll be the day that I die;
This'll be the day that I die."

Well, since Nixon, we've been on our own,
And fiat grows on a rollin' stone,
But that's not how it used to be.
Till Bill Phillips sang for the president,
'Bout a curve that he had just invent-
ed to fine-tune where the gods thought we should be.

Oh, but while old Bill was looking down,
Uncle Milton stole his laurel crown.
The profession was confounded;
Friedman's doctrines were propounded.
And while Lucas read a book on math
The real world's business took a bath,
We wrote the Phillips Curve's epitaph,
The day the dollar died.

We were singin',
Bye-bye, Miss American Pie.
Drove my Chevy to the levee
But the levee was dry.
Them good old boys were drinkin' whiskey and rye
Singin', "this'll be the day that I die;
This'll be the day that I die."

Helter-skelter in a summer swelter,
Inflation blew up our fallout shelter,
Eight, ten percent and risin' still.
It led to strikes and social unrest;
For politicians it became such a test
That Paul Volker was brought in to close the till.

Now the half-time air was sweet perfume
While Reagan played a marching tune.
We all got up to dance,
Oh, but we never got the chance!
'Cause the lobbyists swarmed on the field;
The marching band was quick to yield.
Do you recall what was revealed
The day the dollar died?

We started singin',
Bye-bye, Miss American Pie.
Drove my Chevy to the levee
But the levee was dry.
Them good old boys were drinkin' whiskey and rye
Singin', "this'll be the day that I die;
This'll be the day that I die."

Oh, then we became confused and leery,
With no firm ground of econ theory
And bad ideas 'bout what was wrong.
So come on: Fed be nimble, Fed show verve!

Maestro fooled with the bank reserves
'Cause fiat is the devil's only song.

Oh, and as I watched him play that game
My hands were folded in professional shame.
No angel born in hell
Could break that Satan's spell.

And as the flames climbed high into the night
To light the sacrificial rite,
I saw Wall Street laughing with delight
The day the dollar died.

They were singin',
Bye-bye, Miss American Pie.
Drove my Chevy to the levee
But the levee was dry.
Them good old boys were drinkin' whiskey and rye
Singin', "this'll be the day that I die;
This'll be the day that I die."

I met a man who sang the blues
And I asked him for some happy news,
But he just smiled and said you're toast.
I went down to the sacred store
Where I'd bought some Hayek years before,
But the man there said the Austrians were just ghosts.

And in the streets: the children screamed,
The lovers cried, and the poets dreamed.
But not a word was spoken;
The mainstream's bells were broken.
And the three men needed in this flurry:
Ludwig, Fritz, and my old friend Murray,
Were laughed out of court by the mainstream jury
The day the dollar died.

And they were singin',
Bye-bye, Miss American Pie.
Drove my Chevy to the levee
But the levee was dry.
Them good old boys were drinkin' whiskey and rye
Singin', "this'll be the day that I die;
This'll be the day that I die."

99

A Vulgar Keynesian Visits My Chamber

(I HEARD A NOISE that seemed to come from my chamber
door. I opened it, and then . . .)

Deep into that darkness peering, long I stood there wondering,
    fearing,
Doubting, dreaming dreams some Austrians dared to dream
    before;
But recession was unbroken, and the darkness gave no token,
And the only words there spoken were the whispered words,
    "Spend more!"
These I whispered, and an echo murmured back the words,
    "Spend more!"
Merely these and nothing more.

Back into the chamber turning, all my soul within me burning,
Soon again I heard a yapping somewhat louder than before.
"Surely," said I, "surely that is something at my window lattice;
Let me see then, what thereat is, and this mystery explore—
Let my heart be still a moment and this mystery explore;—
'Tis hot air and nothing more!"

Open here I flung the shutter, when, with many a flirt and
    flutter,
In there stepped a stately Keynesian of benighted days of yore.
Not the least obeisance made he; not a minute stopped or
    stayed he;

But, with Lord Keynes's mien he perched above my chamber
door—
Perched upon a bust of Mises just above my chamber door—
Perched, and sat, and nothing more.

Then this mainstream guest beguiling my sad fancy into
smiling,
By the grave and stern decorum of the countenance he wore,
"Though thy crest be shorn and shaven, thou," I said, "art sure
no craven,
Ghastly grim and ancient Keynesian peddling academic lore—
Tell me what thy best advice is on this sad recession's shore!"
Quoth the Keynesian, "Just spend more."

Much I marveled this ungainly boob to hear discourse so
plainly,
Though his answer little meaning—little relevancy bore;
For we cannot help agreeing that no living human being
Ever yet was cursed with seeing a Keynesian above his chamber
door—
Bird or beast above the sculptured bust above his chamber door,
Saying only "Just spend more."

But the Keynesian, sitting lonely on the placid bust, spoke only,
Those three words, as if all his advice he did outpour.
Nothing further then he uttered—not a feather then he
fluttered—
Till I scarcely more than muttered "Other loons have flown
before—
On the morrow he will leave me, as recovery hopes have flown
before."
Then the fool said, "Just spend more."

Index

About the Author

ROBERT HIGGS is Senior Fellow in Political Economy for the Independent Institute and Editor at Large of Independent's quarterly journal *The Independent Review.*

He is the recipient of numerous awards, including the Gary Schlarbaum Award for Lifetime Defense of Liberty, Thomas Szasz Award for Outstanding Contributions to the Cause of Civil Liberties, Lysander Spooner Award for Advancing the Literature of Liberty, Friedrich von Wieser Memorial Prize for Excellence in Economic Education, Templeton Honor Rolls Award on Education in a Free Society, and Premio Juan de Mariana.

Dr. Higgs is the editor of Independent Institute books *Opposing the Crusader State, The Challenge of Liberty, Re-Thinking Green, Hazardous to Our Health?* and *Arms, Politics, and the Economy,* plus the volume *Emergence of the Modern Political Economy.*

He is also the author of *Delusions of Power, Depression, War, and Cold War, Neither Liberty Nor Safety, Politická ekonomie strachu (The Political Economy of Fear,* in Czech), *Resurgence of the Warfare State, Against Leviathan, The Transformation of the American Economy 1865–1914, Competition and Coercion: Blacks in the American Economy, 1865–1914,* and *Crisis and Leviathan.*

A contributor to numerous scholarly volumes, he is the author of more than 100 articles and reviews in academic journals. His popular articles have appeared in *The Wall Street Journal, Los Angeles Times, Providence Journal, Chicago Tribune, San Francisco Examiner, San Francisco Chronicle, Society, Reason,* AlterNet, and many other publications and Web sites, and he has appeared on Fox News, NPR, NBC, ABC, C-SPAN, CBN, CNBC, America's Talking Television, Radio America Network, Radio Free Europe, Talk Radio Network, Voice of America, Newstalk TV, the Organization of American Historians' public radio program, and scores of local radio and television stations. He has also been interviewed for articles in the *New York Times*, *Washington Post*, *Terra Libera*, *Investor's Business Daily*, UPI, *Orlando Sentinel*, *Seattle Times*, *Chicago Tribune*, *National Journal*, *Reason*, *Washington Times*, WorldNetDaily, *Folha de Sao Paulo*, Newsmax, *Financial Times*, *Al-Ahram Weekly*, Creators Syndicate, and elsewhere.

Dr. Higgs has spoken at more than 100 colleges and universities and at the meetings of such professional organizations as the Economic History Association, Western Economic Association, Population Association of America, Southern Economic Association, International Economic History Congress, Public Choice Society, International Studies Association, Cliometric Society, Allied Social Sciences Association, American Political Science Association, American Historical Association, and others.

He received his Ph.D. in economics from the Johns Hopkins University, and he has taught at the University of Washington, Lafayette College, Seattle University, and the University of Economics, Prague. He has been a visiting scholar at Oxford University and Stanford University, and a fellow for the Hoover Institution and the National Science Foundation. He is also an honorary professor of economics and history at Universidad Francisco Marroquín in Guatemala.

Independent Studies in Political Economy

For further information:
510-632-1366 • orders@independent.org • http://www.independent.org/publications/books/